What readers are saying about
iOS SDK Development

Being a successful iOS developer means maintaining laser-like focus on the details that are specific to your app. The best way to do this is to write as little code as possible. Apple's frameworks provide an incredible starting point, but you have to understand what they do, how they work, and why they're designed the way they are. I can scarcely think of anyone more qualified to teach you the ins and outs of Apple's iOS SDK than Bill Dudney and Chris Adamson. Their all-new, updated book, *iOS SDK Development*, is a must-read, plain and simple.

➤ **John C. Fox**, Creator of MemoryMiner and Co-Host, iDeveloper Live

A programmer looking to branch out into iPhone or iPad development couldn't ask for a better guide to getting started. Chris and Bill are excellent teachers, and that really comes through in these pages.

➤ **Dave Klein**, Founder of CocoaConf and Author of *Grails: A Quick-Start Guide*

Never have I read an iOS book that so thoroughly guides the reader through the development cycle of an iOS app. I recommend this book to anyone learning the iOS platform.

➤ **Jeffrey Holland**

In short, this is one of the best iOS books I have read. It might require some outside homework for someone totally new to programming, but most people coming to iOS will be existing developers (like me) that are getting sick of PHP and .NET.

➤ **Joel Clermont**

iOS SDK Development

Chris Adamson
Bill Dudney

The Pragmatic Bookshelf

Dallas, Texas • Raleigh, North Carolina

Many of the designations used by manufacturers and sellers to distinguish their products are claimed as trademarks. Where those designations appear in this book, and The Pragmatic Programmers, LLC was aware of a trademark claim, the designations have been printed in initial capital letters or in all capitals. The Pragmatic Starter Kit, The Pragmatic Programmer, Pragmatic Programming, Pragmatic Bookshelf, PragProg and the linking g device are trademarks of The Pragmatic Programmers, LLC.

Every precaution was taken in the preparation of this book. However, the publisher assumes no responsibility for errors or omissions, or for damages that may result from the use of information (including program listings) contained herein.

Our Pragmatic courses, workshops, and other products can help you and your team create better software and have more fun. For more information, as well as the latest Pragmatic titles, please visit us at *http://pragprog.com*.

The team that produced this book includes:

Brian P. Hogan (editor)
Potomac Indexing, LLC (indexer)
Molly McBeath (copyeditor)
David J Kelly (typesetter)
Janet Furlow (producer)
Juliet Benda (rights)
Ellie Callahan (support)

Printed in the United States of America.
ISBN-13: 978-1-934356-94-4
Printed on acid-free paper.
Book version: P1.0—November 2012

Contents

Acknowledgments

This book starts with all the people who asked for it. The relevance and accuracy of our previous edition, *iPhone SDK Development*, diminished as Apple piled on language innovations like blocks, tool changes like Xcode 4, and all sorts of neat stuff to play with. Readers of the first edition wondered when we'd get an update out, or they'd send us screenshots of Xcode 4 and say, "How do I make my windows look like the screenshots in your book?" It didn't take long for us to think that our old book was doing a disservice to new readers and cried out for a up-to-date do-over.

Writing a book is a huge undertaking. But of course it's not just the authors that worked hard. Our editor, Brian Hogan, was an invaluable partner in the tasks of bringing this book home with just the right amount of encouragement and chiding to get us over the hump and of rescuing this book when we were foolishly targeting two different audiences and not reaching either of them. So thanks to Brian for his work throughout this process and converting sometimes-messy prose into something our readers could understand.

We have a number of individual thanks to hand out in this edition. Jonathan Penn turned us onto UI Automation testing (covered in Section 9.3, *User Interface Testing*, on page 219) with his talks at CodeMash and CocoaConf, which is no small feat given our long-held skepticism about the testability of GUIs.[1] Graham Lee tipped us off to Xcode 4.3's undocumented support for command-line testing, though we couldn't get it running as well as we'd like —maybe in Xcode 5. Finally, we couldn't write a sidebar called "Don't Ship Programmer Art" (in Chapter 10, *The App Store and Beyond*, on page 233) and then post iTunes Connect screenshots with our own ugly handmade icon for the sample Recipes app, so we brought in Scott Ruth of Brave Bit App Studio to bring the bling.[2] He's a designer-turned-programmer (with the help of the

---

1.   http://cocoamanifest.net
2.   http://www.bravebit.com

Pragmatic Studio's iOS programming courses), and you'll see his pixels near the end of the book.

From Chris Adamson

It's been comfortable working again with the Prags and their innovative and practical publishing system. Building—and more importantly, updating—programming books with this system is a breeze, and writing markup is second nature to developers like us. For what it's worth, I wrote a bunch of my stuff on an iPad at a standing desk with a dock keyboard and the Textastic app (http://www.textasticapp.com). It's inspiring to think that we're writing about how to build the tools we use every day; maybe someone reading this book will write my next favorite app.

I'm grateful to my family for putting up with both my absence and my stress through one more book and to all the readers of the first edition who wrote in or posted on the forums as they got their first apps up on the store. That's the kind of thrill that keeps us going.

Obligatory end-of-book tune check: this time it was Sarah Slean, Rich Aucoin, Coeur de Pirate, Fitz and the Tantrums, and Metric. Up-to-date stats at http://www.last.fm/user/invalidname.

From Bill Dudney

I'd like to thank the many folks who have been to the Pragmatic iOS Studios (http://pragmaticstudio.com/ios). Your questions, insights, and struggles have been an inspiration for much of the material in this book. I always love walking into a class early on the first day and feeling the energy of people excited to learn something new. Listening to the questions and watching the victories helped me immensely in understanding how to present iOS to developers new to the platform.

Any mention of the Studios requires a heartfelt thanks to my co-teachers, Daniel Steinberg and Matt Drance. I learn something new every time I deliver the class with them.

My family put up with a distracted father and husband all too often throughout the writing of this book. But I'd like to say a special thanks to my wife, Sarah, for all her help in editing my first, second, and all-too-often third drafts. I'd also like to thank a 2,000-year-old Jewish carpenter for touching my life and making it so much more than it might have been.

From Both of Us

Finally, we'd both like to thank Steve Jobs for having given up so much of his life to pursue something he believed in. Computers should be easy to use. He inspired a team of brilliant people to work beyond what they ever thought they could do. And they delivered some great things: the Macintosh in 1984, the NeXT in 1988, the iMac in 1998, and the iPhone in 2007. He did not settle for anyone doing less than his or her best. He was one of a kind and the world is a brighter place for him having been in it.

Some people ask us if the "gold rush" is over. As Bill always says, it's just beginning, but instead of a gold rush we are in the midst of another economic revolution. iOS, and therefore mobile, is defining a whole new way that we can use computers to keep us better connected to things that matter. Even with 700,000-plus apps in the store, we have only begun to scratch the surface of what is possible. The iOS platform is crying out for you to make something spectacular—please let us know when you do!

Introduction

When we wrote the first edition of *iPhone SDK Development*, we knew we weren't writing something like *The C Programming Language* that would live on unchanged for decades. But was two years on the shelf too much to ask for?

Apparently so! And we're not complaining. Since the release of our first book in early 2009, the platform has surged in popularity and prominence. In the intervening years, the platform has added a whole new device family in the iPad, sold millions of units, and changed its name from *iPhone OS* to *iOS* to better reflect its multiple uses and perhaps to leave the door open to future devices.

The SDK has also grown in breadth and depth, adding new features, new frameworks, and new tools. Since the first book, Apple has changed compilers and has radically overhauled Xcode, the primary iOS development environment. As we did our day-to-day work with all this new stuff, we'd sometimes look over the book and notice each time that more and more of it was out-of-date. The Xcode screenshots, the callbacks to selectors instead of blocks, the exposure of private variables and method names in the public header—all this stuff we weren't using ourselves anymore—it all seemed so...so *2009*.

A New Start and a Do-Over

If you happen to have read the previous book and then you flip through this one, you'll notice something: we have copied over *absolutely nothing* from the old book. This one is 100 percent new. As we looked at all the changes to the platform—between Xcode 4, iOS 6, and the iPad—we decided that so much had changed that we would be better off starting off fresh. This freed us to embrace everything that's new, making a complete cut with the past and writing a truly up-to-date book.

And there's so much that's new! The radically overhauled Xcode 4 is the first version of the development tool that's truly built for iOS development, rather than having iPhone concepts bolted onto a Mac IDE. It completely rethinks how developers work with projects, and its sensible conceptual divisions make finding its functionality more predictable. In code, the revolutionary new Automatic Reference Counting frees developers from the drudgery of manual retain and release calls, a routine that if mishandled would lead to memory leaks or crashes. With multicore processors like the A5 comes a need for practical concurrent programming, something the iOS SDK answers with Grand Central Dispatch, a technology that allows programmers to divvy up small bits of code and data as "blocks" and let the system decide how best to run them.

In fact, it's possible to have too much of a good thing, and the iOS 6 SDK is a good example. In our first book, we worked to present most of the interesting things you could do with the platform and watched as our 250-page book grew to nearly 600 pages, blowing through deadline after deadline. And that was just for iPhone OS 3. To cover all the subsequent changes in iOS versions 4 through 6 at the same depth, we'd be in the thousands of pages. And that's not very "pragmatic."

So we've adjusted our focus for this edition. This book is about setting you off on the right foot: understanding the fundamentals, getting comfortable with the tools and the concepts, and developing good habits. We've put a particular emphasis on the last of these, looking for the kinds of things that aren't just handy classes or compiler tricks but instead are the values and routines that will help produce better apps. To that point, you'll find we spend time talking about topics like internationalization, testing, debugging, and source code management. We're also adopting modern iOS development practices, such as using Objective-C properties exclusively instead of using traditional instance variables and getting private methods out of public header files.

Our goal is for this book to serve as a prerequisite for all the other iOS titles from the Pragmatic Bookshelf, such as *iOS Recipes: Tips and Tricks for Awesome iPhone and iPad Apps [WD11]* by Paul Warren and Matt Drance and *Core Data [Zar12]* by Marcus S. Zarra. And, of course, it should provide a good grounding for any future titles that dig further into the many frameworks of iOS.

But more importantly, you should come away from this book with a firm grasp of the most essential iOS APIs—the UIKit GUI framework and the essential utilities of the Foundation framework—and enough of a sense of where things are and how things work to be able to grab the documentation for interesting-looking features and be able to figure it out.

So Here's the Plan

With that goal in mind, let's look at how we're going to get there. We'll start by getting Xcode from the Mac App Store, and by the time we're done we'll be ready to upload our own apps to the iOS App Store. Here's a road map to the journey:

- Chapter 1, *Tweetings and Welcome to iOS 6*, on page 1, starts by downloading and installing the SDK and beginning work on a first app, which uses iOS 6's new Social framework to send a tweet telling the world that our journey is underway. We'll use Xcode's visual tools to build a user interface and connect it to our first code.

- Chapter 2, *Programming for iOS*, on page 27, gets into the specifics of coding by introducing the Objective-C programming language and the two frameworks we use most frequently in iOS apps: Foundation and UIKit.

- Chapter 3, *Asynchronicity and Concurrency*, on page 57, addresses the issues of how and when our code is run, showing how many of the iOS APIs use asynchronous callbacks and employing the Grand Central Dispatch system to handle concurrent execution of our code.

- Chapter 4, *View Controllers*, on page 77, turns our attention back to the UI and looks at how iOS apps are built on a strong Model-View-Controller (MVC) foundation, which will let us make our code more resilient and easier to maintain.

- Chapter 5, *Table Views*, on page 95, continues to build our UI arsenal by bringing in the flexible and widely used table view, the linchpin of most iPhone apps that need to present lists of data.

- Chapter 6, *Storyboards and Container Controllers*, on page 119, is where we'll learn how to build a visual road map of the many screens of an app and how to build much of the logic of that navigation and presentation automatically.

- Chapter 7, *Documents and iCloud*, on page 155, gives us the tools we need to save our user's work to the filesystem as well as to Apple's new iCloud service.

- Chapter 8, *Drawing and Animating*, on page 189, lets us bring our own pixels to the game using the Core Graphics framework to draw images and shapes and use Core Animation to give them life.

- Chapter 9, *Testing and Fixing Apps*, on page 207, addresses the things that can go wrong when we build and run our apps and how we use the SDK's tools both to make them right and to make sure they don't go wrong again.

- Chapter 10, *The App Store and Beyond*, on page 233, completes our journey by changing our outlook from learning to doing. We'll start maintaining our code for the long haul, running it on the device, submitting it on the store (without getting rejected), and managing it after it's in users' hands.

Expectations and Technical Requirements

The technical requirements for iOS development, in general terms, are pretty simple: a reasonably new Mac, running the most-recent production version of Mac OS X. The specific version numbers increment ever upward; check out Xcode on the Mac App Store for the latest requirements. For this edition, our baseline is Xcode 4.5 and the iOS 6 SDK (included with Xcode 4.5), running on Mountain Lion (10.8.2).

We also expect readers of this book to be proficient programmers in at least one object-oriented language. That can be one of the many curly-brace descendants of C (C++, C#, or Java), or an OO scripting language like Ruby or Python. In the previous edition, we assumed some previous familiarity with C and its memory-management concepts (pointers, malloc(), and so on), but we found many readers didn't have it. For this edition, we are providing a catch-up appendix for readers who've never had to master these challenges. If the * and & memory operators are unfamiliar, or perhaps terrifying, Appendix 1, *Wait! I Forgot (or Never Learned) C!*, on page 259, will lay out the C essentials needed to work with Objective-C, the primary language of iOS development.

Online Resources

This book isn't just about static words on a page or screen. It comes with a web page, http://www.pragprog.com/titles/adios, where you can learn more and access useful resources:

- Download the complete source code for all the code examples in the book as ready-to-build Xcode projects.

- Participate in a discussion forum with other readers, fellow developers, and the authors.

- Help improve the book by reporting errata, such as content suggestions and typos.

If you're reading the ebook, you can also access the source file for any code listing by clicking on the gray-green rectangle before the listing.

And So It Begins

We're now ready to begin digging into the iOS 6 SDK. In the next chapter, we'll tool up, familiarize ourselves with the development environment, and write our first app. We'll revise this app over the course of the first few chapters as our skills grow and we learn new tricks.

Anytime you get stuck, check against the source code from the book's page or join us in the forum to let us know what's going on.

Let's go!

Tweetings and Welcome to iOS 6

With all the advances in the tools and frameworks in iOS 6, it's a great time to be starting our journey into iOS app development. In fact, we should tell all our friends what we're up to. In this first chapter, that's exactly what we're going to do. For our first example, we're going to build an app to send out a tweet announcing that we've written our first iOS app. We'll get set up with the SDK and start our first project. First, we'll build the user interface using Apple's visual GUI builder, and then we'll switch into coder mode to implement the app's logic. By the end, we'll have a simple app that will send a real live tweet out to the Internet proclaiming our accomplishment.

First, we need to equip ourselves for the journey.

1.1 Tooling Up

To develop iOS 6 apps, we use Xcode 4. While "Xcode" generally refers to the *integrated development environment* (IDE) (in which we develop code and user interfaces and run a build process to generate the actual apps), it can also mean the entire collection of material we'll need to build iOS applications. When we download Xcode, we get not only the Xcode app itself but also the software development kits (SDKs) for iOS and Mac OS X, which contain documentation, frameworks, helper applications, and more.

Xcode is available for free via the Mac App Store. The Xcode 4.5 application is actually a bundle that contains the Mac and iOS SDKs, starter documentation, and helper applications that we'll use later. For the curious, we can snoop around the contents of the bundle with Finder's Show Package Contents command to see what's inside the hefty 6 GB app. Fortunately, this bundling is an implementation detail that we don't need to worry about: everything we'll need to build the apps in this book is accessible via Xcode's user interface.

The Mac App Store will put Xcode in the /Applications directory. It's a good idea to drag it from there to the Dock so it's always handy.

Let's start building a first app with Xcode; we'll learn about its ins and outs along the way.

1.2 Our First Project

To start building our app, launch Xcode from the /Applications directory or from the Dock. It may need to do some one-time-only setup work the first time it runs, such as asking permission to install components like the "Mobile Device framework." When Xcode finally comes up, it shows the greet window seen in Figure 1, *Xcode greeting window*, on page 2. The right side, initially empty, shows a list of recently opened projects, while the left has buttons to start a new project, set up source control, explore the documentation, or visit Apple's developer site. You can start a new project by clicking the "Create a new Xcode project" button here, or you can dismiss the window and then use the menu sequence File→New→New Project... (⇧⌘N).

Figure 1—Xcode greeting window

When we create a new project, a window opens and immediately slides out a sheet that asks us what kind of project we want to create. This project template sheet, shown in Figure 2, *Xcode project templates*, on page 3, has a list on the left side of project categories divided into iOS and Mac OS X sections. Since we're building an iOS application, we'll select "iOS Application" and then look at the choices in the main part of the frame. We can click each to see a general description of what kind of app to start on. For our first example, we'll select Single View Application.

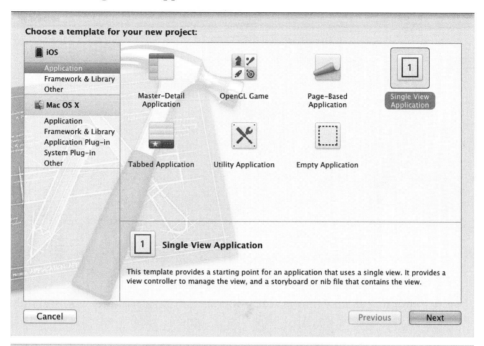

Figure 2—Xcode project templates

After clicking Next, the sheet shown in Figure 3, *Xcode project creation options*, on page 4, asks us for details specific to the project. Some of these change based on the project type; in general, this is where we need to provide names and other identifiers to the app, indicate which device formats (iPhone and/or iPad) it's for, decide whether or not to set up unit tests right away, and so on. For our first app, here's how we should fill out the form:

- *Product Name*—A name for the product with no spaces or other punctuation. For namespacing reasons (see below), we'll prepend our names with *PRP*, so use PRPFirstProjectTweeter here.

- *Organization name*—This can be a company, organization, or personal name, which will be used for the copyright statement automatically put at the top of every source file.

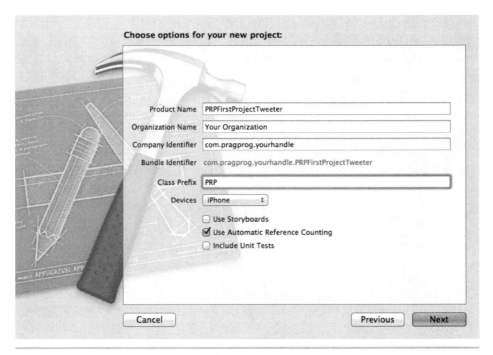

Figure 3—Xcode project creation options

- *Company Identifier*—This is a reverse-DNS style stub that will uniquely identify our app in the App Store, so if someone else creates a PRPFirstProjectTweeter the two apps won't be mistaken for each other because they'll each have a unique product identifier, which is the auto-generated third line of the form. If you have your own domain, you can use it for the company identifier; otherwise, just invert your email address, such as in com.company.yourhandle.

- *Class Prefix*—Objective-C, which we'll use to code our app, has no namespaces for its classes, meaning that if we define class Foo and we import a third-party framework that also defines a Foo, we will confuse the compiler and fail to build. The accepted workaround is to preface all classes with an upper-case prefix; Apple's classes use two letters, and they recommend that third-parties use three. In *iOS Recipes [WD11]*, Paul Warren and Matt Drance chose the prefix PRP for *Pragmatic Programmers*, and we'll do the same here.

- *Device Family*—This determines whether the template should set us up with an app that's meant to run on an iPhone (and iPod touch) or iPad or be a "universal" app with a different layout for each. Not all templates offer all three options. For this app, and for most of the apps in the book, we'll use the iPhone style since it runs on all iOS devices.

- *Use Storyboard*—Leave this unchecked. We'll learn about this style of development in Chapter 6, *Storyboards and Container Controllers*, on page 119.

- *Use Automatic Reference Counting*—This is an Objective-C language option that will greatly simplify our work. For now, just check it. We'll look at how it works in *Automatic Reference Counting*, on page 31.

- *Include Unit Tests*—Projects can be set up with unit tests from the get-go. We'll hold off for now and look at unit testing in Section 9.1, *Unit Testing*, on page 207.

After clicking Next, we choose a location on the filesystem for our project. There's also an option for creating a local Git source code repository for our files; we'll look at source control in Section 10.1, *Protecting Our Code with Source Control*, on page 233, so we can leave it unchecked for now. Once we specify where the project will be saved, Xcode copies over some starter files for our project and reveals them in its main window.

The Xcode Project Workspace

Xcode 4 radically simplifies the many-windows approach of its earlier versions and puts almost everything developers need into two windows. One of these is the one that just opened for us: the project workspace. This window provides our view into nearly everything we'll do with a project: editing code and user interfaces, adjusting settings for how the project is built and run, employing debugging tools, and viewing logged output.

The project workspace is split into five areas, although four of them can be hidden with menu commands. These areas are shown in an "exploded" view in Figure 4, *Parts of the Xcode project workspace*, on page 6. The project workspace is split up as follows:

Toolbar The toolbar at the top of the window offers the most basic controls for building projects and working with the rest of the workspace. The leftmost buttons, Run and Stop, start and stop build-and-run cycles. Next is the scheme selector, which chooses what to run and in what environment (more on this in *Projects, Targets, and Schemes*, on page 21). A Breakpoints button turns breakpoints on and off, which we'll use in Section 9.2, *Debugging Our App*, on page 217. Next comes an iTunes-like status display that shows the most recent build and/or run results, including a count of warnings and errors generated by a continual background

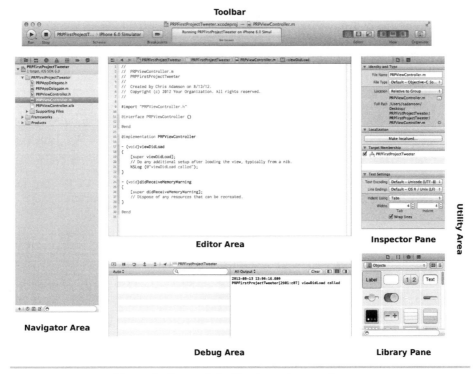

Figure 4—Parts of the Xcode project workspace

analysis of the code. The Editor buttons let us switch between three different kinds of editors, as explained below. After this, three View buttons allow us to show or hide the Navigator, Debug, and Utility areas (see below). Finally, an Organizer button brings up the Organizer window, which addresses multiproject concerns like device management, documentation, and source control repositories. The toolbar can be hidden with the View menu, but we find it too useful to ever want to hide.

Navigator Area The left pane (which may be hidden if the leftmost View button in the toolbar is unselected) offers high-level browsing of our project's contents. It has a mini-toolbar to switch between seven different navigators. The file navigator (⌘1) shows the project's source and resource files and is therefore the most important and commonly used of the seven. Other navigators let us perform searches (⌘3), inspect build warnings and errors, inspect runtime threads and breakpoints, and more.

Editor Area The main part of the project workspace is the Editor area. This is the only view that cannot be hidden. Its contents are set by selecting a file in the Navigator area, and the form the editor takes depends on the file being edited. For example, when a source file is selected, we see a typical source code editor. But when a GUI file is selected, the Editor area becomes a visual GUI editor. The Editor button in the toolbar switches the editor pane between three modes: standard, which is the default editor for the type of file that's selected; assistant, which shows related files side-by-side; and version, which uses source control to show current and historical versions of the file side-by-side, a "blame" mode that shows the committer of each line of code, or a log of commit comments alongside the code. The Editor area also contains a jump bar, a bread-crumb-style strip at the top that shows the hierarchy of the thing being edited; for a source file, this might go "project, group, file, method." Each member of the jump bar is a pop-up menu that navigates to related or recent points of interest.

Utility Area The right side of the project workspace is a utility area that provides detailed viewing and editing of specific selections in the Editor area. Depending on the file being edited, the toolbar atop this area can show different tools in its Inspector pane. Basic information about a selected file and quick help on the current selection are always available. For GUI files, there are inspectors to work with individual UI objects' class identities (⌥⌘3), their settable attributes (⌥⌘4), their size and layout (⌥⌘5), and their connections to source code (⌥⌘6). We'll be using all of these shortly. At the bottom of the Utility area, a library pane gives us click-and-drag access to common code snippets, UI objects, and more.

Debug Area The bottom of the window, below the Editor area and between the Navigator and Utility areas, is a view for debugging information when an app is running. Its tiny toolbar has a segmented button that lets us switch between a debugging view that lets us inspect memory when stopped on a breakpoint, a text view of logging output from the application, or a split view of both.

So that's how Xcode presents our initial project to us, but what can we do? Well, there's a big round Run button, and it's not like it's disabled. Let's try running the app. Make sure the scheme is "iPhone Simulator" (as opposed to "iPad Simulator" or the name of an actual device), and click Run. The status area will add a progress bar that fills up as it builds all the files and bundles them into an app, and when it's done, it will launch the iOS Simulator. The Simulator is another OS X application, which looks and behaves more or less like a real iPhone or iPad. When our app runs in the Simulator, the main screen disappears and is replaced by a big gray box that fills the Simulator screen.

1.3 Building Our User Interface

That gray box in the Simulator is our app. It's not much, but then again, we haven't done anything yet. Let's start building our app for real. Press Stop in Xcode to stop the simulated app, and then take a look at the project in Xcode.

If the file navigator isn't already showing on the left side of the project workspace window, bring it up with ⌘1. The file navigator uses a tree-style hierarchy with a blue Xcode document at the top, representing the project itself as the root. Under this are files and folders. The folder icons are *groups* that collect related files, such as the views and logic classes for one part of the app; groups don't usually represent actual directories on the filesystem. We can expand all the groups to see the contents of the project, as seen in Figure 5, *Default files in PRPFirstProjectTweeter project*, on page 8.

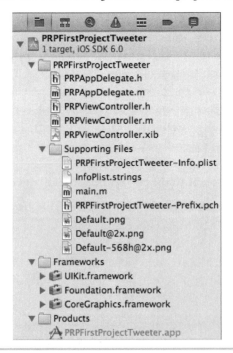

Figure 5—Default files in **PRPFirstProjectTweeter** project

Different project templates will set us up with different files. For the view-based app, we get four source code files in the PRPFirstProjectTweeter group, along with a PRPViewController.xib. These are the files we'll be editing. The supporting files help build and run our app, but we won't need to edit them directly. Frameworks represents the iOS frameworks our app will call into at runtime: UIKit and Core Graphics for the user interface and Foundation for essential classes like arrays and strings. Finally, the Products group shows the files our build will create: in this case, PRPFirstProjectTweeter.app.

So if the PRPFirstProjectTweeter group is where we're going to start our work, where do we begin? Usually in iOS apps, we begin with the user interface. By focusing on what the user sees and how he or she interacts with it, we keep our focus on the user experience and not on the data models and logic behind the scenes. On iOS, we typically build our user interfaces visually and store them in *nib files*. The project has one nib file, PRPViewController.xib (the .xib extension means "XML nib"), so let's click it.

Introducing Interface Builder

When we click the nib, the Editor area switches to *Interface Builder* (IB) mode, the visual editor for GUIs. IB shows a single iPhone-size view, complete with a simulated status bar with battery indicator at its top in a draggable frame on a graph paper–type background. The left side of the editor area has three nondescript icons in a tall vertical strip: a translucent cube, an orange cube with a *1*, and a dashed gray square. We can mouse over them and get pop-overs with their identities: File's Owner, First Responder, and View. Near the bottom of the strip, there's a gray right arrow; click this and the strip expands out to mini-icons with labels and section headers collecting these icons as Placeholders and Objects. We find this mode much more useful, and we will use it throughout the rest of the book. Figure 6, *Editing the user interface with Interface Builder*, on page 10, shows the Interface Builder mode with the placeholder/object strip expanded.

So we have a gray view, which looks just like what came up when we ran the app in the Simulator. Let's start building the UI. To keep it simple, we're going to add a single UI element: a button that says "I finished the project." Our goal will be to make the app send out a tweet when we tap this button.

Let's start by creating the button. We get the default UI widgets from the Object library, which is in the bottom part of the Utility area. Show the utility area with the rightmost of the toolbar's View buttons, and then go to the toolbar in the bottom pane and click the box-shaped icon (third from the left) to bring up the Object library. There's a keyboard shortcut for this, but it's pretty obscure: ^⌥⌘3. The Object library shows icons or names for all the common UIKit user interface views, along with some other object types. Find the "Round Rect" button and click and drag it into the gray view.

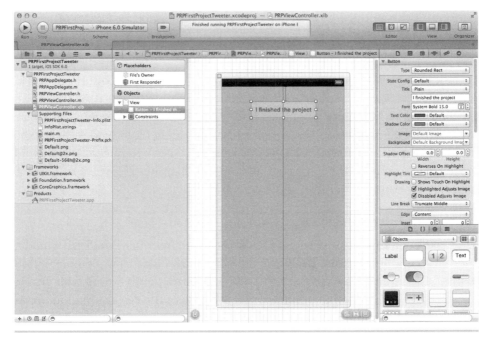

Figure 6—Editing the user interface with Interface Builder

This gives us a plain white button inside our app's view. Without a title, the user won't know what it's for. We can double-click the button and type a title directly into it. However, the title isn't the only thing we can change in this button. Making sure that the button is selected (that is, that it shows resize handles), bring up the Attributes inspector by clicking the "slider playhead" icon at the top of the Utility area or by pressing ⌥⌘4.

The Attributes inspector, shown in Figure 6, *Editing the user interface with Interface Builder*, on page 10, lets us view and edit many of the traits of a selected object. For a button, that means its title, font, colors, shadows, and so on. Buttons have multiple states, meaning they can have different titles, colors, and other attributes, depending on whether they're disabled, being clicked, and so forth. Make sure that "State Config" says Default, and then for Title, type in I finished the project. When we tab out of this field or click anywhere else, the title is immediately applied to the button.

However, our title is now much larger than the button's size will permit, so the title gets truncated with an ellipsis (…) in the middle. We need to widen it! We could just resize the button with its handles—and ordinarily we would do just that because it's so easy, but for the sake of learning something new, let's make use of another inspector. The Size inspector is available under the ruler icon in the utility area or by typing ⌥⌘5. This lets us enter exact values for the button's location as *x-y* coordinates and its size as width and height. Set the width to about 220 and the button should look a lot better. We can also resize with the handles and move the button around by dragging, and the Size inspector will update itself.

While we're at it, let's drag the button toward the edges of the view. As we approach, dashed lines appear, which indicate Apple's recommended margins and spacing. A vertical dashed line also appears when the button crosses the center of the view, so we more easily center our button. Go ahead and center it and place it in the top half of the view.

Interface Builder Connections

We can play with appearance and layout all we like, but sooner or later, we should ask ourselves, "How do we get the button to do something?" After all, our goal is to send a tweet when the user taps the button. But look as we might through the Attributes inspector, there's nothing like an "onClick" field. What we need to do instead is to tie our GUI back into our code.

In iOS, we tie our GUI objects together with our code by means of *connections*. These are relationships set up in Interface Builder, though we have to change our code to create one. So let's go look at the code. In the file navigator, Xcode set us up with four source files in the PRPFirstProjectTweeter group: these are two Objective-C classes, one called *PRPAppDelegate* and the other called *PRPViewController*. Each has an .h header file and an .m implementation file. We'll get into the Objective-C language in the next chapter, but what we need to understand at this point is that the header file is where we declare the public interface to a class and the implementation is where we write the code that actually does stuff.

So we have two classes and this user interface nib. How do we connect them? As it turns out, Xcode has already set up some connections for us. With PRPViewController.xib still selected, click the File's Owner object from the left side of Interface Builder and then visit the Identity inspector, the third button in the toolbar at the top of the utility area (also reachable with ⌥⌘3). File's Owner represents the object that will load the nib file with the user interface. The first field in the Identity inspector, Class, identifies File's Owner as PRPViewController. So that's the first piece of the puzzle: the PRPViewController class, one of the two classes we have source files for, "owns" the user interface nib.

Now go over to the Connections inspector, the rightmost button on the utility area toolbar (⌥⌘6). In the first section, Outlets, there are two bubbles called view and View, connected by a line. If we mouse over the bubbles, the big screen view in the Content area highlights in blue. What this is showing us is that the PRPViewController has a connection to this view that we've been playing with. We can also click View in the objects list on the left, and we'll see the other side of the connection: the Connections inspector now has a section called *Referencing Outlet*, with linked bubbles view and File's Owner.

This kind of connection is called an *outlet*, and it represents a reference from a variable in the source code to a specific object in the nib. This means the class has a variable called view that is connected to this specific UI object, and as a result, we can call methods on the view to do stuff with it. The other kind of connection is called an *action*, and it goes the other way, from an event in the nib to a method in the source code. And that's exactly what we need: a way for a button tap to tell the code to do something. But how do we get Interface Builder to make the connection?

IB needs to know that there is a method to connect to somewhere in the source of PRPViewController. Select the PRPViewController.m file in the file navigator, and notice as the Content area switches over to a source code editor. In it, we see the template has provided trivial implementations of a handful of methods (this number has been shrinking over the years, and in Xcode 4.5, only two methods are stubbed out, viewDidLoad and didReceiveMemoryWarning). Anywhere between the @implementation and @end lines—perhaps the bottom, where it will be easier to find—enter the following empty method definition:

Tweetings/PRPFirstProjectTweeter01/PRPFirstProjectTweeter/PRPViewController.m
```
-(IBAction) handleTweetButtonTapped: (id) sender {
}
```

This defines an instance method called handleTweetButtonTapped: that takes one argument, sender, and has a return type of IBAction. The return type is key. While IBAction is actually equivalent to void, meaning the method doesn't return a value, Interface Builder uses the return type to recognize the method as something that can accept an incoming action connection.

Save the file with ⌘S and go back to PRPViewController.xib. We're now ready to connect the button in the nib to the method in the source file. We can choose any of several ways to do this:

- We can select the button and bring up the Connections inspector (⌥⌘6). In the list of sent events, drag from the dot next to Touch Up Inside over to File's Owner. When the mouse button is released, a pop-up menu over File's Owner will list all of its known actions, which for now is just handleTweetButtonTapped:. Click this to make the connection, which will then be shown with linked bubbles in the Connections inspector, as illustrated in Figure 7, *Creating a connection in Interface Builder*, on page 13.

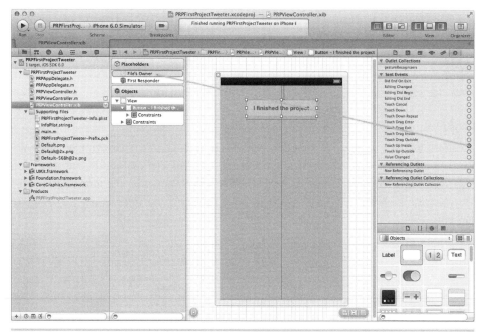

Figure 7—Creating a connection in Interface Builder

- Instead of visiting the Connections inspector, we can control-click or right-click the button to bring up a heads-up display (HUD) menu of the button's connections and drag from the Touch Up Inside event in that menu.

- We can start the connection from the other end by selecting File's Owner and bringing up the Connections inspector or by right-clicking or control-clicking it to show its HUD. Either way, the list of connections has a section for Received Actions, which contains handleTweetButtonTapped:. We can drag from that dot over to the button, where we'll get a pop-up menu with actions to connect to (we'll want Touch Up Inside).

- If we use the toolbar's "assistant" button (the middle of the three Editor buttons), we can view the nib and source code side by side and control-drag a connection from the button to the source method itself.

Once made, a connection is shown in the source code by a filled-in bubble next to the method signature. The connection can be broken by clicking the X button in its bubble in the Connections inspector, so feel free to try these different approaches by breaking and remaking the connection.

1.4 Coding the App

Now that we've added a button to our view and wired it up, we can run the app again. The app now has the "I finished the project" button and we can even tap it, but it doesn't do anything. In fact, we don't even know if we've made our connections correctly. One thing we can do as a sanity check is to log a message to make sure our code is really running. Once that's verified, then we can move on to implementing our tweet functionality.

Logging

On iOS, we can use the C function NSLog() to write a string out to the system's log file. We can implement our action to just log a message every time the button is tapped and thereby verify that the connections are working. Select PRPViewController.m in the file navigator (⌘1) to edit its source code and rewrite handleTweetButtonTapped: like this:

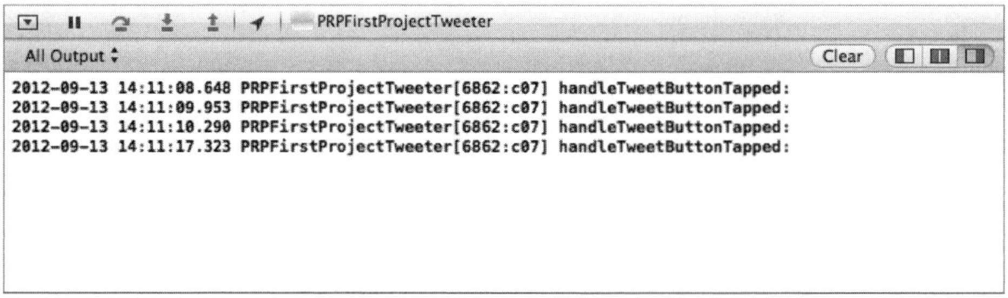

Figure 8—Logging to the Xcode Debug area

Tweetings/PRPFirstProjectTweeter01/PRPFirstProjectTweeter/PRPViewController.m

```
-(IBAction) handleTweetButtonTapped: (id) sender {
NSLog (@"handleTweetButtonTapped:");
}
```

Run the app again and tap the button. Back in Xcode, the Debug area automatically appears at the bottom of the project workspace once a log or error message is generated, as seen in Figure 8, *Logging to the Xcode Debug area*, on page 14. Every time the button is tapped, another time-stamped entry is written to the log and shown in the Debug area. If the Debug area slides in but looks empty, check the three rightmost buttons on the Debug Area mini-toolbar; these switch between a variables view (populated only when the app is stopped on a breakpoint), a console view where log messages appear, and a split between the two. Another way to force the console view to appear is to press ⇧⌘C.

So now we have a button that is connected to our code, enough to log a message that indicates the button tap is being handled. The next step is to add some tweeting!

Digging Into the Docs

The ability for apps to send and receive tweets was new in iOS 5, and is bolstered with Facebook support in iOS 6, but how would we know how to use it? This calls for some documentation.

Xcode's documentation viewer is part of the Organizer window, which addresses cross-project concerns like source control, device management, and documentation. Bring up the organizer with the toolbar button or by pressing ⇧⌘2. The organizer has five toolbar buttons, the last of which is Documentation. When we click the Documentation button, the view switches to a navigator on the left and a content view on the right. The navigator has a mini-toolbar to switch between three modes: browsing by expanding topic trees, searching for keywords, and returning to previously created bookmarks.

However, when we try to browse the documentation, we may be challenged to sign in with an Apple ID. If you haven't joined the developer program at http://developer.apple.com/, the only way to see the docs is to download a local copy. This is a good thing for all of us to do anyway, so we'll have a local copy to refer to when we don't have Internet access. In Xcode's preferences, click the Downloads icon and then the Documentation tab. This pane, shown in Figure 9, *Downloading documentation with Xcode preferences*, on page 16, lists the available doc sets and whether they're installed or need to be downloaded. If the current version of iOS—6.0 as of this writing—doesn't say "Installed," then just click the Install button to download it to your Mac.

Back in the Organizer, click the magnifying glass icon to bring up the search navigator, shown in Figure 10, *Viewing documentation in Xcode Organizer*, on page 17. The search navigator lets us type in a term to search for in the documentation for the installed platforms (potentially multiple versions of iOS and Mac OS X) as well as in the documentation for Xcode itself. This documentation is kept up-to-date by periodically downloading updates from Apple, although this requires being a member of one of Apple's free or paid developer programs and signing in with an Apple ID. Since we only want to search iOS 6 documentation, use the Doc Sets menu to turn off all the doc sets other than iOS 6. If this menu isn't visible, click the magnifying glass in the search field and select Show Find Options. Since we don't know exactly what we're looking for, set the match type to Contains.

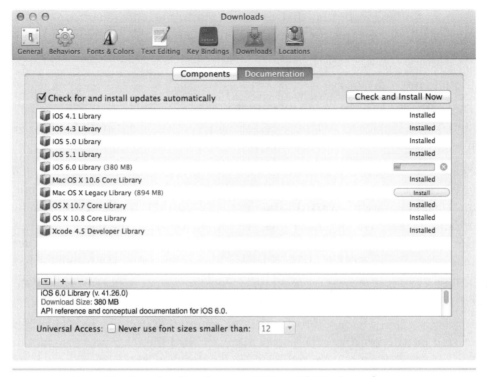

Figure 9—Downloading documentation with Xcode preferences

What are we looking for exactly? Since we want to send a tweet, we can enter tweet as the search term and find some useful results, such as a canSendTweet method, a SLComposeViewController class, and even a sample code project called Tweeting. But we can do a little better in iOS 6. Search for twitter, and one of the results will be the constant SLServiceTypeTwitter. Select this result and the documentation will follow the link to the middle of a class called SLServiceRequest, with SLServiceTypeTwitter defined as follows:

> A string constant that identifies the social networking site Twitter

Scroll to the top of this file to see the essential traits of this SLRequest class: what class it inherits from (NSObject), what versions of iOS provide it (iOS 6 and up), and what framework it's a part of. In this latter item, the term Social.framework is a clickable link, so follow it to the top-level documentation of the "Social Framework Reference," which begins as follows:

> The Social framework lets you integrate your application with supported social networking services. The framework provides a template for creating HTTP requests and provides a generalized interface for posting requests on behalf of the user.

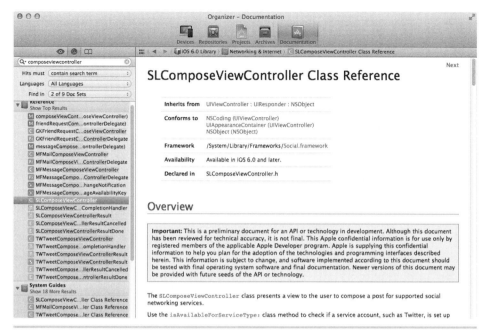

Figure 10—Viewing documentation in Xcode Organizer

Well, this is a win. Rather than just being able to tweet, we've found a framework that provides access to a variety of social networking services. Let's definitely use that. Scroll down to the class listing and discover that there are just two classes: the SLRequest in which we found the SLServiceTypeTwitter constant and an SLComposeViewController. Click the link to the latter and take a look at its documentation, which begins like this:

> The SLComposeViewController class presents a view to the user to compose a post for supported social networking services.

> Use the isAvailableForServiceType: class method to check if a service account, such as Twitter, is set up and reachable before presenting this view to the user.

This looks particularly promising. We can use this SLComposeViewController to post to Twitter, and presumably our same code will work just as well for other social networking services.

Calling Up the SLComposeViewController

With the help of this SLComposeViewController, we're ready to lay down some code. In PRPViewController.m, rewrite the method as follows:

Whatever Happened to the Twitter Framework?

Beta readers will remember that this section previously discussed the TWTweetRequestView-Controller, which was part of iOS 5's "Twitter" framework. In iOS 6, the "Social" framework offers a nearly identical set of features and APIs and supports not only Twitter but also Facebook and Sina Weibo. The new framework is also clearly meant to be expanded in the future with support for other social networking services.

Since the Social framework does everything the Twitter framework did and more, we've switched the examples in the first few chapters to use the new framework.

Tweetings/PRPFirstProjectTweeter01/PRPFirstProjectTweeter/PRPViewController.m

```
Line 1  -(IBAction) handleTweetButtonTapped: (id) sender {
            if ([SLComposeViewController isAvailableForServiceType: SLServiceTypeTwitter]) {
                SLComposeViewController *tweetVC =
                [SLComposeViewController composeViewControllerForServiceType:
     5           SLServiceTypeTwitter];
                [tweetVC setInitialText:
                 @"I just finished the first project in iOS SDK Development. #pragsios"];
                [self presentViewController:tweetVC animated:YES completion:NULL];
            } else {
    10          NSLog (@"Can't send tweet");
            }
        }
```

We've replaced our one-line C logging statement with several lines of Objective-C, which is what iOS uses for most of its high-level APIs, such as UIKit and the Social framework. Let's tease out how this code works. We call methods in Objective-C by using square braces, putting the object (or class, for a class method) first and then the method name and arguments. To start with, on line 2 we ask the SLComposeViewController class if it's even possible to send tweets: it might not be if a given social network isn't set up to post.

If we can send tweets, then we allocate and initialize a new [SLComposeViewController on lines 3–5, and we assign it to the variable tweetVC, which gets the *character, because it, like all Objective-C objects, is a C pointer.

On lines 6–7, we set the initial text of the tweet to "I just finished the first project in iOS SDK Development. #pragsios" by calling the setInitialText: method on tweetVC. The leading @ identifies the string as an Objective-C NSString as opposed to a typical null-terminated C string.

This is all we need to do to prepare the tweet, so on line 8, we show the tweet composer by telling self (our own PRPViewController) to presentViewController: with the newly created and configured tweetVC, setting the animated: parameter to YES, which makes the tweet view "fly in." The third parameter, completion, specifies code to execute once the view comes up; we don't need that, so we send NULL.

Finally, if canSendTweet returned NO, the else block on lines 9–11 logs a debugging message that we can't send tweets. As our skills improve, we'll want to actually show the user a message in failure cases like this.

And that's it. We did all the work in IB to create the button and have it call this method when tapped, so we should be able to just build and tweet at this point, right? Let's try running the app. Click the Run button and see what happens.

Disaster—the project doesn't build anymore! Instead, we get a bunch of error messages in red displayed alongside our code, as seen in Figure 11, *Build errors shown in source code editor*, on page 19. Worse, depending on the width of the window, the errors are likely truncated. What are we supposed to do?

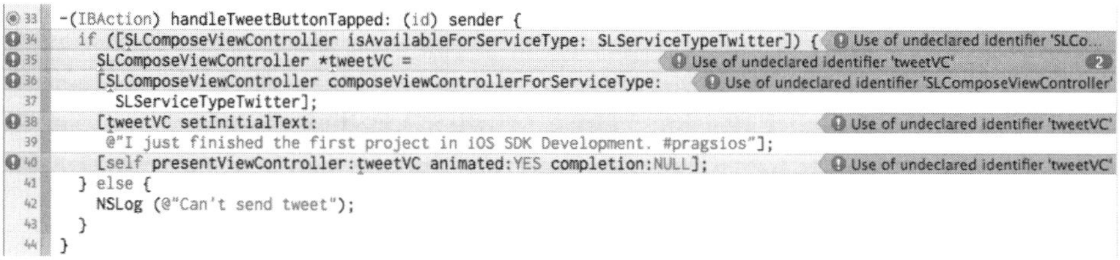

```
33  -(IBAction) handleTweetButtonTapped: (id) sender {
34      if ([SLComposeViewController isAvailableForServiceType: SLServiceTypeTwitter]) {  ⓘ Use of undeclared identifier 'SLCo...
35          SLComposeViewController *tweetVC =                              ⓘ Use of undeclared identifier 'tweetVC'          2
36              [SLComposeViewController composeViewControllerForServiceType:   ⓘ Use of undeclared identifier 'SLComposeViewController'
37              SLServiceTypeTwitter];
38          [tweetVC setInitialText:                                         ⓘ Use of undeclared identifier 'tweetVC'
39              @"I just finished the first project in iOS SDK Development. #pragsios"];
40          [self presentViewController:tweetVC animated:YES completion:NULL];   ⓘ Use of undeclared identifier 'tweetVC'
41      } else {
42          NSLog (@"Can't send tweet");
43      }
44  }
```

Figure 11—Build errors shown in source code editor

Broken Builds

Let's get a more detailed look at what's going on. Visit the log navigator using the rightmost button in the Navigator area toolbar, or just type ⌘7. This replaces the list of files with a list of our builds and runs, with the most recent at the top. Click the top Build PRPFirstProjectTweeter, and the Content area shows a build log, as seen in Figure 12, *Build errors shown in log viewer*, on page 20. The first few files build successfully, as indicated by green checkmarks, but PRPViewController.m fails with a bunch of errors. Most of them are Use of undeclared identifier 'SLComposeViewController'.

This error means that the compiler doesn't know we're using the iOS 6 Social framework, and therefore it doesn't recognize the SLComposeViewController. Xcode project templates only set us up to use the most common frameworks, and anything else has to be added manually. By convention, a framework's headers can be found via the relative path Framework/Framework.h. So to tell the compiler about the Social framework, add the following line near the top of PRPViewController.m, before the @interface line:

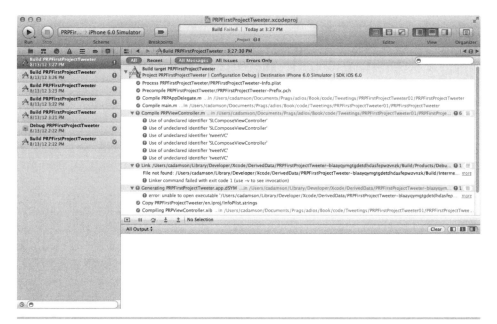

Figure 12—Build errors shown in log viewer

Tweetings/PRPFirstProjectTweeter01/PRPFirstProjectTweeter/PRPViewController.m
```
#import <Social/Social.h>
```

The #import directive tells the compiler to read in another file, usually a header file with function and/or method declarations. The angle brace syntax tells the compiler to search common paths (specifically, the SDK's framework directories) for the Social.h file. Notice that the Xcode template has already provided our file with an #import "PRPViewController.h", so the implementation file can find its own headers. Importing the Social framework's headers also gives us code completion for its various classes and methods.

Anyway, this should fix everything, right? Let's build again.

And...it's still busted. We're down to just one error, and if we look at it in the log viewer, PRPViewController.m has built successfully. Now we have a new problem, something called "Link":

```
Undefined symbols for architecture i386:
  "_OBJC_CLASS_$_SLComposeViewController", referenced from:
      objc-class-ref in PRPViewController.o
  "_SLServiceTypeTwitter", referenced from:
      -[PRPViewController handleTweetButtonTapped:] in PRPViewController.o
ld: symbol(s) not found for architecture i386
clang: error: linker command failed with exit code 1 (use -v to see invocation)
```

Clang? Linker? What's going on? To figure this out, we should take a broader look at what's happening in our build.

Projects, Targets, and Schemes

In the file navigator, click the root of the tree, PRPFirstProjectTweeter, seen in Figure 13, *Editing an Xcode project and targets*, on page 21.

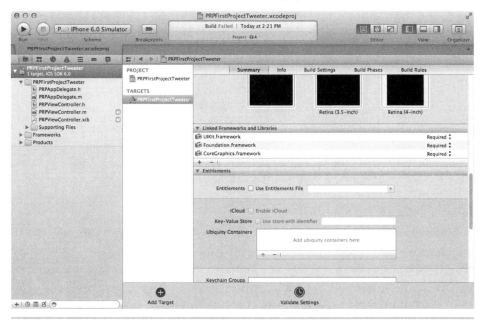

Figure 13—Editing an Xcode project and targets

This changes the editor into a project editor view, where we configure the project and how it's built. On the left side of the editor, there's an icon for the project, followed by a list of targets. A target defines the steps to make a particular product, usually by using some or all of the files in the project. Our code has only one target: building the PRPFirstProjectTweeter app. However, we could have multiple targets for things like building a "lite" version of an app that has only a subset of the full app's capabilities. Unit test suites can also be implemented as targets, as we'll see in Section 9.1, *Unit Testing*, on page 207. Targets are also used when we tell Xcode to run our app: next to the toolbar's Run and Stop buttons, the scheme selector lets us pick a combination of a target (in our case, the PRPFirstProjectTweeter app is the only choice) and an environment to run in, such as the Simulator or a connected iOS device.

When we click the project icon or any of the targets on the left side of the editor, the view presents the settings we can adjust for the project or target.

There are tabs at the top of this view, with labels like Info and Build Settings. The target has a Summary tab, in which we can set things like the app's version number and its icon and startup image. These will come with sensible defaults, although it may make sense to set the version to a prerelease value like 0.1 so we can save 1.0 for the first full release.

Scroll down in this summary to find the Linked Frameworks and Libraries section, shown in the aforementioned Figure 13, *Editing an Xcode project and targets*, on page 21. This shows which frameworks are linked as part of the build process. What does that mean? Well, to build an app target, Xcode needs to go through several steps. First it *compiles* the source code to machine code. Next, it *links* symbolic references in the code to library calls to the actual code libraries, creating an executable binary. With all that resolved, it *copies* needed files—the executable, nib files, resources like images and sounds—into a special folder called an application bundle, which is the runnable app. This flow is graphically represented by the target's Build Phases tab, which lists the files involved in each step.

Adding Frameworks to the Build

By default, most Xcode project templates link in three frameworks: UIKit, which provides the application life cycle and the common UI widgets; Core Graphics, a 2D drawing framework that provides the coordinate system used by UIKit; and Foundation, which provides essential classes like strings, collections, data wrappers, and so on. And this takes us back to the error: the linker said it had a problem with the reference to the SLComposeViewController from the Social framework.

Let's add the Social framework to the set of frameworks that the linker knows about. Click the plus (+) button at the bottom of the Linked Frameworks and Libraries section. This slides out the libraries and frameworks sheet shown in Figure 14, *Adding a framework to an Xcode project*, on page 23. Scroll down to find Social.framework and add it to the project. This adds the Social framework to the list in the summary and adds a Social.framework toolbox icon to the file navigator. We can drag this toolbox to the Frameworks group, but it's purely cosmetic and not necessary.

There's a simple rule of thumb for all of this. Anytime we use a class that's not in UIKit, Core Graphics, or Foundation—something we can check by looking at the documentation for the class we want to use, which indicates its library or framework—we need to #import the library or header to satisfy the compiler and add it to the list of linked libraries and frameworks to make

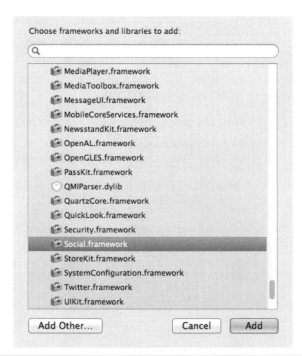

Choose frameworks and libraries to add:

MediaPlayer.framework
MediaToolbox.framework
MessageUI.framework
MobileCoreServices.framework
NewsstandKit.framework
OpenAL.framework
OpenGLES.framework
PassKit.framework
QMIParser.dylib
QuartzCore.framework
QuickLook.framework
Security.framework
Social.framework
StoreKit.framework
SystemConfiguration.framework
Twitter.framework
UIKit.framework

Add Other...   Cancel   Add

Figure 14—Adding a framework to an Xcode project

the linker happy. We'll be sure to point this out going forward, although most of this book will be limited to UIKit and Foundation.

Tweeting at Last

Now try running again. This time the build completes without errors, and the app will launch in the Simulator. Try clicking the button; it likely shows an error alert saying that no Twitter accounts have been configured, with buttons offering to take you to Settings or to cancel.

To fix this, we use the Simulator as we would a real iPhone: tap the Settings button (or use the home button to switch out of the app and launch the Settings app, and then go into the Twitter settings). In Settings, configure a Twitter account with name and password and tap the Sign In button. Once done, double-tap home and switch back to PRPFirstProjectTweeter. This time when you tap the button, the Tweet composer should come up, as seen in Figure 15, *Sending a tweet with SLComposeViewController*, on page 24. Edit the text if desired and then click Send. Go visit your Twitter page on the Web with a browser—for style points, go ahead and use Safari in the Simulator—to see your brand-new tweet, posted for all the world to enjoy and admire.

Figure 15—Sending a tweet with **SLComposeViewController**

1.5 Tweet, Sweet Success

In this chapter, we've gotten our first project built, launched, and sending data to the Internet. We downloaded and installed Xcode, created a view-based project, and started customizing it. We customized the user interface, connected a UIButton in the View's nib file to a method in our PRPViewController class, and implemented that method to show iOS 6's default tweet-composer UI (though we did have to work through a small build issue in order to use the Social framework). When it was all done, with just a little bit of code and UI tweaking, we ended up with an app that sends tweets. Not bad for one chapter's work.

Now that we've had our first experience with the tools that the SDK gives us, we're going to use the next chapter to learn more about the Objective-C language that iOS uses for its high-level frameworks, and in the process we'll make our app more interesting and more functional.

For Further Thought

Here are a few things to think about or try out to expand your understanding of the stuff we've covered in this chapter. The questions don't necessarily have "correct" answers. Please join us on the forums at http://forums.pragprog.com/ to discuss your ideas about them.

1. In PRPViewController.xib, try changing the font, color, and size of the button by using the Attribute and Size inspectors.

2. Cut the action connection from the button to the handleTweetButtonTapped:, and then reconnect it with the various techniques described in *Interface Builder Connections*, on page 11. Do you like some techniques more or less than others?

3. Cut the action connection and then replace the IBAction return type with void, like this:

   ```
   -(void) handleTweetButtonTapped: (id) sender {
   ```

   Notice that it's no longer possible to connect the button's Touch Up Inside event to the method. Why not?

4. Add a second button to post to your Facebook account (if you have one). You'll probably want to connect the button to a new action method (perhapshandleFacebookButtonTapped:), in which you'll need to use the SLService-TypeFacebook when creating the SLComposeViewController.

CHAPTER 2

Programming for iOS

In a single chapter, we've learned enough about the iOS SDK to write a simple app that can send tweets on our behalf to the Internet. Still, we did have to take it on faith that the code we used to create the SLComposeViewController would do what we needed it to. Now that we've gained some familiarity with our tools, it's time to do the same with the language and libraries.

In this chapter, we're going to look at the fundamentals of coding an iOS app: programming with Objective-C and calling the default frameworks, UIKit and Foundation. As we go, we'll make a series of enhancements to our Twitter app. We'll add the ability to see our twitter.com page, internationalize the app for other languages and locales, and see how the language and tools work together to make us more productive.

Staged Projects

As we build our sample projects in this book, we will often write simple code, only to rewrite it with more ambitious code later as our knowledge increases.

All the different versions would be hard to put in one source file. So in the downloadable book code, we often have multiple copies of each project, each representing a different stage of its development. The different stages use numbered folders, like PRPFirstProjectTweeter01, PRPFirstProjectTweeter02, and so on. These folder names also appear in the captions for each code example in the text.

2.1 Introducing Objective-C

So what is Objective-C and why are we using it? The Objective-C programming language is an extension to the C language, providing object orientation and other higher-level programming concepts. Objective-C still relies on C for basic things like flow control (while, break, return, and the like) and basic mathematical and logical operators (such as +, sin(), and |). For readers not familiar with C, we've provided a brief catch-up in Appendix 1, *Wait! I Forgot (or Never Learned) C!*, on page 259.

The difference is that C isn't object-oriented: it has no concept of classes and objects, nor of methods called on those objects. That's what Objective-C provides. Objective-C is a highly pragmatic language, productive for developers while still offering the performance of compiled CPU-native code, something proven out by its use in Apple's Mac and iOS frameworks (to say nothing of the hundreds of thousands of apps on the App Store).

As with C, Objective-C classes typically use a header file and an implementation file. The header presents the publicly accessible parts of the class, like methods and properties. We use the @interface in the header file to declare the class and its inheritance. For the PRPViewController, we use the colon character (:) to declare it as a subclass of UIViewController.

```
@interface PRPViewController : UIViewController
```

The other class that Xcode provided for our project is PRPAppDelegate. While we'll discuss its responsibilities later, note that it has a different declaration:

```
@interface PRPAppDelegate : UIResponder <UIApplicationDelegate>
```

This means that the class is a subclass of UIResponder, but it also implements the UIApplicationDelegate protocol. A *protocol* is a named collection of methods that classes may implement, similar to Java's interface. In this case, it means PRPAppDelegate handles callback methods related to the life cycle of the application and its interaction with the system. By default, protocol methods are optional, but they can be made mandatory, which means that a class will have to implement those methods if its @interface declares that it implements the protocol.

2.2 Methods and Messaging

In the previous chapter, we handled the tap on our button using Interface Builder (the visual GUI builder mode) to connect the button's Touch Up Inside event to a method in the file PRPViewController.m. The method has the following signature:

```
-(IBAction) handleTweetButtonTapped: (id) sender;
```

Let's break this down into parts:

- The - character identifies this as an instance method called on a specific object instance. To create a class method, which applies to the class as a whole instead of to an instance, we would use +.

- The parentheses indicate the return type of the method. IBAction is something of a special case: while it is technically equivalent to C's void, meaning the method doesn't return anything, we use it to indicate that the method can receive connections in Interface Builder.

- handleTweetButtonTapped: is the name of the method. This method takes one parameter, as indicated by the colon (:) character. A method that takes no parameters does not use the colon, while one that takes multiple parameters names each parameter and adds a colon. For example, we could have handleTweetButtonTapped:event: for a method call that provides more information about the touch event that prompted the call. Written in this format, with just the method and parameter names but not the return or parameter types, we have a *selector*, a string that uniquely identifies one method. Selectors will be important later when we need to treat the method itself as an object.

- (id) sender is the single parameter to our method. The parentheses declares the type, while sender is the parameter name. The id type is the root of all Objective-C objects and is in fact just a C typedef. As a result, all Objective-C objects are C pointers to this id type. Usually, we'll use more specific types than this, but in the case of an event handler, the sender could be anything, so this parameter is very loosely typed.

We call these "methods" out of habit, but Objective-C is actually doing something more interesting under the covers. Technically, method calls are actually messages sent between objects by Obj-C's lightweight runtime environment. This gives Obj-C the flexibility of many scripting languages, because it's possible to construct messages at runtime and send them to objects; we don't *have* to resolve everything at compile time. Another advantage of Obj-C messaging is that a message sent to a nil object quietly does nothing, whereas in languages like Java, calling a method on a null object raises a runtime exception. This spares us from having to test an object for nil before calling a method on it; if the object *is* nil, nothing bad will come of sending it a message. Deliberately setting objects to nil is a common idiom among Objective-C programmers for saying "I'm done with this thing and I don't want to think about it anymore," and many converts from other languages find it a relief to not always have test objects for non-null.

Let's look back in the method body to see how we called methods.

```
if ([SLComposeViewController isAvailableForServiceType: SLServiceTypeTwitter]) {
```

We started with a class method call, [SLComposeViewController isAvailableForServiceType: SLServiceTypeTwitter], to verify that the Social framework will even let us send a tweet (it could be prohibited by parental controls or other limitations). If so, we continue with our tweet composition. The square braces indicate that we're sending an Obj-C message, with the SLComposeViewController class as the target that receives the message and isAvailableForServiceType as the selector that defines the message which takes the constant SLServiceTypeTwitter as its parameter.

2.3   Memory Management

Knowing that we can send a tweet, we then create an instance of SLCompose-ViewController:

```
SLComposeViewController *tweetVC =
[SLComposeViewController composeViewControllerForServiceType:
  SLServiceTypeTwitter];
```

The SLComposeViewController class uses a convenience "factory"-style method to generate new instances. This is actually somewhat atypical: normally we have to use a two-step process called "alloc and init." For example, back in iOS 5, the Twitter-only TWTweetComposeViewController would be created like this:

```
TWTweetComposeViewController *tweetVC =
  [[TWTweetComposeViewController alloc] init];
```

This is the recipe we usually use for creating objects. First, we call the alloc on the class we want an instance of. This method allocates memory for the object and returns a pointer to it as an id. However, the object is not ready to use until we call the instance method init. Classes override init to set up their initial state. Some classes will define additional initialization methods that take arguments, like GUI classes that offer an initWithFrame: to initialize a view and set up its initial location and size. When a class has several initializers, it is common to refer to the one that takes the most arguments as the *designated initializer* and to implement other initializers as just calling the designated initializer with default values.

At any rate, by convention, an object is ready to use once it has been alloc'ed and init'ed. And in the case of SLComposeViewController, the entire process is hidden behind the factory method composeViewControllerForServiceType, which could (and, in fact, *does*) return instances of service-specific subclasses of SLComposeView-Controller.

So, we've created our object, but when do we get rid of it? C programmers will recall that the hardest part of malloc()'ing some memory is knowing when to free() it. Many modern languages use garbage collection, which requires the runtime to figure out which objects are no longer needed and can be freed.

That liberates the developer from worrying about memory at the expense of CPU time (to perform the garbage collection) and predictability (in that we can't predict when GC will run or how many cycles it will take away from the app's primary functionality).

Instead, Objective-C uses a system of reference counting to manage memory. Each object has a reference count associated with it. When an object is alloc'ed, the count is set at 1. Any other object that uses this object and wants to keep it from being freed can call retain to increase the count by 1. We may also copy an object to get a new object, copied from the original, with a reference count of 1. When we're done with an object, we can call release to decrease the count by 1, and when the count reaches 0, the object is freed from memory.

Having said that, our code from the last chapter never releases the SLCompose-ViewController or any other objects. So, does this mean we're just leaking memory, allocating objects that are never freed? Fortunately, we're not this foolish.

Automatic Reference Counting

Starting in iOS 5, the iOS SDK introduced automatic reference counting (ARC), which liberated us from the manual retain/release cycle that was previously required. Simply put, ARC figures out where all the retain and release calls should go and silently adds them as part of the compile.

ARC figures out memory management by turning what had been conventions for method naming into enforceable rules. For example, methods with alloc, copy, or new are assumed to return objects that must be memory managed; other methods don't. One curious side effect of this is that we can't use new in the name of a variable (like newName), since new as a method name is a little-used synonym for a combined alloc and init, and this confuses ARC.

ARC is enabled by default for new projects and is backward-compatible all the way back to iOS 4.3. So the only reason to turn it off and go back to manual memory management would be if we needed to run with an earlier version of iOS. In this book, we will *always* leave ARC on.

This isn't the end of the ARC story—we will have more work to do when we venture out of Objective-C and call the SDK's lower-level C APIs—but it's enough to assuage our concerns as we get rolling.

2.4 Managing an Object's Properties

Now that we've gone back and figured out how our object allocation and method calls work in the last chapter's code, let's put this knowledge to work and add some new functionality to the app. Our original app lets us send a tweet, but there's no way to tell if we were successful. We'll gradually improve that throughout this chapter and the next. For starters, let's use iOS's built-in web browser to bring up our Twitter page inside the app.

Select PRPViewController.xib to bring it up in Interface Builder. We're going to add a "reload" button at the top and a web view to fill up most of the bottom of our view. Using the Object library (^⌥⌘3) at the bottom right, drag a new button under the existing one, and give it the title "Show my tweets." Then drag out a web view—its icon in the Object library resembles the Safari app icon—and put it on the bottom portion of the view, using the resize handles to drag it out to the margins. The completed view should look like Figure 16, *Adding a UIWebView to View*, on page 32.

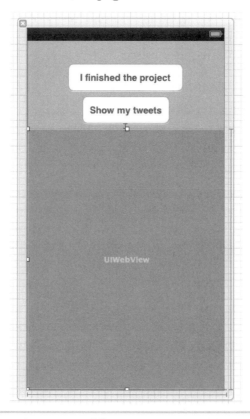

Figure 16—Adding a UIWebView to View

For this to work, we need to write another event-handler method, one that handles a tap on "Show my tweets." That method will need to load the user's Twitter page in the web view. But wait: How do we make a call from this event-handler into the web view we just created in the nib?

In the last chapter, we talked about outlets, which are used to connect variables in our code to objects in the nib. Preceding a variable with the IBOutlet modifier tells Interface Builder that a variable can serve as an outlet. So that begs the question of how to declare variables in Objective-C. The traditional way is to declare instance variables in the header file in between curly braces that immediately follow the @interface declaration, like this:

```
@interface PRPViewController : UIViewController {
        IBOutlet UIWebView *twitterWebView;
}
```

But *don't* write that. We won't be using instance variables in this book because Objective-C gives us something better: properties.

In Objective-C, properties are a combination of an instance variable, getter and setter methods to access it, and declared conventions for threading and memory management. That's potentially a lot of boilerplate code to write, but fortunately, the compiler will do it for us. Let's begin by adding a property declaration to PRPViewController.h. This goes anywhere between the @interface and @end:

Programming/PRPFirstProjectTweeter02/PRPFirstProjectTweeter/PRPViewController.h
```
@property (nonatomic, strong) IBOutlet UIWebView *twitterWebView;
```

The end of this line is just like the instance variable: it declares class UIWebView (with the IBOutlet modifier that lets us connect to it with Interface Builder) and the name twitterWebView. To the left of that, we use the compiler directive @property, along with attributes for the property in parentheses: (nonatomic, strong). These attributes define how the property can be used. The possible attributes address three concerns:

Access Properties are either readwrite (the default) or readonly.

Threading Properties are either atomic (the default, which doesn't have an actual keyword), meaning they can only be accessed by one thread at a time, or nonatomic, which can be faster because the code won't have to test for thread safety. For any UIKit property, we can always set nonatomic, because UIKit methods and properties should only ever be accessed from the main thread, the one that started the app. With that convention, there's no point enforcing thread safety in the property: there should never be two threads attempting to set the property, since main is the only one that should access it at all.

Memory Management If a property is an Objective-C object (as opposed to a C type), the property declaration indicates how it should be memory managed. The default is assign, which means that the property is just a pointer and does not participate in memory management. Often, we want to use retain, increasing the object's reference count by 1 when assigned, so that it is not released without our knowledge. Another option is copy, which is appropriate if the property could change on us. We often want to copy things like strings or arrays because they have mutable subclasses and we usually want to hold on to the value we received at assign-time, rather than a value that could change on us.

ARC adds two new memory-management attributes: strong and weak. We use these in cases where two objects have each other as properties, which could lead to a circular reference where neither object can be freed because each refers to the other. The strong property is an "owning" reference, meaning that it retains its object. weak is like assign in that it doesn't affect its object's retain count. However, when the object of a weak property is freed, the property becomes nil, making it safe to call methods on (unlike the assign property, where the reference becomes a dangerous dangling pointer). We prefer weak to assign in order to pick up the safety of these zeroing weak references, and we also prefer strong over the equivalent retain.

Once we declare the property, there are three ways to actually implement it in code:

- Create an instance variable and add appropriately named setter and getter methods. In this case, they would be twitterWebView for the getter and setTwitterWebView: for the setter.

- Use the @dynamic directive to turn off the compiler warning, and then provide implementations for the getter and setter methods through exotic runtime techniques like class introspection.

- Let the compiler do it for us by using the @synthesize directive.

Starting in Xcode 4.4, properties are automatically synthesized by default, so we don't need to do anything else to start using twitterWebView, unless we want to do something special (to know when we'd do that, see *Why Would I Ever Not Just @synthesize My Properties?*).

To access the property, we use dot notation, similar to a C struct. That means we can read the property with a call of the form object.property and set it with object.property = value.

Now that we've synthesized the twitterWebView property, we're ready to use it in our code. We'll write an event handler for "Show my tweets" that loads the user's Twitter page into the web view. The docs show us that UIWebView has a

Joe asks:

Why Would I Ever Not Just @synthesize My Properties?

There are two primary reasons for not using auto-@synthesize: either we want to do something special with the instance variable, or we're not able to provide it at compile-time. The latter is the rare @dynamic case. It's esoteric, so we won't be considering it further.

When we omit the @synthesize statement, Xcode provides it for us in this form:

@synthesize twitterWebView = _twitterWebView;

This means the instance variable is called _twitterWebView. The underscore helps us easily distinguish between the variable and its representation as a property, which is really just a getter method called twitterWebView and a setter called setTwitterWebView.

But why would we want access to the instance variable at all? If we want to override the getter or setter to provide side effects—such as updating the user interface when you set a different model object for it to display—then we would have to reassign the _twitterWebView instance variable ourselves in the override and then do our side-effect stuff. Using the instance variable directly can also be useful for lower-level APIs that need to access our data as C pointers.

Finally, if we needed our code to be buildable on Xcode 4.3 or earlier, we'd have to do our own @synthesize to support those older versions. However, in this book, we will always omit the @synthesize statement.

loadRequest: method that we can use, provided we use a string to create an NSURL and from that an NSURLRequest. So in PRPViewController.m we write the following method:

Programming/PRPFirstProjectTweeter02/PRPFirstProjectTweeter/PRPViewController.m

```
Line 1  -(IBAction) handleShowMyTweetsTapped: (id) sender {
     2      [self.twitterWebView loadRequest:
     3       [NSURLRequest requestWithURL:
     4        [NSURL URLWithString:@"http://www.twitter.com/pragprog"]]];
     5  }
```

On line 2, we use our property by calling self.twitterWebView. This gets the web view object and lets us call the loadRequest: method on it. The rest is just setting up a suitable NSURLRequest for the call; obviously, the yourtwittername in the URL string should be replaced by an actual Twitter handle.

For this to work, we need to make our connections in IB: from the web view to its IBOutlet and from the event to the IBAction. Switch to PRPViewController.xib, and control-click the "Show my tweets" button to show a HUD with the list of sent events. Connect Touch Up Inside to File's Owner, where another HUD allows us to select handleShowMyTweetsTapped: as the method to receive this event. Next, control-click File's Owner to show its outlets and drag a connection from the twitterWebView property to the web view in the UI, as shown in Figure 17, *Connecting the twitterWebView outlet*, on page 36. We could also make connections with the Connections inspector (⌥⌘6), but we will tend to use control-clicking and the HUDs they pop up.

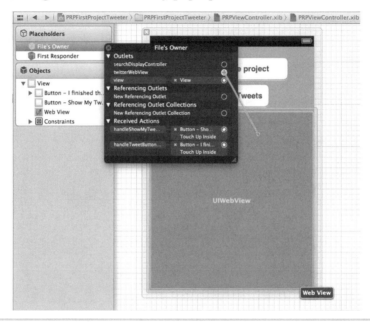

Figure 17—Connecting the twitterWebView outlet

Having made these connections, we're ready to go, so click the Run button to launch the updated app in the Simulator, and then click the "Show my tweets" button. The event sent by the new button goes to the handleShowMyTweetsTapped: method, and its code makes a reference to the self.twitterWebView property, which we just connected, to load up the Twitter page in the web view, as shown in Figure 18, *Programmatically populating a UIWebView*, on page 37. If it doesn't look like the figure, don't panic—we'll fix our user-interface layout in the next section.

2.5 Auto Layout and the iPhone 5

Hopefully, our UI looks good right now. We expect it to look like we laid it out in Interface Builder, but it may look like Figure 19, *PRPFirstProjectTweeter with bad layout*, on page 38, in which the top button has disappeared off the

Figure 18—Programmatically populating a UIWebView

top of the screen, and (although it's hard to tell) part of the web view has gone off the bottom. What happened here?

The seeds of this problem were planted when we first started the project. In IB, click View at the top of the Objects list and then visit the Attributes inspector (⌥⌘4). The first entry is "Simulated Metrics," which defaults to the value "Retina 4 Full Screen." This is the setting for the size of the view as shown in Interface Builder, and its default dimensions are those of the new iPhone 5: 320 points wide by 528 points tall (note that in iOS, sizes are measured in abstract points, which map 1:1 to actual pixels on older screens and 1:2 on Retina displays). The iPhone 5 is much taller than earlier iPhones

Figure 19—PRPFirstProjectTweeter with bad layout

and iPod Touches, so by designing our user interface for the iPhone 5 size, we've made it too tall for the older devices.

We can investigate this in the Simulator by using the menu command Hardware→Devices and choosing between "iPhone" (the non-Retina iPhone 3GS and earlier), "iPhone Retina (3.5-inch)" (the iPhone 4 and 4S), and "iPhone Retina (4-inch)" (the iPhone 5). Each time we change the device, we need to run the app again from Xcode, and we may need to use the Window→Scale menu to fit the Retina simulators onto our screen (keyboard shortcuts ⌘1, ⌘2, and ⌘3 scale to 100%, 75%, and 50%, respectively). The app looks right on the "iPhone Retina (4-inch)" and wrong on the others.

And this brings up a challenge for us: how can we design a user interface that looks good when the screen size can be different based on the device? We could reduce the damage by changing the simulated metrics to the 3.5-inch screen and fitting everything in that space. That would leave a big gap at the bottom of the 4-inch screen, but at least we wouldn't lose anything. We could even take this a step further and pretend to be an old app that was never updated for the iPhone 5, one that gets black bars inserted at the top and bottom of the 4-inch screen for a sort of "letterboxing" effect.

The way a project indicates that it's ready for iOS 5 is found in the target's Summary tab: there are three image wells here for "launch images" that show a "splash screen," or the initial layout of the app while iOS starts it up. If the launch image for "Retina (4-inch)" is missing, iOS assumes the app doesn't understand 4-inch layouts and letterboxes it. So we *could* just delete that image and pretend to be a pre–iPhone 5 app. But let's not chicken out on the iPhone 5. Let's make our app look good on 3.5-inch *and* 4-inch iPhones and iPod touches.

Using Auto Layout

Let's use iOS 6's new *Auto Layout* to describe how we want our user interface elements to be laid out and resized based on a runtime determination of the screen dimensions.

To use Auto Layout, we don't want to think in terms of exact coordinates but instead to define how we want the views and subviews laid out and resized. Auto Layout works with a system of constraints: we declare what rules must be followed and let Auto Layout figure out the rest.

Xcode figures out some of the constraints for us. If we moved the second button close enough to the first one to get the dashed guideline to show up, it assumes we want to maintain that distance between the buttons, creates a constraint that says "maintain this vertical distance between these buttons," and shows the constraint with a blue I-beam between the buttons. The Objects list also shows constraints with colored icons: purple for inferred constraints, which are created for us by IB as we drag and resize, and blue for user constraints, those that we've explicitly created.

Depending on the specific moves you've made to add, resize, and customize the buttons and web view, the inferred constraints may be enough to make Auto Layout work correctly for both screen sizes. It's going to be different for every reader. In the interests of making sure it always works, let's spell out exactly what we need. We want the following to be true:

- The buttons should maintain a constant distance from the top of the screen and from each other.

- The top of the web view should maintain a constant distance from the bottom of the second button and should stretch all the way to the bottom of the screen.

- The heights of the buttons should not change. The height of the web view *may* change (in fact, as the only element in the view with a variable height, it will have to).

Figure 20, *Inferred constraints in the Objects list*, on page 40, shows one possible set of inferred constraints for the current user interface (again, yours may be different).

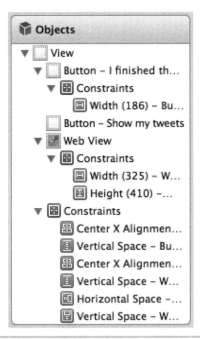

Figure 20—Inferred constraints in the Objects list

Notice that constraints are hierarchical: the main view has six inferred constraints, while the "Show my tweets" button has none. The button doesn't have any constraints of its own because its coordinates and size are implicit from other constraints. Click the button and visit its Size inspector (⌥⌘5, shown in Figure 21, *Inferred constraints in the Size inspector*, on page 41) to see all the constraints at all levels that determine its layout. You'll find it useful to keep an eye on both ways of showing the constraints.

Figure 21—Inferred constraints in the Size inspector

Creating User Constraints

Let's start by clicking on the top button, "I finished the project." This will show its current constraints in the Size inspector as well as show I-beams in the Interface Builder view for its spacing and sizing constraints. We need to keep this object a fixed distance from the top. If you dragged the button to the guideline (or if you do so now), there will already be a vertical space constraint, shown in the Size inspector as "Top Space to Superview Equals Default." But let's assume that we didn't get that constraint for free and that we want some nonstandard distance from the top. At the bottom right of the Interface Builder area, there's a capsule-shaped set of buttons that pop up Auto Layout menus. The middle segment is the *Pin menu*, which gives us the ability to set fixed distances in our UI (in other words, to "pin" edges of our views to one another). From this menu, select the "Top Space to Superview" item, shown in Figure 22, *Creating a vertical spacing constraint with the Pin menu*, on page 42.

This creates a new user constraint, shown with a blue icon and labeled in the Size inspector as "Top Space to Superview Equals 36" (or some other value). It also appears in IB as a new I-beam from the top of the button to the top of the view and is thicker than the I-beams that represent the inferred constraints.

Creating this user constraint also turns some of the other inferred constraints into user constraints, indicated by the icon's color change from purple to blue. The difference is important because user constraints take priority over inferred constraints when Auto Layout tries to figure things out at runtime. For this reason, we can turn an inferred constraint into a user constraint. For example, if we'd set the top button at the guideline and picked up an inferred constraint, we could use the gear menu in the Size inspector to turn

Figure 22—Creating a vertical spacing constraint with the Pin menu

that into a user constraint, which would make it a higher priority and prevent it from being changed by editing other constraints.

Setting the button's distance to the top of the screen was our first requirement. Next we need to attend to the second button. We said earlier that we wanted to keep this a constant distance from the top of the screen, but really we want it to have a constant distance from the first button. Since the top button is now pinned to the top of the view, that constraint height *plus* the first button's height *plus* the height of a gap between the two will equal the proper y-coordinate for the second button (and if Apple ever changes default button heights, it will adapt gracefully). If we used the guidelines when adding the second button, then this distance already exists as a constraint. If not, shift-click to select both buttons, and use the Pin menu's Vertical Spacing to create a new user constraint. The same goes for the space between the second button and the web view: if we used the guidelines, then a vertical spacing constraint already exists; otherwise, shift-click them and create one now.

Now we just need to deal with the web view. Dragging its handles to the bottom of the screen may already have created a constraint. If not, select it and use the Pin menu's "Bottom Space to Superview."

There's one more possible problem at this point. Select the web view and bring up its Size inspector. Look at its constraints. Because we resized it, there may be a height constraint that says "Height equals 420" (or some other value). This is going to be a problem because we said that we needed the web view's height to vary based on whether we're on a 3.5-inch screen or a 4-inch one. If we fix the height, then Auto Layout will get in trouble: between the fixed heights of our vertical spacing and the web view, nothing can give when we find ourselves on a 3.5-inch screen. If this happens, Auto Layout will let us know by way of a log message printed to the Console area, like this:

```
2012-09-17 10:06:26.150 PRPFirstProjectTweeter[2641:c07] Unable to
simultaneously satisfy constraints.
    Probably at least one of the constraints in the following list is one
you don't want. Try this: (1) look at each constraint and try to figure out
which you don't expect; (2) find the code that added the unwanted constraint
or constraints and fix it. (Note: If you're seeing
NSAutoresizingMaskLayoutConstraints that you don't understand, refer to the
documentation for the UIView property translatesAutoresizingMaskIntoConstraints)
```

And after a list of NSAutoresizingMaskLayoutConstraint and NSLayoutConstraints, there will be a message that Auto Layout will attempt to recover by breaking constraint with one of the constraints in the list. Auto Layout may also have to use nonstandard sizes for some elements, such as crushing the height of the buttons down to 0. And yes, that looks as bad as it sounds.

Something's got to give. Fortunately, it's an easy choice: we don't *want* the web view to have a fixed size. We want it to vary based on the other constraints. So, select the web view, go to its Size inspector, find the Height constraint, and use the gear menu to delete it.

Now that we've provided a set of vertical layout constraints that can be attained on both a 3.5-inch and a 4-inch device, our UI will work in either form factor. Try running it, and use the Simulator's Hardware→Device menu to switch between the two Retina sizes. Figure 23, *Using Auto Layout on 4-inch (left) and 3.5-inch (right) Retina simulators*, on page 44, shows our app in the Simulator running on both sizes, stretching or shrinking the web view as appropriate.

Also notice that the Simulator removes the simulated iPhone frame for certain device and scale combinations so that the contents can fit on the desktop screen.

Our takeaway here is that when we lay out our user interfaces we need to take into account the extra pixels afforded by the iPhone 5 (or, looking at it from a future point of view when the iPhone 5 is ubiquitous, the loss of pixels when running on older devices). We can do this by thinking about what parts of our UI can expand and contract vertically—empty spaces and stretchable elements like web views, images, and text views are good candidates—then codifying our layout as a set of constraints. Interface Builder will help build

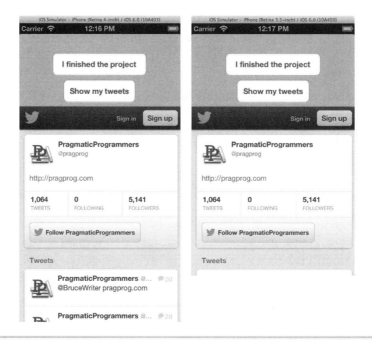

Figure 23—Using Auto Layout on 4-inch (left) and 3.5-inch (right) Retina simulators

constraints as we resize and drag our UI elements around, but it's ultimately up to us to make sure the layout logic holds up.

2.6 The iOS Programming Stack

Now we're rolling: we can visually create automatically-resizing GUIs in nib files, connect them to methods and properties in the view controller class that owns the view, and write code in Objective-C to do stuff. Life is good.

Except that we're still taking a lot on faith when it comes to actually calling stuff in our code. We can search the documentation for cool-looking methods all day, but maybe we should make sure we understand where all these classes are coming from and how they're organized first.

The iOS SDK divides its functionality into a set of frameworks. We saw this in the last chapter when we inspected the project's build phases and added Social.framework to the frameworks that were already part of the project. Conceptually, we can divide the SDK's frameworks into four layers:

Cocoa Touch Layer The top-level abstractions over applications and their UIs (UIKit) and integration with system-provided features like mapping (MapKit) and Game Center (GameKit).

Media Layer Graphics, sound, and video frameworks.

Core Services Frameworks for essential, non-UI functionality, like file-system access, in-app purchase (StoreKit), motion- and orientation-sensing (CoreMotion), and so on.

Core OS Low-level frameworks and libraries needed by the upper layers, including the BSD libraries that are the core of iOS and Mac OS X.

In this book, we will spend most of our time working with the frameworks that are included by default in the Xcode project templates: Foundation and UIKit.

2.7 Building Views with UIKit

The UIKit framework provides the building blocks of touch-based applications for iOS. That means it's responsible both for the concept of what an app *is* and how it interacts with the rest of the system, as well as for providing a suite of user-interface views.

The UIApplication class is the point of contact between our code and the rest of the system. By accessing its sharedApplication object, we can open other apps by URL, receive remote events from Apple's Push Notification service, and set a number for our app icon's badge. But a lot of apps don't do any of these things, so we don't often use UIApplication directly. Instead, the Xcode template sets up a UIApplicationDelegate class for us to customize; this class gets callbacks when common events occur, like the app being started up or opened via URL from another app or when it's sent to the background by the user tapping the home button.

The delegate pattern is frequently used in the iOS SDK, often as an alternative to subclassing. The idea is that for certain responsibilities, usually the custom behaviors specific to an app, an object can delegate its behaviors to another object. In this case, the UIApplication class handles the activities that are common to all applications, but for cases where different apps will want to do different things, it makes callbacks to our PRPAppDelegate. Delegates don't need to be their own classes like this: they are often classes with other purposes that just implement one or two methods (usually collected as a protocol) in order to serve as a delegate.

Views

Many of the UIKit classes are views, which are the onscreen touch objects in our user interface. We've been using these in our Twitter example: our UI has a single view that fills the screen and has three subviews: two buttons and the web view. There are many other view classes available, like switches, tables, sliders, and so on.

The top-level UIView defines the common functionality of all views. All views have visual properties, such as a backgroundColor, an alpha variable, and hidden and opaque flags. As we've already seen, a view can contain other views (which are accessible via a subviews property and can be added with convenience methods like insertSubview:atIndex:), and it can access whatever view it's a subview of via the superview property. Subviews are layered on top of one another by drawing them in the order of the subviews array, with the view at index 0 at the bottom, then index 1 on top of it, and so on.

Views also have frame and bounds properties that indicate their size and location. Each of these properties is a CGRect, a C struct that defines an *x-y* origin (of type CGPoint) and a width-by-height size (of type CGSize). The difference is that the bounds values are in the view's own coordinate system, while the frame is in its superview's coordinate system. Setting either property changes the other as needed, and these interact with two related visual properties, transform and center.

 Joe asks:
When Am I Going to Want to Subclass UIView?

Short answer: sometime between next year and *never*.

It's not like UIView resists subclassing. Far from it: just implement drawRect: (probably via the Core Graphics framework) to draw the view, maybe handle the inherited UIResponder methods to deal with touch events (or use the much handier UIGestureRecognizer APIs), and we'd have a perfectly good custom view.

However, this isn't something we often need to do. We only have to create a custom view when we want to provide an interface that's profoundly different from what's already in UIKit. And this gets at a larger truth: whereas some other platforms are customized through subclassing, UIKit and most of the rest of the iOS SDK is meant to be used as-is. Classes expose common points of customization through techniques like settable properties and callbacks to delegate methods. We don't have to subclass UIButton; we set its title and appearance properties and provide methods to handle taps on it.

There are cases where subclassing is the go-to technique, such as the custom UIViewControllers that manage the behavior of one screen of our app. But when presented with an arbitrary class, plan on using what it exposes before committing to writing a subclass.

Along with views, UIKit provides the UIViewController class, which is meant as the place where we put the logic for our user interfaces. The view controller also has a number of life-cycle callbacks, telling it when its view is loaded from the nib and when the view will appear or disappear as a result of navigating to different parts of the app. We will look more at this relationship in Chapter 4, *View Controllers*, on page 77.

Finally, UIKit provides classes for objects that are commonly needed by user interfaces, such as UIFont and UIImage. Taken together, the UIKit classes provide an extensive and extensible user interface toolkit.

Accessibility in UIKit

UIKit offers deep support for accessibility, the ability of a user interface to adapt to a user's needs, such as limitations in vision, hearing, and touch. Every UIView has accessibilityLabel and accessibilityHint attributes, along with accessibililtyTraits that describe the view's behavior, that the system can use to better expose it to users who need help. For example, blind users can turn on the Voice Over feature to have the iOS speech synthesizer speak the names of UI elements, using the provided accessibility values if they have been set. These attributes can all be customized in Interface Builder or in code.

Many developers don't customize their UIs for accessibility and actually don't need to: the default behavior of iOS makes typical UIKit applications highly accessible. But it's good karma—and a legal requirement in some cases—to test the accessibility of our apps and customize accessibility properties as necessary.

2.8 Using the Foundation Classes

But it can't all be about the visuals, can it? Somehow we have to get the heavy lifting of our apps done. For common programming needs, the iOS SDK provides Foundation, a framework in the Core Services layer that offers common functionality that nearly all apps will use.

We've used a little bit of Foundation without specifically #import-ing it, since Foundation is itself imported by UIKit (recall that Foundation.framework was among the linked frameworks when we looked at the build phases in *Projects, Targets, and Schemes*, on page 21). We used Foundation's string class, NSString, both in our NSLog() statement and in composing the default tweet.

Strings

NSString is a proper Obj-C class that offers many advantages over plain C strings: an NSString has a declared encoding and has deep support for Unicode glyphs. NSString is also used for file-system paths—there is no NSFile—so the class has methods for composing and parsing out path segments.

We can create a static NSString with the @"" syntax, as in @"foo". The @ character distinguishes it from the plain C string, which is just a character array and not an object. We can also create complex strings via string formatters, in which we provide a "format string" with replacement identifiers like %d and %@, followed by a list of arguments to fill in these values. For example, we could call the following:

```
NSString *myString = [[NSString alloc]
  initWithFormat: @"My name is %@. I have written %d apps.",
    @"Chris", 2];
```

The result of this is that myString is My name is Chris. I have written 2 apps. The %@ is the replacement identifier for Objective-C objects; the value that is inserted is whatever is returned from the object's description, which for an NSString like @"Chris" is the string itself.

Collections

Another essential feature of programming frameworks is collections. In Foundation, the essential collections are NSArray and NSDictionary. The NSArray is an Objective-C class that provides the typical services of an array: keeping objects in order, providing a count of its objects, testing to see if an object is in the array (containsObject:), returning a sorted copy of its contents, and so on.

The NSDictionary offers key-value mapping. If we use NSStrings for the keys, then we can retrieve values with valueForKey:, and for other kinds of keys we use objectForKey:.

Members of collections must be Objective-C objects. Foundation provides classes to wrap C primitives as objects, such as NSNumber for numeric types, NSData for byte buffers, and NSValue for any value, even a pointer. An NSNull object is also available to represent the absence of a value, since nil can't be added to the collections.

We can create collections programmatically with methods like NSAarray's initWithObjects: and NSDictionary's initWithObjects:forKeys:. For iOS 6, Xcode 4.5 supports a literal syntax that offers a more expedient way to create arrays and collections. To create an array, we can just enclose its members in square braces and precede them with the @ symbol (similar to the way we use @ for NSString literals). That means we can create an array of strings like this:

```
NSArray *appNames = @[@"Foto Brisko", @"Road Tip", @"BounceIt"];
```

For an NSDictionary, we use a colon to separate each key from its value, use commas to separate the name-value pairs, and wrap the whole thing in curly braces preceded by the @. For an NSDictionary that maps app names to their prices (as NSNumbers), we could write the following:

```
NSDictionary *appPrices = @ {
  @"Foto Brisko": @2.99,
  @"Road Tip" : @2.99,
  @"BounceIt" : @0.99
};
```

Notice how the @ symbols on the values create NSNumber objects suitable for the collection. Without that character, these would be C floats that couldn't be used as NSDictionary values.

The base NSArray, NSDictionary, and NSString classes are immutable: once set, their contents cannot be changed. All of them have mutable subclasses: NSMutableArray, NSMutableDictionary, and NSMutableString. The existence of the mutable subclasses is why we sometimes want to use copy on properties in our classes. If we had an NSString property, it would be legal to set it with an NSMutableString value, and unbeknownst to our code, the value of the string could change after it was assigned. To get the NSString to behave as a normal, immutable string, we copy it into a plain NSString at assign-time.

Joe asks:
What's the Difference Between initWithFormat: and stringWithFormat:?

In many cases, Foundation classes have a class method that duplicates an alloc/init pair. For example, instead of writing [[NSString alloc] initWithFormat:@"..."], we can write [NSString stringWithFormat:@"..."].

The difference is that objects created with the class method are *autoreleased*, meaning they go into a pool of objects that gets released at some point in the future, usually at the bottom of the main run loop.

Before ARC, autoreleasing was a big deal because a method that created an object on behalf of a caller needed to use autoreleasing; it couldn't release the object before returning or else the object would be freed from memory before the caller even got it. But the method usually was in no position to "own" the object or know when to release it either. Autoreleasing solved these kinds of problems.

Thankfully, with ARC, this kind of memory management head scratching goes away, and there isn't a reason to prefer or avoid the class constructors. We use them a lot because they save a little typing—that's all.

We've talked a lot about the potential uses of the UIKit and Foundation frameworks and spent some time away from the code. Let's pull together some of their combined strengths to improve our app.

2.9 Internationalization

Both Foundation and UIKit do their part to support internationalization, the ability of code to adapt to local conventions in different parts of the world. These concerns include things like language, time and date formatting, and currency symbols and separators. If we properly adopt internationalization—hereafter abbreviated as i18n for the first and last letters of the word and the 18 in between—then our Twitter-sender will be as useful to a French-speaking user as an English one. We'll wrap up this chapter by doing exactly that.

Let's identify what parts of our app are currently English-only. When the UI appears, there are two buttons in English, and when the user taps the first button, we fill in the tweet composer with an English message. Both of those need to change.

When we internationalize an app, we create a *localization* for each *locale* we want to support. The locale is a combination of language and geographic region (which lets us distinguish between, say, the variants of Portuguese spoken in Brazil and Portugal), though we can omit the region and focus only on language issues. The localization is a collection of strings, currency formats, graphics, sounds, and other resources that are specific to one locale.

Starting in Xcode 4.4, we declare supported localizations at the project level. Choose the PRPFirstProjectTweeter from the top of the file navigator, and to its right, the PRPFirstProjectTweeter project (as opposed to the target of the same name). Click the Info tab to show the project's current localizations. This should show that for your default language two files are currently localized. Press the plus (+) button at the bottom of this section to show a list of common locales and choose one. For our screenshots, we'll use French (locale fr)—choose any language you're familiar with. If you don't know another language, one useful technique is to use a made-up language like pig latin or Ubbi Dubbi. Either way, we'll be able to find text that needs internationalization by switching the runtime language and looking to see that all the onscreen text changes.

Once we've picked a language, a sheet slides out showing the files in the project that are internationalizable—currently PRPViewController.xib and Info-Plist.strings—and asks for a "reference language" for each. The only choice is your current language (English for us), so just click "Finish." This adds French to the list of project localizations, as shown in Figure 24, *Multiple localizations for an Xcode project*, on page 51.

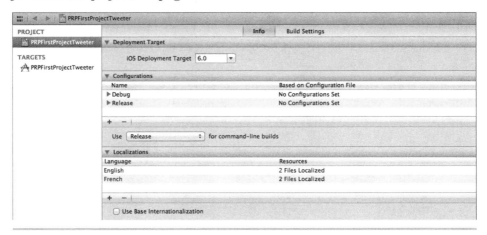

Figure 24—Multiple localizations for an Xcode project

Once a language has been added to the list of localizations, nib files in the project navigator become containers with disclosure triangles, as seen in Figure 25, *Multiple localizations for a nib file*, on page 51. The new localization of a given nib is a copy of the default language nib, which means it's a good idea to finalize the UI before localizing so we don't have to make UI changes across multiple localized nibs. Now that we have a French version of the nib, PRPViewController.xib (French), select it and change the labels of the buttons. For French, "I finished the project" becomes "J'ai fini le projet," and "Show my tweets" becomes "Voir mes Tweets."

Figure 25—Multiple localizations for a nib file

That internationalizes our user interface...almost. When the user composes a tweet, we still set up the tweet composer with an English string. That's something we do in code, with an NSString. So we need a way to i18n that too.

Like UIKit, Foundation is also i18n-aware and has functions and methods for dealing with locale-specific data. One of the simplest options is to use NSLocalizedString(), a macro that behaves like a C function and which retrieves

> ### Joe asks:
> ## Could I Create My User Interface in Code?
>
> It's possible to create a UI programmatically by instantiating all the UIView, UIButton, and other view objects with alloc/init calls, customizing them by setting properties or calling methods, and adding them as subviews. There's nothing that Interface Builder can do that can't also be done in code.
>
> However, Apple strongly recommends against building UIs in code, and internationalizing a UI is one of the best arguments for using nibs. If a given language doesn't lay out cleanly, maybe because its text tends to be wider or narrower than the default language or because the localization prefers a different reading direction, like right to left, this can be addressed by just resizing components or laying them out differently. Reworking the UI doesn't change the connections to the code and therefore doesn't change behavior.

a localized equivalent for a given string. It takes two arguments: a key to look up the localized string and a comment that we don't need. So we will rewrite the line in handleTweetButtonTapped, where we set the initial text of the tweetVC like this:

Programming/PRPFirstProjectTweeter03/PRPFirstProjectTweeter/PRPViewController.m

```
[tweetVC setInitialText: NSLocalizedString (
  @"I just finished the first project in iOS SDK Development. #pragsios",
  nil)];
```

All we've done is wrap the string we were already using with a call to NSLocalizedString(). The convention in Foundation is that we use our default language value as the key when looking up localizations. If we fail to find a localized equivalent, we'll fall back to this string. This makes for an easy i18n recipe: anytime we're about to write a hard-coded string that the user will see, we write NSLocalizedString (hard-coded-string, nil) instead—the worst that can happen if we do nothing else to internationalize is that we'll see our original hard-coded string.

Now we need to provide a lookup table of string values for our localization. We do this with a strings file. In the project file, click the Supporting Files group and use the menu command File→New→File... (⌘N). In the dialog, choose the Resource group and select Strings File. When prompted for a file name, we *must* use the name Localizable.strings for Foundation to find our localizations.

This creates a Localizable.strings file for our default language, which we don't actually need localizations for. What we need to do now is to add a French localization to the strings file. Select Localizable.strings, bring up the File inspector (⌥⌘1), and in the Localization section, click the Make Localized button. This slides in a sheet asking, "Do you want to localize this file?" and offering a pop-up menu of languages. The file, in its current form, will be moved to the selected language's "lproj folder," meaning that we are declaring the current language for this file, to which we will then add further localizations. Choose English and click OK. This alone only gives us an English localization of Localizable.strings, but the Make Localized button is now replaced by check boxes for all the localizations defined in the project. Click French to add the French localization.

As with the nib, the strings file will now have a disclosure triangle that exposes English and French versions of the file. Edit the French version as follows, with the English string in quotes, an equals sign, a French equivalent, and a semicolon. We've added a line break to suit the book's formatting; this isn't necessary for the file to work.

Programming/PRPFirstProjectTweeter03/PRPFirstProjectTweeter/fr.lproj/Localizable.strings
```
"I just finished the first project in iOS SDK Development. #pragsios" =
"Je viens de terminer le premier projet en iOS SDK Development. #pragsios";
```

Let's try this out. Using the Simulator, visit the Settings application and switch languages by navigating through General→International→Language and then choosing "Français." Go back to Xcode and run the app in the Simulator. When the app comes up, the buttons will now be in French. Tap "J'ai fini le projet" and the tweet composer will appear, prepopulated with French text, as seen in Figure 26, *Localized programmatic text*, on page 54. Notice that all the elements provided by UIKit are automatically localized as well: the Cancel and Send buttons become the "Annuler" and "Envoyer buttons," respectively.

Going forward, we are not going to take the time to localize all of our example apps. However, we will use NSLocalizedString() anywhere that we're hard-coding a user-visible string, because that's all it takes to internationalize the string and it's easy to provide a given localization later on: just create a Localizable.strings file.

2.10 Wrap-Up

In the first chapter, we had to take a lot on faith about Objective-C and the iOS frameworks in order to get started with the tools. In this chapter, we've dug deeply into the language and libraries, revealing how they work and why. We started by demystifying the square braces and other idiosyncrasies of Obj-C, including how it manages memory and why ARC takes away most of

Figure 26—Localized programmatic text

our need to worry about it. Then we looked at the two most important frameworks in the iOS SDK, UIKit and Foundation, and got comfortable with views and collections, both of which we'll be using frequently from here on out. Finally, we brought the power of UIKit and Foundation to bear on a cross-cutting concern, internationalization, using UIKit's nib-loading ability to bring up a locale-appropriate GUI and Foundation's localized string support to let us call up i18n'ed strings at runtime.

Now we have some newfound confidence in how to write code, but in the new multicore era, there are important considerations about *how* and *when* it runs. In the next chapter, we'll look at how iOS lets us write blocks of code that can run at arbitrary times or even at the same time.

For Further Thought

Here are a few things to think about or try out to expand your understanding of the stuff we've covered in this chapter. The questions don't necessarily have "correct" answers. Please join us on the forums at http://forums.pragprog.com/ to discuss your ideas about them.

1. What's an easy way to tell the difference between a C function call and an Objective-C method invocation?

2. Figure out the various subclasses returned by [SLComposeViewController composeViewControllerForServiceType:] by using the NSLog() function and the class method, which return the class of an object.

3. Is it legal to combine Objective-C's property-accessor dot operator with C's struct-accessor dot operator in the same expression? Here's one way to try it out: in *Views*, on page 45, we mentioned that every UIView, such as a view controller's view, has a frame, expressed as a CGRectstruct. So...self.view.frame.origin.x? Does it work? If it does, can you tell which dots denote properties and which denote members of a struct?

4. We've seen the Delegate pattern earlier, in which a delegate object receives callbacks from some other object. Let's say object A has a property for helper object B, and B has a property for A as its delegate. To avoid a circular reference, we should make one of these properties weak. Which one?

5. Take a look at the documentation for NSDictionary. If you had to loop through a dictionary and do something with each key-value pair, how many different ways could you do it?

CHAPTER 3

Asynchronicity and Concurrency

It's very easy for us to look at an app and think it moves through the code in a straight line: first it does Step One, then Step Two, then Step Three, and so on. After all, this is how programming has worked since the era of vacuum tubes and punch cards. But then again, an iPhone isn't much like UNIVAC, or like Babbage's Difference Engine for that matter. For starters, some of the tasks our iOS devices perform take varying amounts of time; if Step Two is going to wait ten seconds for something to happen, could we perform some other work in the meantime? And the multicore CPUs like Apple's A6 can literally do two things at once, so shouldn't we be thinking of how to keep both those cores busy and productive?

In this chapter, we're going to look at how our code is run and how we can take advantage of recent advances in the iOS dialects of Objective-C and C to write code that takes advantage of *asynchronicity*, the ability of code to run when some unpredictable event demands it, and *concurrency*, the ability of several pieces of code to run at the same time.

3.1   Encapsulating Concurrent Code with Blocks

As it stands right now, our Twitter app lets us compose a tweet, view our Twitter page, and operate in multiple languages. But when we compose a tweet and click Send, nothing happens. We have to manually click the "Show my tweets" button to see if the tweet went out. Surely we can improve that behavior.

If we take a look at the SLComposeViewController in the documentation, we find a property called completionHandler, described as "the handler to call when the user is done composing a post." So that's good: we could use this to reload the web view once the tweet has been sent. Notice that, like the event handlers for the buttons, this is an asynchronous concern: we are providing code that gets called only when an unpredictable user-interface event demands it.

Let's get ready by doing a little refactoring. We will want to reload the web view either in response to a user tapping the reload button or when he or she finishes composing a tweet. That calls for moving the reload logic into its own method, reloadTweets, which can then be called from handleShowMyTweetsTapped: and from our completion handler.

Prior to Xcode 4.4, we needed to declare the method signature prior to any calls that actually use it, and this is still a useful practice for backward compatibility. We could declare the method in the header file, but that exposes it publicly, and it's really more of an implementation detail. What we need is a C-style forward declaration in the .m file, but Objective-C doesn't support them. What we use instead is a class extension, which looks like a second @interface declaration but goes inside the implementation file. In PRPViewController.m, an empty class extension has been stubbed out for us; edit it to look like this:

```
Concurrency/PRPFirstProjectTweeter04/PRPFirstProjectTweeter/PRPViewController.m
@interface PRPViewController()
-(void) reloadTweets;
@end
```

This extends the previous declaration of the PRPViewController interface, the one in the .h file, by adding another method declaration, reloadTweets. This method can be called anywhere in the .m file, but it isn't exposed to outsiders.

Speaking of exposure to other classes, there's no good reason that the twitter-WebView should be publicly visible, and we certainly wouldn't want a caller to be able to reassign it to an object other than the one we created in our nib.

Fortunately, class extensions can also contain property declarations. So cut the @property line from the PRPViewController.h header file, and paste it into the .m file's class extension, which should now look like this:

```
Concurrency/PRPFirstProjectTweeter04/PRPFirstProjectTweeter/PRPViewController.m
@interface PRPViewController()
-(void) reloadTweets;
@property (nonatomic, strong) IBOutlet UIWebView *twitterWebView;
@end
```

Now that we've hidden the property, let's get back to our original refactoring. Go to the bottom of the file and refactor the event handler to call reloadTweets:

```
-(IBAction) handleShowMyTweetsTapped: (id) sender {
  [self reloadTweets];
}

-(void) reloadTweets {
  [self.twitterWebView loadRequest:
   [NSURLRequest requestWithURL:
    [NSURL URLWithString:@"http://www.twitter.com/yourhandle"]]];
}
```

Categories

Class extensions can be seen as a special case of categories, one of Objective-C's most clever features. Categories allow us to add methods to any class, even classes we don't own, like those in the iOS SDK frameworks.

For example, consider that NSArray has a lastObject method, but it doesn't have one to get the first object. [myArray objectAtIndex:0] isn't equivalent, because it throws an exception for empty arrays. With a category, we could write a safe firstObject method by declaring a category of new methods on NSArray like this:

```
@interface NSArray (MySafeMethods)
-(id) firstObject;
@end
```

By convention, this header would go in a file called NSArray+MySafeMethods.h, and the implementation would go in a corresponding .m. The implementation can't add instance variables to the class, so there are limits on what we can do in a category.

Unlike a category, a class extension *can* provide instance variables in that it supports property declarations. In fact, now that the Xcode compiler can find method calls without the forward declaration that a class extension provides, the private declaration of properties is probably the most significant use of class extensions.

Now we just need to call reloadTweets when the user sends the tweet, which we get from this completionHandler. The docs tell us that the handler is of type SLComposeViewControllerCompletionHandler, so we follow the link to that typedef and it looks like this:

```
typedef void (^SLComposeViewControllerCompletionHandler)
        (SLComposeViewControllerResult result);
```

What...the...heck?

The carat character tells us we're not in Kansas anymore. This indicates a new C-language extension introduced by Apple called a *block*. A block is an object that contains both executable code and program state. The idea is much like that of a closure: the code inside the block receives a copy of the variables that were in scope when the block was created.

For this typedef, the void tells us that the block does not return a value, and it accepts a SLComposeViewControllerResult called result as a parameter. The result is an enum with values that tells us whether the SLComposeViewController was dismissed with the Cancel or the Done button.

So to reload the web view, we need to create a block that checks to see that the result is SLComposeViewControllerResultDone, and if so, calls reloadTweets. We create a block with the carat (^) character, like the documentation did. We rewrite handleTweetButtonTapped: as follows:

```
Concurrency/PRPFirstProjectTweeter04/PRPFirstProjectTweeter/PRPViewController.m
Line 1  -(IBAction) handleTweetButtonTapped: (id) sender {
          if ([SLComposeViewController isAvailableForServiceType: SLServiceTypeTwitter]) {
            SLComposeViewController *tweetVC =
            [SLComposeViewController composeViewControllerForServiceType:
     5       SLServiceTypeTwitter];
            [tweetVC setInitialText: NSLocalizedString (
              @"I just finished the first project in iOS SDK Development. #pragsios",
              nil)];
            tweetVC.completionHandler = ^(SLComposeViewControllerResult result) {
     10       if (result == SLComposeViewControllerResultDone) {
                [self dismissViewControllerAnimated:YES completion:NULL];
                [self reloadTweets];
              }
            };
     15     [self presentViewController:tweetVC animated:YES completion:NULL];
          }
        }
```

The new part is lines 9 through 14. We create a block with the ^ and the parameter list from the documentation and then enclose our code in curly braces. On line 10, we test the value of the result parameter. If it's SLCompose-ViewControllerResultDone, then we know the tweet was sent (and not cancelled) and we get to work. We start with a call to [self dismissViewControllerAnimated: YES completion:NULL] on line 11, which takes a view controller to dismiss (self) and a completion block to execute when the dismissal animation completes (the empty block NULL means we do nothing special).

We didn't have to explicitly dismiss the SLComposeViewController before we added the custom completionHandler, but now that we're using a SLComposeViewController-CompletionHandler, its documentation tells us that "the completion handler is called while the SLComposeViewController is still visible and *it is responsible for dismissing the view controller*" (emphasis ours).

To fill in the web view, we call [self reloadTweets] on line 12. The interesting part of this line is where we get self from, since it isn't passed into the block as a parameter. It's a variable in scope at the time of the block's creation, so the code in our block can call it directly. For that matter, our block could also refer to the sender parameter that was sent as a parameter to handleTweetButton-Tapped:, because that's another variable that's in scope when the block is created.

Notice the odd syntax on line 14 (};). The closing curly brace ends the block that started on line 9, and the semicolon ends the assignment of this block to the property tweetVC.completionHandler. This may be harder to read than it is to write; syntax-aware code completion in Xcode helps a lot with blocks.

Run this and send a tweet. Shortly after Send is tapped, the Social framework sends the tweet and then executes the block, which automatically reloads the web view without any further action by the user.

The iOS SDK uses blocks in several interesting ways. The pattern seen here, the *completion handler*, is a clean way of determining what should happen when a long-running action like network access or media I/O completes. We actually had an option to use blocks way back in the first version of this project: the third argument of presentViewController:animated:completion: specifies a completion handler block to execute once a modal view controller's view has been shown. We've used NULL because we don't need to do anything special once the tweet composer appears. Foundation's collection classes also make substantial use of blocks. NSArray has a method enumerateObjectsUsingBlock: that runs a block against every member of an array, and NSDictionary has similar methods that run a block on every key-value pair. We can also use a block as the sorting criteria for the contents of an NSArray and the keys of an NSDictionary.

3.2 Grand Central Dispatch

One of the most important features of blocks is that they allow us to break down code into small pieces that can be run concurrently, that is to say at the same time. For example, Foundation's sorting methods take a flag that indicates whether the block is safe from side effects if multiple copies of it are invoked at the same time. Concurrency is particularly important on multicore systems like the Apple A6 (used in the iPhone 5) and the A5 (used in the second- and third-generation iPads), as it makes it easier for the system to give each core something to do, rather than performing all the work for an application on a single core using a traditional single-threaded model.

To some developers, this sounds like threading, which is a widely-understood solution to concurrency that's supported in many languages. In fact, Objective-C does let you create NSThreads, though it's somewhat easier to use a related API, the NSOperation. However, the problem with threads is that while it's obvious that multiple threads offers a way to make code concurrent, it's hard to know how many threads to use. If two threads are good, are three even better? Not necessarily, since there's a CPU expense involved in "context switching" between threads. In fact, an ideal threading arrangement for one CPU architecture may not work well on another, and we still want to run well on old devices with single-core CPUs or be ready for future devices with quad-core.

iOS solves the concurrency problem with Grand Central Dispatch, a system-level technology that optimizes CPU use by monitoring how busy the cores are and balancing work between them. In the GCD model, there are multiple queues of work, each with tasks to execute. The tasks are either C function calls or blocks. GCD can then determine which tasks to execute based on the priority of the queue, whether the tasks are suitable for concurrent execution, how busy the CPUs are, and other considerations. To the application developer, concerns about threads and optimization pretty much disappear; we just send blocks to concurrency-aware APIs and let the system figure it out.

GCD provides functions to create queues and to put work on them. The one we'll use the most is dispatch_async(), which takes a reference to a queue and a block to execute on it. The async in the function name means that the call doesn't wait for the block to finish executing; the related dispatch_sync() will actually wait (or, to be cute, it blocks on the block). Mostly, we'll want to use dispatch_async() so our app doesn't wait and instead can move on to other work.

3.3 Concurrency and UIKit

GCD introduces a complication for using UIKit, since all calls to UIKit are required to be on the app's main thread, the one that started the app. This is why we can declare all UIKit properties as nonatomic: they can be thread-unsafe because there's only one thread that should ever call them. But with GCD, we don't know what thread is calling our blocks, so we shouldn't be calling into UIKit from a block that could be called from an unknown thread. And to think we were supposed to not have to worry about threads anymore!

Let's tease this problem out by intentionally getting ourselves in trouble, but for a good reason. Right now, our app is largely dependent on the Twitter page for showing tweets. We'd really like to own that data ourselves so we can customize how we present it, search and sort it, and so on. The iOS Social framework has a SLRequest that we can use to make remote calls to Twitter and get responses we can parse in our own client. We'll get rid of the web view and replace it with a plain UITextView, a multiline text view. It won't be as pretty at first, but we'll be able to control its contents more than we ever could with Twitter's web page.

Switching to a Text View

In PRPViewController.xib, delete the web view by selecting it and pressing the Delete or Backspace key. Deleting the web view also breaks File's Owner's connection to the twitterWebView property, which is what we want. With the web view deleted, drag a UITextView from the Object library (^⌥⌘3) into the space vacated by the web view. We will want this view to start out empty and be read-only, so select the text view, bring up the Attributes inspector (⌥⌘4), delete the default "Lorem ipsum" text, and uncheck the Editable box.

Like the web view it replaces, we also want Auto Layout to grow or shrink this text view as needed to accommodate 3.5-inch and 4-inch screens. Once we've placed and resized the text view, we need to check its constraints in the Size inspector to ensure there's a "Bottom Space to Superview" constraint to lock its bottom to the bottom of the superview. Then we need to create a user constraint if IB didn't already create an implicit constraint for us, and if a fixed-height constraint has been created automatically, we delete it.

Since we'll be populating this text view from code, we'll need an outlet to it. In PRPViewController.m, delete the line declaring the twitterWebView and replace it with a declaration of a twitterTextView, like this:

Concurrency/PRPFirstProjectTweeter05/PRPFirstProjectTweeter/PRPViewController.m

```
@property (nonatomic, strong) IBOutlet UITextView *twitterTextView;
```

Now we need to connect the outlet: control-click File's Owner and drag a connection from twitterTextView to the text view in the UI. Unfortunately, we have to rebuild and reconnect the UI in all of our localized .xib files and create all the needed Auto Layout constraints. So, redo this in the French localization, or just delete the French version at this point and keep in mind our advice that we always want to finish our UI *before* we start localizing. This illustrates why.

Calling the Twitter Web Service

Now let's get into calling Twitter's web service and putting the results in our new text field. The SLRequest has properties for the URL to call, the request parameters to provide, and the HTTP method (GET or POST) to use. There's also an init that takes all of these. Once our request is ready, we call performRequest-WithHandler:, which takes a block that's called when the request is done. The docs remind us that "this handler is not guaranteed to be called on any particular thread," and since the handler will need to populate the text view, this is the part where we're going to get in trouble with the rule that UIKit can only be called from the main thread.

We can do all our work in the block, but for clarity we're going to break it into a separate method handleTwitterData:urlResponse:error:, which we can add to our class extension (as of Xcode 4.4, we don't *have* to, but defining our internal interface like this is useful for organizing our own code). Here's the full class extension with both our methods and the twitterWebView property:

Concurrency/PRPFirstProjectTweeter05/PRPFirstProjectTweeter/PRPViewController.m
```
@interface PRPViewController ()
-(void) reloadTweets;
-(void) handleTwitterData: (NSData*) data
            urlResponse: (NSHTTPURLResponse*) urlResponse
                  error: (NSError*) error;
@property (nonatomic, strong) IBOutlet UITextView *twitterTextView;
@end
```

Notice that when we break lines, Xcode aligns the colons of multiargument calls. This is an Objective-C coding convention that we'll stick with whenever the book's formatting allows it.

Now we're ready to rewrite reloadTweets. This requires a little research into the Twitter web service API. To get a given user's tweets, we load the URL http://api.twitter.com/1/statuses/user_timeline.json, passing in a screen_name parameter. The .json file extension tells Twitter to send us JSON-formatted data, as opposed to .xml or .rss. Foundation has classes to parse JSON and XML, but the JSON parsing (introduced in iOS 5) is much easier to use, so we'll ask for that.

Now that we understand everything we need to make the Twitter request—the SLRequest, the URL for the Twitter web service we want, and the screen_name parameter needed by that web API—we're finally ready to write our new version of reloadTweets.

Concurrency/PRPFirstProjectTweeter05/PRPFirstProjectTweeter/PRPViewController.m
```
Line 1 -(void) reloadTweets {
  -   NSURL *twitterAPIURL = [NSURL URLWithString:
  -     @"http://api.twitter.com/1/statuses/user_timeline.json"];
  -   NSDictionary *twitterParams = @ {
  5     @"screen_name" : @"pragprog",
  -   };
  -   SLRequest *request = [SLRequest requestForServiceType:SLServiceTypeTwitter
                                    requestMethod:SLRequestMethodGET
                                              URL:twitterAPIURL
  10                                     parameters:twitterParams];
  -
```

```
 -      [request performRequestWithHandler:^(NSData *responseData,
 -                                            NSHTTPURLResponse *urlResponse,
 -                                            NSError *error) {
15          [self handleTwitterData:responseData
 -                       urlResponse:urlResponse
 -                             error:error];
 -      }];
 -  }
```

We start with the URL and the parameters that the SLRequest will need. Lines 2–3 set up the URL, while lines 4–6 create a dictionary of parameter name-value pairs using the new NSDictionary literal syntax. With those, we can create the SLRequest on lines 7–10, which also takes the request method SLRequestMethod-GET and a constant for the Twitter service type.

We actually perform the request with a call to performRequestWithHandler: on lines 12–18 specifying three block parameters, which we copied over from the SLRequestHandler documentation. The block's body (lines 15–17) just passes them to the handleTwitterData:urlResponse:error: that we defined in the class extension, which we will need to write next.

Calling Back into the Main Queue

When the Twitter response comes back, our block will call handleTwitterData:url-Response:error:. The NSData parameter is the raw response data from Twitter that we need to parse. Fortunately, since we asked for JSON data, we can use Foundation's NSJSONSerialization class to get the result as an array of dictionaries (which themselves may contain dictionaries). Then all we have to do is iterate over the array and append the text view with each new tweet.

But this is where we get into trouble with UIKit: the block is on an unknown thread, so to touch twitterTextView, we need to have a way to do so back on the main thread.

Grand Central Dispatch works with queues, not threads, but it has a special "main queue" that is associated with the app's main thread. We get this queue with the GCD function dispatch_get_main_queue(). To run code in a specific queue, we can use GCD's dispatch_async(), which takes a queue and a block of work to perform on that queue. Now we've got all the pieces we need to unpack the Twitter data on an arbitrary thread and write to the text area on the main thread:

Concurrency/PRPFirstProjectTweeter05/PRPFirstProjectTweeter/PRPViewController.m

```
Line 1  -(void) handleTwitterData: (NSData*) data
 -            urlResponse: (NSHTTPURLResponse*) urlResponse
 -                  error: (NSError*) error {
```

```
     NSError *jsonError = nil;
5    NSJSONSerialization *jsonResponse =
     [NSJSONSerialization JSONObjectWithData:data
                                      options:0
                                        error:&jsonError];
     NSLog (@"jsonResponse: %@", jsonResponse);
10   if (!jsonError &&
         [jsonResponse isKindOfClass:[NSArray class]]) {
       dispatch_async(dispatch_get_main_queue(), ^{
         NSArray *tweets = (NSArray*) jsonResponse;
         for (NSDictionary *tweetDict in tweets) {
15         NSString *tweetText = [NSString stringWithFormat:@"%@ (%@)",
                                   [tweetDict valueForKey:@"text"],
                                   [tweetDict valueForKey:@"created_at"]];
           self.twitterTextView.text = [NSString stringWithFormat:@"%@%@\n\n",
                                        self.twitterTextView.text,
20                                       tweetText];
         }
       });
     }
   }
```

This starts by creating an empty (nil) NSError on line 4 and passing its address to the JSONObjectWithData:options:error: on lines 5–8. If this NSError is set to a non-nil value or if the object we get back is not an NSArray, then our request has failed and we don't want to try to parse the response (handled by the if on lines 10–11).

If we do have a good response, then we're going to update the UI, so on line 12 we use dispatch_async() to start a block that will be run on the main thread, making it safe for use with UIKit. We iterate over the dictionaries in the array (lines 13–21), pulling out the values for the text and created_at keys and putting these objects into an NSString with stringWithFormat: on lines 15–17. By the way, there are many other interesting fields in the Twitter response; try adding a NSLog (@"%@", tweets); to the code and viewing the Xcode console to see all the stuff we get back.

Once we have this string, we append it to the text view on lines 18–20. UITextView doesn't actually have an "append" method, so what we do instead is create a new string with the twitterTextView's current text, the new tweetText, and two line breaks, and we set that as the new text for the text view. The result is shown in Figure 27, *Parsed tweets in a UITextView*, on page 67.

Setting the twitterTextView's text property is the only reason we had to jump through these GCD hoops. That's the only call to UIKit in the SLRequest's completion handler. But disaster was awaiting if we didn't. To try it out, comment out the dispatch_get_main_queue()() line and the }); line that closes it.

Figure 27—Parsed tweets in a UITextView

This will result in running the block on whatever thread performs the SLRequest callback. The result is a crash, with the following written to the console:

```
2012-08-14 19:15:04.203 PRPFirstProjectTweeter[24838:1303]
bool _WebTryThreadLock(bool), 0xa391900: Tried to obtain the web lock
from a thread other than the main thread or the web thread. This may
be a result of calling to UIKit from a secondary thread. Crashing now...
```

This kind of concurrency problem usually only shows up when you call into UIKit from an arbitrary thread. It's not a problem for simple apps that just react to user input, because event handlers are called from the main thread and can therefore safely call into UIKit. However, whenever we use the completion handler design pattern, we're going to want to ask ourselves if we can safely assume that we'll always be called on the main thread. Fortunately, GCD's dispatch_async() with dispatch_get_main_queue() is a simple recipe for putting a block of work back on the main thread.

Joe asks:
I Heard Twitter Was Changing Its API?

Days before we handed this book off to production, Twitter announced significant changes to its web API. The most alarming of these is that by March 2013, *all* API requests will require authentication. Since we're not authenticating our request for user_timeline.json, there's a good chance this will stop working.

Fortunately, iOS 6's Twitter support makes it pretty easy to authenticate with Twitter for these requests (posting a tweet with the SLComposeViewController is by its nature authenticated). The SLRequest has an account property of class ACAccount, which we set to authenticate our request with that account's credentials.

To show the authentication approach, we've created an alternative version of the previous stage of the project in the downloadable code as PRPFirstProjectTweeter05_A. We start by adding an #import <Accounts/Accounts.h> to the top of PRPViewController.m, and then we go to the project's Build Phases and add Accounts.framework, just like we did when we added the Social framework.

A tour of the documentation shows us that to get an ACAccount we need to create an ACAccountStore and call its accountsWithAccountType: method. The account object is tied to an instance of the store, so we're going to want to keep both of them around for as long as the view controller is valid. That argues for making both of them properties, so let's define them in the class extension:

```
Concurrency/PRPFirstProjectTweeter05_A/PRPFirstProjectTweeter/PRPViewController.m
@property (strong) ACAccountStore *accountStore;
@property (readonly, strong) ACAccount *twitterAccount;
```

We can actually do something neat for the account property: lazy loading. With this approach, we don't expend the effort to create twitterAccount until we need to, and we cache the result. There's a common Cocoa pattern for this, and it involves overriding the getter method. To do that, we need to manually @synthesize our twitterAccount property inside the @implementation:

```
Concurrency/PRPFirstProjectTweeter05_A/PRPFirstProjectTweeter/PRPViewController.m
@synthesize twitterAccount = _twitterAccount;
```

Now we can write the getter method, which must have the same name as the property: twitterAccount. To lazy-load, we check to see if the _twitterAccount instance variable is nil. If it is, we talk to the Accounts framework and populate it. Either way, we return _twitterAccount as the last step. Here's how we do it.

```
Concurrency/PRPFirstProjectTweeter05_A/PRPFirstProjectTweeter/PRPViewController.m
Line 1  -(ACAccount*) twitterAccount {
            if (! _twitterAccount) {
```

```
        self.accountStore = [[ACAccountStore alloc] init];
        ACAccountType *twitterAccountType = [self.accountStore
                                    accountTypeWithAccountTypeIdentifier:
                                    ACAccountTypeIdentifierTwitter];
        NSArray *twitterAccounts = [self.accountStore
                                accountsWithAccountType:twitterAccountType];
        if ([twitterAccounts count] > 0) {
            _twitterAccount = [twitterAccounts objectAtIndex:0];
        }
    }
    return _twitterAccount;
}
```

It's a little involved, but that's because the Accounts framework supports multiple accounts across multiple account types. So after our nil check on line 2, we populate the accountStore property on line 3. Then we have to create an object for the Twitter account type, which we do on lines 4–6. That allows us to use accountsWithAccountType to get all the Twitter accounts as an NSArray on lines 7–8. If we get anything back, we assign the first member of the array to _twitterAccount on line 10; a more elaborate app would show users all their Twitter accounts and let each user choose one. Whether this has assigned _twitterAccount or left it as nil—we would get no accounts back if none are configured—we return its current value on line 13.

Now that our property will look up the account at the very moment we need it, all we have to do is ask for it. Set the request's account property to our twitterAccount just before the call to performRequestWithHandler:, like this:

Concurrency/PRPFirstProjectTweeter05_A/PRPFirstProjectTweeter/PRPViewController.m
```
request.account = self.twitterAccount;
```

When we hit this line, our override of the property getter runs, gets the Twitter account we need, and gives it to the request. Another advantage of lazy loading is that if the property remains nil because there's no account configured, the user could leave the app, switch to Settings to configure a Twitter account, and come back to our app, and the getter would try again and succeed this time.

And while this seems like extra work, authenticating gives us access to nearly all of the Twitter API. For example, rather than getting an arbitrary user's public timeline with user_timeline.json, we could get the authenticated user's home timeline by rewriting the first few lines of reloadTweets like this:

Concurrency/PRPFirstProjectTweeter05_A/PRPFirstProjectTweeter/PRPViewController.m
```
NSURL *twitterAPIURL = [NSURL URLWithString:
  @"http://api.twitter.com/1/statuses/home_timeline.json"];
NSDictionary *twitterParams = @ {
};
```

All this does is change the request URL to use home_timeline.json and eliminate the screen_name parameter, since the user whose timeline we're getting is implicit in which authenticated account we use for the call.

3.4 Sorting with Blocks

We've had to learn some pretty challenging concepts in order to retrieve Twitter data and show it in our own UI. For a real Twitter client, it would be worth it, because we'd be able to use and show much more data than is exposed by the mobile Twitter web page. Let's finish up by looking at some things we can do with the data, tasks that blocks and Foundation make really simple.

When we parsed the Twitter data with the NSJSONSerialization class, we got an NSArray of NSDictionary objects, each with key-value pairs for things like text, created_at, source (the app used to create the tweet), coordinates, various in_reply_to_ fields, and so on. There's also a user whose value is another NSDictionary with lots of interesting fields to pick out, like a description and a profile_image_url that we could use to provide more info about each tweet's author.

Since we have all this data, let's perform a simple manipulation: sorting it. NSArray offers several methods for sorting. One that's directly relevant to our experience is sortedArrayUsingComparator:. If we look up this method in the docs, we'll find the argument is an NSComparator, a block that takes two objects of type id and returns an NSComparisonResult constant to indicate how they should be ordered: NSOrderedAscending, NSOrderedDescending, or NSOrderedSame.

So all we have to do is write a block that knows how to sort two NSDictionary objects from the tweets array using whichever key (text and created_at, and so on) interests us. Let's rewrite handleTwitterData:urlResponse:error: as follows:

```
Concurrency/PRPFirstProjectTweeter06/PRPFirstProjectTweeter/PRPViewController.m
Line 1  - (void) handleTwitterData: (NSData*) data
     -              urlResponse: (NSHTTPURLResponse*) urlResponse
     -                    error: (NSError*) error {
     -    NSError *jsonError = nil;
     5    NSJSONSerialization *jsonResponse =
     -    [NSJSONSerialization JSONObjectWithData:data
     -                                    options:0
     -                                      error:&jsonError];
     -    if (!jsonError &&
    10        [jsonResponse isKindOfClass:[NSArray class]]) {
     -       dispatch_async(dispatch_get_main_queue(), ^{
     -         NSArray *tweets = (NSArray*) jsonResponse;
     -         tweets = [tweets sortedArrayUsingComparator:
     -                  ^NSComparisonResult(id obj1, id obj2) {
    15                     NSString *tweet1 = [obj1 valueForKey:@"text"];
     -                     NSString *tweet2 = [obj2 valueForKey:@"text"];
     -                     return [tweet1 compare:tweet2];
     -                  }];
     -         for (NSDictionary *tweetDict in tweets) {
```

```
20        NSString *tweetText =
   -      [NSString stringWithFormat:@"%@ (%@)",
   -       [tweetDict valueForKey:@"text"],
   -       [tweetDict valueForKey:@"created_at"]];
   -      self.twitterTextView.text = [NSString stringWithFormat:@"%@%@\n\n",
25                                    self.twitterTextView.text,
   -                                  tweetText];
   -    }
   -  });
   - }
30 }
```

In this version, we use sortedArrayUsingComparator: on line 13 to replace tweets with a sorted version of its contents. The NSComparator, which performs the logic used by the sort to compare array members, is the block on lines 13–18. Each object to be sorted is an NSDictionary, since that's what's in tweets, the array we're sorting. So, to sort by the text of each tweet, we call valueForKey: on lines 15 and 16 to get the text of each tweet. Notice that we don't have to cast obj1 and obj2 to NSDictionary, because valueForKey: is actually defined in a category on NSObject, so it's always available. Once we have the text of tweet1 and tweet2, we can call NSString's compare: method, which compares two strings and returns the very NSComparisonResult constants that our block needs to return.

Build and run this example, and tap "Show my tweets" in the simulated app. Figure 28, *Tweets sorted alphabetically*, on page 72, shows the output with pragprog as the Twitter user name. The tweets are sorted alphabetically by text, which makes the tweets that start with numbers, certain special characters, and replies appear first in the text view, since numbers, the hashtag (#), and the @ character precede letters in Unicode.

Key-Value Coding

Putting our sort logic in a block is powerful because it lets us write as much or as little logic as we need to perform comparisons. On the other hand, to introduce a second- or third-order sort (like "sort by author name, then date, then tweet text"), the block is going to get pretty busy. This kind of sorting is pretty common, so we could probably do better, right?

Indeed we can. Foundation gives us a remarkable design pattern called *key-value coding* (KVC). To put it simply, it means that things we can get via string keys, like keys in a dictionary, can be chained together in a path with the dot operator. So, if a given tweetDict has a key user whose value is an NSDictionary, and that dictionary has a key name, then we can get the user's name with the method valueForKeyPath:, like this:

```
NSString *userName = [tweetDict valueForKeyPath:@"user.name"];
```

Figure 28—Tweets sorted alphabetically

KVC pays off for us in Foundation's support for sorting. NSArray's various sort methods include sortedArrayUsingDescriptors:, which takes an array of NSSortDescriptors, objects that determine how two objects in an array should be sorted. The sort descriptor is initialized with a key path, meaning that when we have an array of objects, all we have to do is provide the name of the field to sort on as a key path string, and Foundation does the rest.

It gets better, because this isn't just about NSDictionary. Key-value coding is also applied to public properties of objects. Or manually written getter methods. Or even public instance variables (which we're not using in this book, but they still work). If the value keyed by user was not NSDictionary but rather a custom PRPTwitterUser class with a property called name, the above user.name path would work, completely unchanged. In other words, it doesn't matter what the objects in the containment hierarchy are; it only matters that for a given key-path element foo, there's either a public property foo, a method foo, an instance variable foo, or a valueForKey: method that returns a non-nil value when given the string argument foo.

Let's rewrite handleTwitterData:urlResponse:error: one more time. We'll sort the tweets alphabetically and throw in an extra call to put a user name on every tweet (which is a little gratuitous, considering we're getting a single user's timeline, but it's still cool). Here's the rewritten method:

```
Line 1 - (void) handleTwitterData: (NSData*) data
                   urlResponse: (NSHTTPURLResponse*) urlResponse
                         error: (NSError*) error {
       NSError *jsonError = nil;
    5  NSJSONSerialization *jsonResponse =
       [NSJSONSerialization JSONObjectWithData:data
                                       options:0
                                         error:&jsonError];
       if (!jsonError &&
   10      [jsonResponse isKindOfClass:[NSArray class]]) {
         dispatch_async(dispatch_get_main_queue(), ^{
           NSArray *tweets = (NSArray*) jsonResponse;
           NSSortDescriptor *sortByText =
           [NSSortDescriptor sortDescriptorWithKey:@"text" ascending:YES];
   15      NSArray *sortDescriptors = @[sortByText];
           tweets = [tweets sortedArrayUsingDescriptors:sortDescriptors];
           for (NSDictionary *tweetDict in tweets) {
             NSString *tweetText =
             [NSString stringWithFormat:@"%@: %@ (%@)",
   20        [tweetDict valueForKeyPath:@"user.name"],
             [tweetDict valueForKey:@"text"],
             [tweetDict valueForKey:@"created_at"]];
             self.twitterTextView.text = [NSString stringWithFormat:@"%@%@\n\n",
                                          self.twitterTextView.text,
   25                                      tweetText];
           }
         });
       }
     - }
```

On lines 13–14, we create an NSSortDescriptor that sorts on the text key path of whatever objects it receives. We then create an NSArray containing only this descriptor (line 15) and send it to sortedArrayUsingDescriptors (line 16) to replace the tweets array with a sorted copy of itself.

Just to show off deeper key paths, on line 19, we change the string format to take three substitutions, and on line 20, we make the first of these the result of getting the key path user.name. That means we get the value for the key user, and whatever object we get back, we then get the value for the key name. When we run the app this time, as shown in Figure 29, *Tweets sorted alphabetically via key-value coding*, on page 74, the tweets are still sorted by text but now show the user name at the beginning of each line.

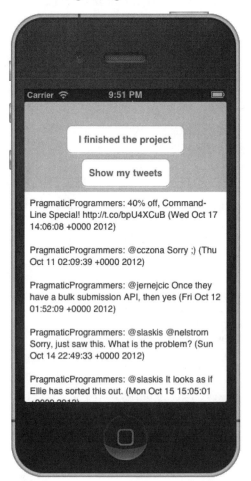

Figure 29—Tweets sorted alphabetically via key-value coding

This last example took us away from concurrency, but it was for a good reason: as appealing as blocks can be as a way to encapsulate our logic, sometimes the frameworks give us even cleaner ways to do what we want.

3.5 Wrap-Up

In this chapter, we took our knowledge of Objective-C and the UIKit and Foundation frameworks and started addressing questions of *how* and *when* our code runs. Apple's design patterns often stress asynchronicity as a means of unblocking the main thread while waiting for input from the user interface or the network, which means we need to write our code as callbacks that run exactly when they're needed. For newer APIs like Twitter, these callbacks are implemented as blocks, so we learned to embrace the ^ character and write these bite-size nuggets of code that can run asynchronously or even concurrently. We'll need blocks again when we use them to perform animations in Chapter 8, *Drawing and Animating*, on page 189. We also looked at how concurrency presents challenges if we're on an unknown thread and have to put UIKit work back on the main thread, and we discovered how Grand Central Dispatch offers a straightforward solution. Finally, we looked at how Foundation uses blocks to let us provide small bits of logic for tasks like sorting and how sometimes blocks aren't the cleanest solution available.

With this introduction complete, we're going to spend the next few chapters in UIKit. We'll start by discovering the UIViewController class and learning why it's so central to providing the logic of our iOS apps.

For Further Thought

Here are a few things to think about or try out to expand your understanding of the stuff we've covered in this chapter. The questions don't necessarily have "correct" answers. Please join us on the forums at http://forums.pragprog.com/ to discuss your ideas about them.

1. We've seen that blocks are used to finish user-interface work, like handling the dismissal of the SLComposeViewController. What are other kinds of tasks with unpredictable timing that might be well suited to using blocks as completion handlers?

2. We mentioned earlier that block-based sorting can be done concurrently, which may improve performance. To try it out in the block-based sorting example (PRPFirstProjectTweeter06), replace the call to sortedArrayUsingComparator: with a call to sortedArrayWithOptions:usingComparator:, passing NSSortConcurrent for the first parameter and our block for the second. The NSSortConcurrent constant asserts that the logic in the block is safe to run concurrently, meaning two instances of it can run at the same time. Does the code in our block look concurrency-safe? Can you think of things that wouldn't be safe?

3. Consider the following code:

    ```
    NSString *myString = @"foo";
    dispatch_async (dispatch_get_main_queue(), ^{
            NSLog (@"%@", myString);
    });
    myString = @"bar";
    ```

    What's the output of this code? Is it always the same?

4. Now consider this code:

    ```
    NSMutableString *myString = [NSMutableString stringWithString:@"foo"];
    dispatch_async (dispatch_get_main_queue(),  ^{
            NSLog (@"%@", myString);
    });
    [myString setString:@"bar"];
    ```

    What's the output of this code? Why is it different than the output from the previous question?

5. In the KVC sort example, how could we easily perform a second-order sort? In other words, if two tweets had the exact same text, how could we then sort them by their created_at values?

CHAPTER 4

View Controllers

In the last chapter, we learned about concurrency with Objective-C and GCD. In this chapter we're going to take a somewhat higher-level view and look at the how-and-why of putting our code together. We're going to start putting together a new example, and in the course of it, we'll make more and more use of view controllers, which are one of the essential building blocks of iOS apps. We'll look at the role they play in apps, what they provide at runtime, and how they help us build better code.

iOS's use of view controllers is part of a design pattern, a reusable solution to a common problem. The term *design pattern* has its origin in architecture. For example, through the ages the arch has been used to make bridges and passages through walls. The arch is a design pattern that successfully solves a problem.

In software, there are many famous design patterns, one of the most important of which is Model-View-Controller, or MVC for short. MVC is a software design pattern that simplifies designing and implementing applications.

The *model* in MVC is the heart of an application. If we can reduce an application's description into a single sentence, we usually find that the nouns represent the model classes and the verbs are the actions the model classes can perform. Consider this application definition statement (ADS) of the Photos app on iPhone:

> Photos is an easy-to-use digital photo editing, organizing, and sharing application for casual and amateur photographers.

The nouns *photo* and *photographer* are the model classes. The verbs *edit*, *organize*, and *share* are the actions that the model needs to perform. As we flesh out an app from the skeleton of an ADS, we will discover more nouns and verbs that describe additional model objects and actions.

The main purpose of the *view* is to expose features the model provides in a way that makes it easy for users to access those features. The view is the way users perceive an application. In any iOS application, what we see and interact with is the view for that application. The table view that presents the list of email messages, the view that presents a single photo...each of these is a view for its respective application.

The *controller* ties the view and the model together. The controller acts as the translator from the generic world of the view to the specific world of the model. For example, the view that presents the list of messages in the Mail app is made up of several generic UIKit classes, including UITableView and UIButton. Behind these generic view classes is a controller that translates between user intentions (expressed by touching the view) and the model actions that perform the requested function. The relationship goes the other way too: when the model changes (for example, when a new email is received), the view is updated accordingly.

This chapter focuses on the *C* in MVC. We are going to build a simple recipes application that has a model, a view, and a controller. iOS has some very specific ideas about how to provide that controller, as it strongly encourages us to organize our logic into view controllers.

UIKit provides the UIViewController class to manage the behavior of a hierarchy of views. On iPhone and iPod touch, this is usually a single "screen" or "page," although on iPad it might also be the contents of a pop-over. It fulfills the role of a controller by mediating between a view, such as those we've been building in Interface Builder, and some kind of data model. iOS also tasks the view controller with other responsibilities that we'll get into soon, but for now, it's enough to know that iOS apps largely consist of views we build in Interface Builder, models we build in code, and UIViewControllers to bridge the two. It's the MVC pattern, and we'll be using it again and again.

4.1 Practicing MVC

Let's put our understanding of MVC to work and build an application. We are going to start simple and use a single view controller that displays one field. We are going to explicitly lay out each of the MVC roles to help build our understanding.

We are going to build a simple application to manage recipes. What, specifically, do we mean by that? Let's start with an application definition statement: "A simple, easy-to-use application to manage lists of recipes for cooking enthusiasts." We have one main noun here, the recipe. That will be our model throughout the rest of this chapter. We'll then display the properties of the model class in a view and then tie the view to the model with a view controller. Later, in Chapter 5, *Table Views*, on page 95, we'll broaden our scope to present a list of recipes, and then in Chapter 7, *Documents and iCloud*, on page 155, we'll look at how to store our recipe model on disk so it persists from run to run.

Let's start with the model. For simple models, it's fine to use an instance of a Foundation class like NSArray or NSDictionary. However, to keep our MVC roles crystal clear, we will create a new class to serve as the model. Then we can build the view in Xcode's Interface Builder tool and finally tie the two together by writing a subclass of UIViewController. In other words: model, view, controller.

Let's start with a new iOS "Single View Application" in Xcode. Create a new project in Xcode with ⌘⇧N. In the "Choose options for your new project" panel, set the Product Name field to Recipes, the Company Identifier field to com.pragprog.adios, the Class Prefix to PRP, and the Device Family to iPhone; uncheck the Use Storyboard and Include Unit Tests check boxes; click the Next button; and save the project.

Model Class

Let's build the model class first. This is the first time we're creating a new class beyond the classes that the Xcode template provides us with, so we use a new technique. First, select the Recipes group from the project navigator in Xcode (⌘1) and select "File→New File..." or type ⌘N. You should have a dialog window like the one in Figure 30, *Choosing a new file template*, on page 80. Make sure to select Cocoa Touch and Objective-C class, and then click the Next button.

The next dialog prompts you to name the class and specify the superclass. Name the class PRPRecipe and make sure to choose NSObject, and then click the Next button. In the last step of the wizard, you'll be asked where to save the new class. Choose the Recipes folder and make sure the Recipes target is selected. The dialog panel should look like Figure 31, *Specifying a new class name*, on page 80.

Through the next few chapters we will be fleshing out the PRPRecipe model class with more detail. For now, we want to keep it simple, so let's just add a title property to our PRPRecipe. Open the header and add the property declaration like this:

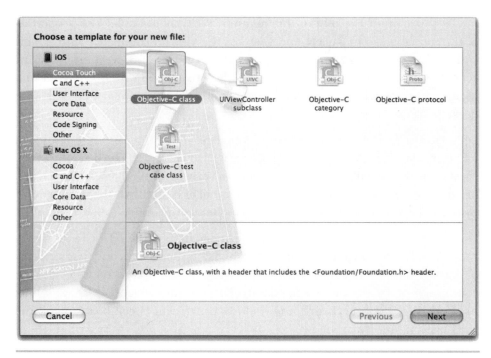

Figure 30—Choosing a new file template

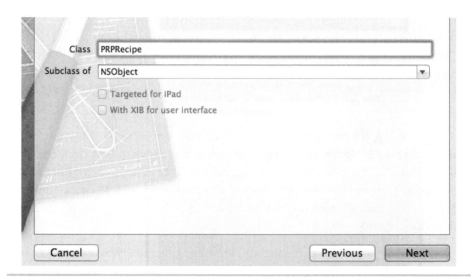

Figure 31—Specifying a new class name

ViewsAndControllers/Recipes_01/Recipes/PRPRecipe.h

```
@interface PRPRecipe : NSObject

@property(nonatomic, copy) NSString *title;

@end
```

This property keeps track of our recipe's titles. Of course, a real recipe would need more information: directions, a list of ingredients, and so on. We will add some of this later, but for providing a model that we can present in a UIViewController, this will do just fine.

The title needs to be set to a reasonable default value. We'll do that by overriding the init method and setting the value, like this:

ViewsAndControllers/Recipes_01/Recipes/PRPRecipe.m

```
- (id)init {
    self = [super init];
    if (self) {
      self.title = @"New Recipe";
    }
    return self;
}
```

Now that we have a model, the next step in our application is to build a view to display it. Eventually, we will want to be able to edit our model object, but in our initial view let's just display it.

The View

As we've seen in earlier chapters, the primary tool we use to create and edit a view is Interface Builder. In Xcode, open the file PRPViewController.xib by selecting it in the file navigator in Xcode.

To display the title we will use a UILabel. To add it to the UI, open the Object library (^⌥⌘3), select the Label object, and drag it into the view. Once in the view, resize the label so that the right side is aligned with the rightmost alignment guide (the blue dashed line that appears as you drag toward the edge of the view). The finished view should look like Figure 32, *Label adding*, on page 82.

Remember in our MVC triad that the model contains the data, the view displays the data and presents the means to interact with the data, and the controller provides the translation between the two. Now that we have the view and the model, it's time to build the controller.

Figure 32—Label adding

Controller

Xcode has already created a skeleton of the controller for us. Let's put some flesh on the bones of this skeleton. Open PRPViewController.h. We'll start by giving the controller a way to access the title label. Add a property to point to the label, like this:

ViewsAndControllers/Recipes_01/Recipes/PRPViewController.h
```
@property(nonatomic, strong) IBOutlet UILabel *recipeTitle;
```

The IBOutlet keyword specifies that the recipeTitle property can be connected via Interface Builder in Xcode to the label we added to the view in the previous section. Specifically declaring the property to be of class UILabel keeps us from making mistakes and connecting to some other type of view.

To get the property "wired up" to the label, we need to connect the two in the nib file, PRPViewController.xib. In Section 1.2, *Our First Project*, on page 2, we made this kind of connection by using the Connections inspector (⌥⌘6). That still works, but let's exercise another technique for the sake of variety and experimentation. We can control-drag from File's Owner to UILabel. To do this, hold the ctrl key while clicking File's Owner and then drag toward the label. As we do this, Interface Builder draws a blue line from the click point to the current mouse position. When the mouse is over the label, lift up and a pop-up window will appear with a list of possible connections. The two steps of this gesture are shown in Figure 33, *Connecting an IBOutlet via ctrl-dragging*, on page 82. Click the recipeTitle item to perform the connection.

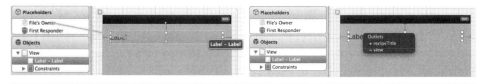

Figure 33—Connecting an IBOutlet via ctrl-dragging

The connection sets up a relationship between our view controller (File's Owner) and the label. By making this connection we are saying "when this label is loaded from the nib file, call setRecipeTitle: on the view controller with the newly loaded object."

Now that we have the label set up and connected, we need to make a way to populate the label with the recipe title. To do that, we need to add another property to our controller. In the header file, add a property declaration like this:

ViewsAndControllers/Recipes_01/Recipes/PRPViewController.h
```
@property(nonatomic, strong) PRPRecipe *recipe;
```

Now the controller has a pointer to keep track of the model it will display. But to make it compile we need to import the PRPRecipe interface, so do that now.

Now the compiler knows about the PRPRecipe class and we can freely use its methods.

Now let's get the title from our recipe and place it into the recipeTitle label. The interesting part is figuring out *when* to do that. There are several methods we could override that would work: we could do it when the view controller is created or when the view loads. However, these approaches will only set the property once. Later, in Chapter 6, *Storyboards and Container Controllers*, on page 119, we are going to reuse this view controller to discuss transitions and navigation, and we'll be changing its contents every time it appears. The viewWillAppear: method is called just before the view is displayed on screen, so it will continue to work as our application evolves.

Let's go to PRPViewController.m and implement the viewWillAppear: method. Change the code to look like this:

ViewsAndControllers/Recipes_01/Recipes/PRPViewController.m
```
Line 1  - (void)viewWillAppear:(BOOL)animated {
     2      [super viewWillAppear:animated];
     3      self.recipeTitle.text = self.recipe.title;
     4  }
```

Since this method is called just before the view controller's view is shown onscreen, we can be sure that any time that the PRPViewController's view is displayed, the recipe's title will be placed into the label.

Model Creation

Now that we have our view controller set up to display the recipe's title properly, it's time to get a particular recipe into this view controller. In this example, we are going to create the model instance in the PRPAppDelegate. Open the PRPAppDelegate.m file and navigate to the application:didFinishLaunchingWithOptions: method.

This method is called just as our application finishes its launching sequence. In other words, the UIApplication object for our application is fully instantiated and is ready to start processing user input by this point. In the code provided by Xcode's single-view application template, the application:didFinishLaunchingWith-Options: method creates the window, along with an instance of our view controller via initWithNibName:options:, which references the PRPViewController.xib that contains the view (and which we've been customizing with Interface Builder). The app delegate then makes our view controller the window's rootViewController (we will look at the rootViewController in detail in Section 4.2, *Working with a View's Life Cycle*, on page 85). That's enough to get the view onscreen, but there's nothing providing a model for the view controller yet. We need to create an instance of PRPRecipe and set that new instance to be the recipe on our view controller instance. To do that, change the code to look like this:

```
ViewsAndControllers/Recipes_01/Recipes/PRPAppDelegate.m
Line 1  - (BOOL)application:(UIApplication *)application
     -  didFinishLaunchingWithOptions:(NSDictionary *)launchOptions {
     -      PRPRecipe *recipe = [[PRPRecipe alloc] init];
     -      recipe.title =  @"Chocolate Chip Cookies";
     5
     -      self.window = [[UIWindow alloc] initWithFrame:[[UIScreen mainScreen] bounds]];
     -      self.viewController = [[PRPViewController alloc]
     -                          initWithNibName:@"PRPViewController" bundle:nil];
     -      self.viewController.recipe = recipe;
     10     self.window.rootViewController = self.viewController;
     -      [self.window makeKeyAndVisible];
     -      return YES;
     - }
```

On line 3 we create the recipe object with the usual alloc and init calls. Next, on line 4, we set the title of the recipe to be Chocolate Chip Cookies. Then on line 9, we set our view controller's recipe, that is, its model, to be the recipe object we just created.

Now it's time to run the app for real. When the app has launched it will look like Figure 34, *Recipes running*, on page 85.

This is a simple but full-fledged MVC application. The model is the PRPRecipe class; there's not much to it yet, but we can surely add more properties to beef it up. The data in the model is pushed into the view by the PRPViewController class, and we built the view with Interface Builder and stored it in a nib.

Figure 34—Recipes running

Now that we have a working example, let's take a step back and look at the life cycle of the view in more detail.

4.2 Working with a View's Life Cycle

To understand the life cycle of a view controller's view property, we need to go back to the beginning of our application and discuss how the view comes into memory.

Let's go back to the application:didFinishLaunchingWithOptions: method in our PRPAppDelegate class. This delegate method is really the beginning of our application's code. Since the template gives us what is needed to get our initial view onscreen, let's focus on that code now and ignore the parts that we added to get the recipe into our view controller. Here is the reverted code for reference.

```
ViewsAndControllers/Recipes_02/Recipes/PRPAppDelegate.m
Line 1 - (BOOL)application:(UIApplication *)application
     2 didFinishLaunchingWithOptions:(NSDictionary *)launchOptions {
     3   self.window = [[UIWindow alloc] initWithFrame:[[UIScreen mainScreen] bounds]];
     4   self.viewController = [[PRPViewController alloc]
     5                          initWithNibName:@"PRPViewController"
     6                          bundle:nil];
     7   self.window.rootViewController = self.viewController;
     8   [self.window makeKeyAndVisible];
     9   return YES;
    10 }
```

First, this method creates a window that will eventually be placed onscreen. The window is the root of the view hierarchy. Next, on lines 4–6 we create our view controller. The first argument is the name of the nib file that should be loaded. It might not look like it, but this is the beginning of our view's life cycle.

The next line sets the window's rootViewController to be our new view controller instance. This is the second important step in the life of our view controller's view because the window displays the view from this VC when it comes onscreen. Next, on line 8, we tell the window to makeKeyAndVisible; this third step eventually causes our view controller's view to become visible. Let's break down these steps into a more detailed discussion.

If you recall, we edited the view earlier. We added the UILabel and made a connection between File's Owner and the label. Let's open the PRPViewController.xib file again and look at it in a bit more depth. Show the Utility view and select the Connections inspector (⌥⌘6). Select the File's Owner object. The Connections inspector will look like Figure 35, *View controller connections*, on page 86.

Figure 35—View controller connections

This is the connection that associates the view in our nib file with our view controller.

Now that we see where the view is specified, it's not clear why that matters or what triggers the loading of the nib file. The important thing to understand here is how lazy view controllers are: they don't really do anything until asked. When a view controller is initialized with the initWithNibName:bundle: method, it does *not* load the nib file; instead, it just records the nib file name in its nibName property and the bundle in the nibBundle. When a view controller is asked for its view, it first looks to see if it already has a view. If it does have a view, it simply returns it. If it does not, then it looks to see if the view controller's nibName is specified. If so, it loads the nib file using the [NSBundle loadNibNamed:owner:options:] method and passing itself in as the owner argument. The NSBundle class loads the nib file, substituting the owner parameter (in this case, the view controller) as the File's Owner object during the load.

The second and third steps the view goes through to get onscreen are closely tied together. First, we set our view controller to be the rootViewController for our window, and then we send makeKeyAndVisible to the window. When the window is displayed via the makeKeyAndVisible, it sends the view message to the rootViewController, which forces the view controller to load its view (as described earlier).

The returned view is then added to the window so that it becomes part of the view hierarchy. And with that, our view is onscreen and visible to our users.

Now that we have seen all three steps in order, let's look at the same process from the last method invoked and how that causes the cascade of events that results in the view being onscreen. When the window is sent makeKeyAndVisible, it asks its rootViewController for its view. The view controller does not have a view yet, so it loads the nib file. The view controller then returns its newly loaded view. The window then adds that view to the view hierarchy.

And voilà! Our view is on the screen.

Intentionally Breaking Things

While we are in the nib file and messing around, let's go on a short journey to see a very common mistake and how it manifests itself, so when you hit it in the wild you are not caught off guard. Let's open the Recipes application that we finished up in Section 4.1, *Practicing MVC*, on page 78. Open the PRPViewController.xib file and select File's Owner. Open the Connections inspector (⌥⌘6) and break the connection to the view by clicking on the little x on the right side of the View element in the inspector. Save the file and click the Run button in Xcode.

Open the console (via ⌘⇧C) and take a look at the output. You should see an error message that looks like this:

```
Recipes[15932:207] *** Terminating app due to uncaught exception
'NSInternalInconsistencyException', reason: '...
loaded the "PRPViewController" nib but the view outlet was not set.'
```

The application crashes, but it's kind enough to tell you why on the console. This message is telling you that the view controller was asked for its view and it did not find it, so it loaded its nib file. After the nib file was loaded, the view was still not set, so the view controller raised the NSInternalInconsistencyException, which terminated the app. The fix, of course, is to go back to the nib file and undo the change we introduced specifically to see this crashing exception. Go back to the PRPViewController.xib file and make the connection from File's Owner to the view object by clicking File's Owner while holding down the Control key and dragging to the view object. When you lift up on the mouse, the connection will be remade. Run again and the application will start just fine.

It is very common to forget to make that connection from the view controller to the view, particularly when you create your own view controller classes (which is why Xcode will offer to create the nib alongside the new class and prewire the view outlet). You should learn two lessons from this diversion. First, make sure to connect your view controllers to their views. And second, the console is a great place to get info about what is going on in an application.

That's the story of how views make it onto the screen. The window knows what to display by asking the rootViewController for its view. Since the VC was created knowing its nib file, it loads that nib file to get the view. That view is placed into the window and is then on the screen.

4.3   Building a Detailed Recipe View

Now that we know how our view gets onscreen, let's flesh out our recipe model a bit so that we have something nicer to look at. Along the way, we'll learn a bit about some of the other subclasses of UIView in UIKit.

Open the PRPRecipe.h header and add a property for the directions and a property for an image of the completed recipe. The code should look like this:

```
ViewsAndControllers/Recipes_03/Recipes/PRPRecipe.h
@interface PRPRecipe : NSObject

@property(nonatomic, copy) NSString *title;
@property(nonatomic, copy) NSString *directions;
@property(nonatomic, strong) UIImage *image;

@end
```

Be sure to use strong rather than copy on the UIImage property: it would waste memory to copy a lot of image data around.

With these two properties in place, we can step up our game for the look of our view. Open the PRPViewController.xib file by selecting it in the project navigator. We want to do three things here: first, make the title use a bold font; second, add a text view so we can display the directions; and third, put an image view on the screen so we can show what the completed recipe looks like.

To change the title to use a bold font, we just need to change the font that the UILabel uses. Select the title label, open the Attributes inspector (⌥⌘4), and click the Change Font button, as seen in Figure 36, *Changing font of a UILabel*, on page 89.

When the pop-up window is visible, select the Font pop-up menu and then select the System Bold item.

Next, let's add a text view to display the directions. To do that, we need to go to the Object library (^⌥⌘3). In the filter field at the bottom of this pane, type "text" to narrow the displayed objects to just the ones with *text* in their name or description.

Click the Text View object and drag it onto the view. Using the Size inspector (⌥⌘5), place it at {20, 50, 280, 100}. In the Attributes inspector (⌥⌘4), turn

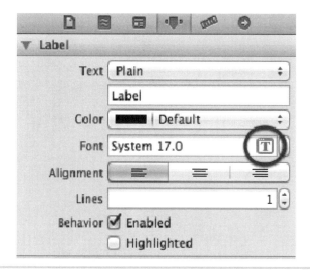

Figure 36—Changing font of a UILabel

off editing, turn off horizontal scrollers, and change the background color to clear.

Next we want to place an image view. In the Search field, type "image," select the Image View, and drag it into the view. Size the view with the Size inspector at {20, 160, 280, 280}. The interface should look like Figure 37, *Updated interface*, on page 90.

Now that we have some new views on the screen to show additional data, we need to wire up the controller to get the data from the model into these views. That means it's time to head back over to PRPViewController.h. Select the file in Xcode and add two new IBOutlet properties, like this:

ViewsAndControllers/Recipes_03/Recipes/PRPViewController.h
```
@property(nonatomic, strong) IBOutlet UITextView *directionsView;
@property(nonatomic, strong) IBOutlet UIImageView *imageView;
```

Now that the view controller has outlets for these two elements of the view, we need to head back to the interface file to make the connections to the text and image views that we added just a couple of paragraphs back. Open PRPViewController.xib again, select File's Owner, and control-click and drag to the text view. Let up on the mouse and select directionsView from the pop-up. Do the same for the image view, but connect it to the imageView outlet. The Connections inspector should look like Figure 38, *Updated connections*, on page 90.

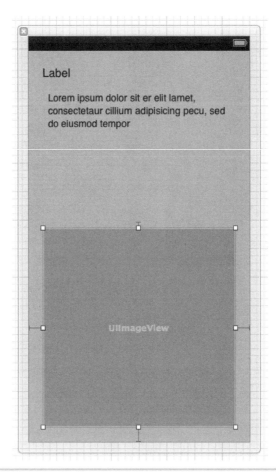

Figure 37—Updated interface

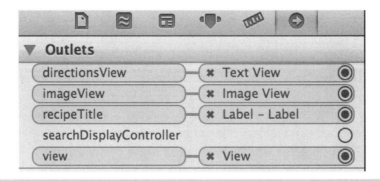

Figure 38—Updated connections

Now we move on to updating the code in our controller to put the data we get from the model into the view. Open the PRPViewController.m and go back to the viewWillAppear: method. We need to grab the directions text from the recipe and place that into the directionsView, and we need to grab the image of the completed recipe and place that into the imageView. The code is very simple; just rewrite viewWillAppear: like this:

```
ViewsAndControllers/Recipes_03/Recipes/PRPViewController.m
Line 1 - (void)viewWillAppear:(BOOL)animated {
     2   [super viewWillAppear:animated];
     3   self.recipeTitle.text = self.recipe.title;
     4   self.directionsView.text = self.recipe.directions;
     5   if(self.recipe.image) {
     6     self.imageView.image = self.recipe.image;
     7   }
     8 }
```

This code is not much different from our previous version of viewWillAppear:. On line 4 we put the directions string from the recipe into the text property of the directionsView, which simply places that string into the text view.

Next, on lines 5–7 we put the image from the recipe into the imageView's image property. We replace the imageView's image only if the recipe's image is set.

Sizing Images

Images are a big part of making iOS applications stand out, but they can be a huge performance drain. An often-overlooked performance issue is the expense of compressing an image. In the sample code the image of the chocolate chip cookies is 280 x 280. The image was purposefully sized that way to match the size of the UIImageView instance in our view. If we were to try to display a 5-megapixel image in a 280 x 280 image view, it would display just the same but the image view would have to do a bunch of work to make the image fit into that 280 x 280 size. In essence it would have to read five million points from the image to fill seventy-eight thousand points on the screen. That is very wasteful, both in terms of performance (how long it takes) as well as power consumption (how much power is drained from the battery). On the iPhone 4 you might not notice the performance hit because it's so fast and we are only displaying one image, but our users would notice the battery drain.

We are done with the heavy lifting, but we still need to put an image and directions into the recipe model object. Remember that we created an instance of PRPRecipe in the PRPAppDelegate's application:didFinishLaunchingWithOptions: method. So let's go back there and update that code. Open the file PRPAppDelegate.m and select the application:didFinishLaunchingWithOptions: method.

The downloadable sample code has an image and some directions for chocolate chip cookies. Feel free to do something similar or just copy what is in the sample code. To add an image file to Xcode, you can drag it from the Finder to the project navigator. When prompted, make sure to check the "Copy items into destination group's folder (if needed)" check box; this keeps the image file with your source files rather than just managing a reference to the original image on your filesystem. Don't forget to resize and crop the image to be 280 x 280.

The updated code should look like this:

ViewsAndControllers/Recipes_03/Recipes/PRPAppDelegate.m

```
Line 1 - (BOOL)application:(UIApplication *)application
       - didFinishLaunchingWithOptions:(NSDictionary *)launchOptions {
       -     NSString *directions = @"Put the flour and other dry ingredients in a bowl,\
       -     stir in the eggs until evenly moist. Add chocolate chips and stir in until even. \
     5     Place tablespoon-size portions on greased cookie sheet and bake at 350° for \
       -     6 minutes.";
       -     PRPRecipe *recipe = [[PRPRecipe alloc] init];
       -     recipe.title = @"Chocolate Chip Cookies";
       -     recipe.image = [UIImage imageNamed:@"cookies.jpg"];
    10     recipe.directions = directions;
       -     self.window = [[UIWindow alloc] initWithFrame:[[UIScreen mainScreen] bounds]];
       -     self.viewController = [[PRPViewController alloc]
       -                            initWithNibName:@"PRPViewController"
       -                            bundle:nil];
    15     self.viewController.recipe = recipe;
       -     self.window.rootViewController = self.viewController;
       -     [self.window makeKeyAndVisible];
       -     return YES;
       - }
```

The directions string is set up on line 6. The backslash character ("\") tells the compiler that the string continues on the next line.[1] On line 9, we create a UIImage from the IMG_1948.jpg image. Feel free to use this image, or take a break from coding and go bake your own cookies and take a picture of them.

Now that our app is complete, click the Run button in Xcode. The running app should look like Figure 39, *Completed recipes app*, on page 93.

Congratulations again! You have a view controller that is capable of showing a recipe, including a photo of what the completed product will look like. Before we go on to the next topic, we need to take a short detour into understanding how view controllers help us to manage the memory used by its view.

---

1. We use this character to suit the formatting of the book; you can keep the string all on one line in your own code.

Figure 39—Completed recipes app

4.4 Wrap-Up

We've successfully completed a real MVC application. Most applications on the app store might be more sophisticated, but they share the same basic structure of this application: a model that contains the heart and soul of the app, a view that presents the information and makes it easy to manipulate, and a controller that translates from the view to the model.

In the next chapter we are going to show a list of recipes, which will be our introduction to table views. We will build on our current example, but we won't be looking at the view controller that we built here again until Chapter 6, *Storyboards and Container Controllers*, on page 119, where we will reuse this view controller when navigating from the list of recipes to the particulars of one recipe.

For Further Thought

Here are a few things to think about or try out to expand your understanding of the stuff we've covered in this chapter. The questions don't necessarily have "correct" answers. Please join us on the forums at http://forums.pragprog.com/ to discuss your ideas about them.

1. Intentionally breaking things is a great way to learn what to expect when you don't intentionally break things. In the nib file for the final part of the example, connect the view parameter from the view controller to the UIImageView and run the app. What happens and why?

2. UIImageView allows you to animate through a series of images. Shoot and resize a couple more images of some cookies. Use those images to create a slide show with the UIImageView. Hint: completing this will require you to dig into the UIImageView docs.

CHAPTER 5

Table Views

Tables are frequently seen in iOS apps because they're an effective way to present a variable amount of data in a familiar format. We'll use them in this chapter to make our recipes app more useful.

Many of the default applications use table views extensively: Mail, Safari, Phone, iPod, iTunes, and more. In fact, there are fewer built-in apps that *don't* use tables than those that do. Even things that you might not think of as table views turn out to be table views, like the message history in Messages and even the grouped pseudo-buttons in Settings.

In this chapter, we'll explore how to present data in a table format by reusing the PRPRecipe model class from Chapter 4, *View Controllers*, on page 77, but instead of displaying a single recipe, we will display a list of recipes. Let's get started.

5.1 The UITableView

First though, let's clear up some terminology. iOS has a different sense of "table" than other platforms do; we're not talking about a two-dimensional grid like an Excel spreadsheet or a Java JTable. Instead, a UITableView is a UIView that presents data as an arbitrarily tall list of cells optionally split into sections of arbitrary lengths.

On iPhone, a table typically takes up the entire screen. This is possible on iPad as well, but they often look bad, so tables are usually shown inside pop-overs on the tablet.

Tables come in two styles: plain and grouped. The plain table is seen in apps like Mail: the cells are rectangular, while the section headers have white text on a gray background and the current section header "parks" at the top of the view while scrolling. In a grouped table, the cells are indented from the edge and have a visible background. The top and bottom cells within a section have rounded "end caps," which make a one-cell section look like a button, and the section headers scroll with the background. Figure 40, *UITableView styles: plain (left) and grouped (right)*, on page 96, shows the difference between the two kinds of tables, which can be set with the style property or with the attribute inspector in IB.

Figure 40—UITableView styles: plain (left) and grouped (right)

5.2 Displaying a List of Recipes

We left our recipes application in the last chapter displaying a single recipe. While that was a great start, what we really want is to keep a whole recipe box on our iPhone. To pull that off, we are going to need several instances of our PRPRecipe model. We will then need a view that is capable of displaying a list of objects, and for that, we'll use a table view. As before, we'll use MVC: if the table is the view and we have a model that holds several recipes, then we need a view controller to combine the two. Let's get started by creating the controller and the view, and then we will create our list of model objects.

Create a Table View Controller

First we need to create a subclass of UITableViewController to translate between our list of recipes and the table view that displays them. UITableViewController is a subclass of UIViewController that defines additional methods that support a table view.

In Xcode with the PRPRecipes project open, let's select the "File->New File…" menu item (⌘N). In the sheet that drops down, we need to choose the "Objective-C class" item and then click Next. Since we are creating a table view controller, we need to choose UITableViewController in the "Subclass of" pull-down. Let's call the new class PRPRecipesListViewController. Be sure that the "With XIB for user interface" check box is also selected. Click Next, and in the next page, choose the Recipes folder and then click the Create button.

You should see three new files in Xcode's project navigator: the PRPRecipesListView-Controller.xib file and the PRPRecipesListViewController header and implementation files (.h and .m).

Create Recipes List

In the previous version of this example, we created a single instance of PRPRecipe to serve as the model, which the controller then used to populate the view. That worked great then, but now we have a list to fill. We could use the one recipe as a table model, but that single item would be lonely. Let's go back to the PRPAppDelegate and modify it to make and keep track of several recipes.

First we need to create a property on the app delegate to hold the list. The natural fit for a list of objects is an NSArray. In Xcode, select the PRPAppDelegate.h file and add a property for the new list, like this:

TableViews/Recipes_04/Recipes/PRPAppDelegate.h
```
@property (copy, nonatomic) NSArray *recipes;
```

Lazy Creation

Let's create the list and then place it into the recipes property. We could do that in the app delegate and assign the view controller's property, or we could create it in the VC's init method. But let's try something different, something lazy.

Often, it's a good idea to create things "lazily," meaning only when we absolutely need them. When we create objects in our program at the last minute, we keep from allocating the memory and doing the work to initialize them until the last possible minute. This typically works in our favor because we don't use memory until we have to. Lazy creation also makes it easier to clean it up when we are done because we know if we delete the objects they will be recreated when we need them.

To implement our recipes method that lazily creates the array, we go to PRPAppDelegate.m and write a new getter method, like this:

TableViews/Recipes_05/Recipes/PRPAppDelegate.m
```
- (NSArray *)recipes {
  if(!_recipes) {
    // create the recipes here
  }
  return _recipes;
}
```

Remember that properties in Objective-C are just declarations that specify the way the get and set methods work. So what we have done here is to provide the get method rather than let the compiler generate it for us (the setter will still be synthesized). The first thing we do here is to check to see if the instance variable (also called an *ivar* for short) backing the property exists. If the ivar exists, then the _recipes array exists and we can simply return it.

If the ivar doesn't exist, we need to create an array, fill it with recipes, and then assign our recipes property to the newly created array. Import the PRPRecipe.h filename and then replace the comment with this code to create the array and add the first two recipes:

TableViews/Recipes_04/Recipes/PRPAppDelegate.m
```
NSMutableArray *localRecipes = [NSMutableArray array];
PRPRecipe *recipe = [[PRPRecipe alloc] init];
recipe.directions = @"0 - Put some stuff in, and the other stuff, then stir";
recipe.title = @"0 - One Fine Food";
recipe.image = [UIImage imageNamed:@"cookies.jpg"];
[localRecipes addObject:recipe];
recipe = [[PRPRecipe alloc] init];
recipe.directions = @"1 - Put some stuff in, and the other stuff, then stir";
recipe.title = @"1 - One Fine Food";
recipe.image = [UIImage imageNamed:@"cookies.jpg"];
[localRecipes addObject:recipe];
```

The code download bundle creates several recipes, as shown in the following screenshots. You are, of course, free to create five or twenty-five recipes in this method; all of them will show up in your tableview.

The final step in our lazy creation code is to assign our localRecipes variable to the recipes property. After the last recipe has been added to localRecipes, add this line of code.

TableViews/Recipes_04/Recipes/PRPAppDelegate.m
```
self.recipes = localRecipes;
```

Since the recipes property is specified to copy its value, writing self.recipes = local-Recipes will make a *copy* of localRecipes and assign it to the _recipes ivar. Making a copy of an NSMutableArray might sound inefficient, but it really isn't. The recipes are not copied, just the data structure to hold onto the list. It is important to make a copy, though, so that we end up with an immutable NSArray rather than its mutable subclass, since some other part of the app could change a mutable array without the view controller knowing about it.

We can add as many recipe instances here as we'd like, and it could be interesting to experiment with the number of recipes and see how the table view reacts. Speaking of the table view, let's go fix up the application:didFinish-LaunchingWithOptions: method to display our new table view instead of the old single recipe view.

Display the Table View

Let's navigate to the application:didFinishLaunchingWithOptions: method in the PRPAppDelegate and change it so that our table view controller is the rootViewController. That will make the table the view that gets shown when the app comes up. Here's the updated implementation:

TableViews/Recipes_04/Recipes/PRPAppDelegate.m

```
Line 1 - (BOOL)application:(UIApplication *)application
     2 didFinishLaunchingWithOptions:(NSDictionary *)launchOptions {
     3    self.window = [[UIWindow alloc] initWithFrame:[[UIScreen mainScreen] bounds]];
     4    self.viewController = [[PRPRecipesListViewController alloc]
     5                       initWithNibName:@"PRPRecipesListViewController"
     6                       bundle:nil];
     7    self.window.rootViewController = self.viewController;
```

The big change here is on lines 4–6. If we were to build and compile now, two undesired things would happen. First, we'd get a compile error that our table view controller is undefined. Second, the compiler would complain about the type mismatch between the viewController property and the type of the object we are assigning. To fix the first issue we need to change the #import statement to import the PRPRecipesListViewController.h instead of the PRPViewController.h in the header file. Next we need to modify the property declaration so the viewController's type matches. When done, the changed header should look like this:

TableViews/Recipes_05/Recipes/PRPAppDelegate.h

```
@class PRPRecipesListViewController;
@interface PRPAppDelegate : UIResponder <UIApplicationDelegate>
@property (strong, nonatomic) UIWindow *window;
@property (strong, nonatomic) PRPRecipesListViewController *viewController;
@property (copy, nonatomic) NSArray *recipes;
@end
```

If we were to build and run the app now, the table view would display, but it would not have any data in it. That's no good! We need to pass the array of recipes off to the table view controller. However, the view controller does not have a way for us to tell it what the recipes are. Right after the line to change the rootViewController, add a line of code like this:

TableViews/Recipes_04/Recipes/PRPAppDelegate.m

```
self.viewController.recipes = self.recipes;
```

Of course this won't compile, since the viewController does not have the recipes property defined on it yet. That's an easy fix though. First, add the property to the PRPRecipesListViewController. Open the header file and add the property declaration @property (strong, nonatomic) NSArray *recipes.

Now our table view controller knows about the list of recipes, but we still need to have it use that list to populate the table view.

A table view relies on an object that implements the UITableViewDataSource protocol to get its data. Fortunately, our PRPRecipesListViewController already implements this protocol as part of the template code for a subclass of UITableViewController. Let's go take a look and change the implementation to work with our new recipes property.

To update the code, we need to edit the implementation file, so open PRPRecipesListViewController.m in Xcode. We've been ignoring it up to this point, but if we were to hit the Run button in Xcode since adding this new controller, we would see two new build warnings. Both of them are coming from this class, warning us that two of the required methods still have the template-provided implementation. The first is numberOfSectionsInTableView:. This method is called by the table view to discover how many sections it has. We will cover sections in Chapter 6, *Storyboards and Container Controllers*, on page 119. For now, just change this method to return a constant value of 1, like this:

TableViews/Recipes_04/Recipes/PRPRecipesListViewController.m

```
- (NSInteger)numberOfSectionsInTableView:(UITableView *)tableView {
    return 1;
}
```

The next warning is coming from the tableView:numberOfRowsInSection: method. This method is called by the table view for each section to determine how many rows will be in that particular section. Since our previous method implementation tells the table there is only one section, the section parameter sent to this method will always be 0. And for that one section, we return the number of rows as the length of the recipes array. Change your code to look like this:

TableViews/Recipes_04/Recipes/PRPRecipesListViewController.m

```
- (NSInteger)tableView:(UITableView *)tableView
 numberOfRowsInSection:(NSInteger)section {
    return [self.recipes count];
}
```

Now our table view knows how many rows it needs to display. The next step is to configure each row to display the correct data. The table view calls the tableView:cellForRowAtIndexPath: method of its data source for every row on the screen. The table view expects this method to return a UITableViewCell (or a subclass) for each row.

The table view is careful to only call this method for the rows that are visible onscreen. So if we had one thousand recipes, the table view would only call this method about ten times, once for each cell that is visible. Then as we scrolled through the list of a thousand recipes, it would ask us to provide another cell each time a row becomes visible.

Now that we know the conditions under which this method is called, all we need to do is update it to set the text to display in the cell. Change your code to look like this:

TableViews/Recipes_04/Recipes/PRPRecipesListViewController.m

```
Line 1  - (UITableViewCell *)tableView:(UITableView *)tableView
            cellForRowAtIndexPath:(NSIndexPath *)indexPath {
    -     static NSString *CellIdentifier = @"Cell";
    -
    5   UITableViewCell *cell = [tableView
                             dequeueReusableCellWithIdentifier:CellIdentifier];
    -     if (cell == nil) {
    -       cell = [[UITableViewCell alloc] initWithStyle:UITableViewCellStyleDefault
                                        reuseIdentifier:CellIdentifier];
    10  }
    -
    -   cell.textLabel.text = [[self.recipes objectAtIndex:indexPath.row] title];
    -   return cell;
    - }
```

We only have to add one line of code to this method to make our list of recipes show up. We get the recipe we are displaying by grabbing the row from the indexPath passed into this method. Instances of NSIndexPath are used to identify a particular cell by its section and row properties. Then, to set the text of a cell, change the text property of the cell's textLabel, as on line 12.

Considering we only have to populate one property, the code provided for this method by the template seems to be doing a lot of extra work. To understand that, we need to look at how UIKit manages cell reuse.

Let's look back at line 3. Here we are declaring a string called CellIdentifier, and on line 6 we use that identifier to ask the table view for a reusable cell. Behind the scenes the table view is keeping track of all the cells that have been returned from tableView:cellForRowAtIndexPath:. When one of them scrolls offscreen, it gets pulled out of the table view and placed into the reuse queue. Then, as our controller is asked to provide cells to the table view via the tableView:cellFor-RowAtIndexPath: method, it asks the table view if there are any reusable cells available. If there is a suitable cell, one whose identifier matches, the table view returns that cell and our method just sets the cell label text. If there is not a cell to return, then we get back nil. In that case, we go to line 9, where we use the same identifier to create a new cell.

Cell reuse allows our app to only have a few cells in memory at a time; more importantly, it keeps us from having to allocate new memory for each cell during scrolling. Reusing cells is the only way we can keep our scrolling animations smooth.

And that's it—we now have our table view and its data source set up to display our list of recipes. Hit Run in Xcode and you should see something that looks like Figure 41, *First table view*, on page 103.

In this section we took the first step into the deep waters of the UITableView, but there is so much left to learn! Let's get started on our next step to table view mastery by looking at how to edit a table view.

5.3 Editing a Table

Users edit items in a table view by adding, removing, or reordering items. Deleting items is ingrained in iOS users: swiping right inserts the Delete button, and tapping the Delete button removes the item. All of that functionality is built into the table view for us to take advantage of. Adding items takes a bit more work. So we will focus on deleting first and put off addition of a new recipe for Chapter 6, *Storyboards and Container Controllers*, on page 119.

By default, table views will not allow items to be deleted. We can make our table view editable by implementing one additional method on PRPRecipesListView-Controller. In fact, the method is already in the class's implementation file; it's just commented out.

Let's go uncomment the method. Open the PRPRecipesListViewController.m file and search for commitEditingStyle:. This is the method we need to implement for our table view to be editable.

Go ahead and uncomment the method. The code should look like this:

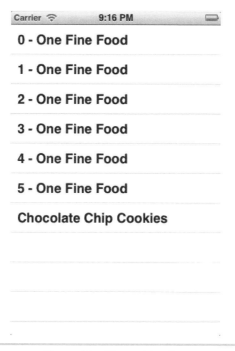

Figure 41—First table view

TableViews/Recipes_06/Recipes/PRPRecipesListViewController.m
```
Line 1 - (void)tableView:(UITableView *)tableView
     2 commitEditingStyle:(UITableViewCellEditingStyle)editingStyle
     3 forRowAtIndexPath:(NSIndexPath *)indexPath {
     4   if (editingStyle == UITableViewCellEditingStyleDelete) {
     5     [tableView deleteRowsAtIndexPaths:[NSArray arrayWithObject:indexPath]
     6                     withRowAnimation:UITableViewRowAnimationFade];
     7   } else if (editingStyle == UITableViewCellEditingStyleInsert) {
     8   }
     9 }
```

On lines 5 to 6, we tell the table view to delete the row we are being asked to remove. We will continue to ignore the UITableViewCellEditingStyleInsert case for now.

Run the application. Once it's running, swipe one of the rows. The Delete button should appear on that row and look something like Figure 42, *Deleting a row*, on page 104.

That was too easy though, wasn't it? We just got our table view to be editable by uncommenting a few lines of code provided to us by the template. Well, it *is* a bit too easy: all we've done is made the view present an editing UI, and

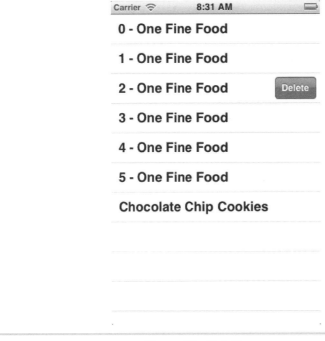

Figure 42—Deleting a row

we have not actually provided any editing capability for our model. To illustrate this, go ahead and tap on the Delete button. *Boom!* The app dies because the view and model are in an incompatible state.

Open the Debug View console (⌘⇧C) and take a look at the output. The table view has printed out a message.

```
*** Terminating app due to uncaught exception 'NSInternalInconsistencyException',
reason:'Invalid update: invalid number of rows in section 0.  The number of
rows contained in an existing section after the update (7) must be equal to the
number of rows contained in that section before the update (7), plus or minus
the number of rows inserted or deleted from that section (0 inserted, 1 deleted)
and plus or minus the number of rows moved into or out of that section
(0 moved in, 0 moved out).
```

Refactoring to Delete

The table view is telling us that one of its internal consistency checks is failing. Of course, we know what the problem is because we ran through this path knowing that we hadn't dealt with editing the model. However, in more complex situations, it might not be so obvious what we've done wrong. This is another great lesson in purposefully breaking things to see what happens, so when the breakage is not on purpose, we recognize what the trouble is.

The trouble here is that the array of recipes that we got from the app delegate (back in *Lazy Creation*, on page 97) is immutable. There are several ways we could fix the problem. At first, it might seem like making the array of recipes into a NSMutableArray might be the way to go. In this simple example, that would work…for now.

In the real world, however, the list of recipes might be coming from a database stored locally on the device and populated by a recurring query to a web service. Simply making our recipes list into a mutable array would make it so we could edit our copy, but that would leave the local database and web service in an inconsistent state. To get ourselves out of this corner we need to do a bit of code surgery.

Having an array of recipes was a great idea to get started: it was simple, quick, and easy to understand. But now that we want to edit the list, it makes sense to build a more abstract representation of our set of recipes and then interact with that. Let's take a cue from the table view and define our own data source, but for recipes.

We are going to define a new @protocol that our PRPRecipesListViewController will interact with to get the recipes as well as to remove the recipes. The first step is to create a new file in Xcode.

With the Recipes group selected in Xcode, create a new file (⌘N). From the first dialog choose Cocoa Touch and Objective-C Protocol, and then click the Next button. Name the protocol PRPRecipesListDataSource and click Next. Make sure the Recipes group is selected and that the Recipes target is checked, and click Create.

Our protocol will abstract the interaction with the list of recipes, so let's define the methods we'll use. We are currently using the array's count method in tableView:numberOfRowsInSection: and the objectAtIndex: in the tableView:cellForRowAtIndexPath: method. So our protocol needs at least two methods: one to provide the count of recipes and another to return a recipe for a given index. But the whole reason we are doing this refactoring in the first place is so we can remove an item. Clearly, we need a third method to remove a recipe at a given index. Here is the protocol definition with our three new methods defined.

TableViews/Recipes_07/Recipes/PRPRecipesListDataSource.h
```
@class PRPRecipe;
@protocol PRPRecipesListDataSource <NSObject>
- (NSInteger)recipeCount;
- (PRPRecipe *)recipeAtIndex:(NSInteger)index;
- (void)deleteRecipeAtIndex:(NSInteger)index;
@end
```

With these three methods in place we can update our PRPRecipesListViewController to use this protocol rather than the array. Open the PRPRecipesListViewController.h file, delete the array property, and add a new property called dataSource. The modified interface should look like this:

TableViews/Recipes_07/Recipes/PRPRecipesListViewController.h
```
#import "PRPRecipesListDataSource.h"

@interface PRPRecipesListViewController : UITableViewController
@property(nonatomic, strong) id <PRPRecipesListDataSource> dataSource;
@end
```

Now let's go update the implementation to use the data source rather than the array. We need to update the tableView:numberOfRowsInSection: method to use the dataSource, like this:

TableViews/Recipes_07/Recipes/PRPRecipesListViewController.m
```
- (NSInteger)tableView:(UITableView *)tableView
 numberOfRowsInSection:(NSInteger)section {
➤    return [self.dataSource recipeCount];
}
```

We have one more table view delegate method to update. Go to tableView:cellForRowAtIndexPath: and update it to use the dataSource's recipeAtIndex: instead of the array's objectAtIndex: method, like this:

TableViews/Recipes_07/Recipes/PRPRecipesListViewController.m
```
Line 1 - (UITableViewCell *)tableView:(UITableView *)tableView
             cellForRowAtIndexPath:(NSIndexPath *)indexPath
  - {
  -     static NSString *CellIdentifier = @"Cell";
  5
  -     UITableViewCell *cell = [tableView
  -                               dequeueReusableCellWithIdentifier:CellIdentifier];
  -     if (cell == nil) {
  -         cell = [[UITableViewCell alloc] initWithStyle:UITableViewCellStyleDefault
  10                                 reuseIdentifier:CellIdentifier];
  -     }
  -
  -     cell.textLabel.text = [[self.dataSource recipeAtIndex:indexPath.row] title];
  -     return cell;
  15 }
```

Now we are almost back to where we started. Our table view controller can get the overall count of recipes and the recipe at a given index. So far, it might seem like a waste to convert from the simple array to this "data source" thing. However, consider what we need to do in the tableView:commitEditingStyle:forRowAtIndexPath: method. Here is the updated code:

```
Line 1 - (void)tableView:(UITableView *)tableView
     2 commitEditingStyle:(UITableViewCellEditingStyle)editingStyle
     3 forRowAtIndexPath:(NSIndexPath *)indexPath {
     4   if (editingStyle == UITableViewCellEditingStyleDelete) {
     5     [self.dataSource deleteRecipeAtIndex:indexPath.row];
     6     [tableView deleteRowsAtIndexPaths:[NSArray arrayWithObject:indexPath]
     7                     withRowAnimation:UITableViewRowAnimationFade];
     8   } else if (editingStyle == UITableViewCellEditingStyleInsert) {
     9   }
    10 }
```

Behind the simple facade of the protocol's deleteRecipeAtIndex: invoked on line 5, we could hide a bunch of complexity. If our recipes did in fact come from some kind of web service, we could implement a network call to delete the recipe behind this simple-looking method.

This brings into focus one of the major points of object-oriented programming: hiding complexity behind simple-to-use APIs. We can already see examples of this in the code provided by the Xcode template. Consider the window's makeKeyAndVisible method for example. Think about all the stuff that has to go on to get something onto the screen: drawing all the content, pushing it to the GPU, compositing it onto the screen, and so on. And we don't have to think about any of it. When we build our own code, we'd do well to adopt similar designs, like hiding complexity and making it look simple. Our PRPRecipesListDataSource gives us the ability to do just that.

However, right now there is no complexity because we've not provided an implementation for the protocol. Let's fix that next.

In Xcode, select the Recipes group and click "New File…" (⌘N). Choose Cocoa Touch and Objective C Class and click the Next button. Name the class PRPRecipesSource, choose NSObject as the superclass and click Next again. Make sure the Recipes group is selected and that the Recipes target is checked, and click Create.

In the PRPRecipesSource.h file, add the PRPRecipesListDataSource protocol to the class declaration, like this:

```
#import "PRPRecipesListDataSource.h"

@interface PRPRecipesSource : NSObject <PRPRecipesListDataSource>

@end
```

As a reminder, this means that the PRPRecipesSource implements the PRPRecipes-ListDataSource protocol, meaning we implement some or all of its declared methods. For this declaration to compile, make sure to import the header for the PRPRecipesListDataSource protocol.

Now on to implementing the source. In this implementation we are not going to do anything fancy like talk to a web service: we are going to continue to use a simple array. But since the PRPRecipesListViewController that will talk to this model doesn't know we are using a simple array, we are free to flesh out our data source implementation at any time without having to change the view controller. That flexibility is the real power of doing good object-oriented design.

The first thing we want to do is add a property in the PRPRecipesSource.m implementation file in a class extension to keep track of our array of recipes. Add a class extension to the top of the file, like this:

TableViews/Recipes_07/Recipes/PRPRecipesSource.m
```
@interface PRPRecipesSource()
@property(nonatomic, strong) NSMutableArray *recipes;
@end
```

We have the property; now we want to lazily create the array of recipes. That should sound familiar—we covered it back in *Lazy Creation*, on page 97. For this example, all we need to do is move the implementation of the recipes method from the PRPAppDelegate class over to this class. While we are in the PRPAppDelegate.m file, change the implementation of application:didFinishLaunchingWithOptions: to set the viewController's dataSource, like this:

TableViews/Recipes_07/Recipes/PRPAppDelegate.m
```
self.viewController.dataSource = [[PRPRecipesSource alloc] init];
```

Now we need to implement the three methods required by the protocol as follows:

TableViews/Recipes_07/Recipes/PRPRecipesSource.m
```
#pragma mark Recipe List Data Source Methods
- (NSInteger)recipeCount {
  return [self.recipes count];
}

- (PRPRecipe *)recipeAtIndex:(NSInteger)index {
  return [self.recipes objectAtIndex:index];
}

- (void)deleteRecipeAtIndex:(NSInteger)index {
  [self.recipes removeObjectAtIndex:index];
}
```

The implementation of the protocol is simple. But now that the implementation is hidden behind our protocol, we can choose to make them as complex as we'd like without the table view controller ever needing to know.

Now we have everything in place to perform the delete, so let's run the app. When we hit the Delete button, instead of crashing, the row now animates away and the model is updated.

5.4 Working with Cell Styles

What we have so far is sufficient, but only just: we can see the list of recipes, but the rows are not compelling visually. Fortunately, there are several table cell styles built into UIKit; let's consider one as an alternative.

Go back to the PRPRecipesListViewController.m and let's look at the tableView:cellForRowAtIndexPath: method. One of the first things we can do here to spruce up our table view is add the image from the recipe to the cell.

TableViews/Recipes_08/Recipes/PRPRecipesListViewController.m

```
Line 1 - (UITableViewCell *)tableView:(UITableView *)tableView
              cellForRowAtIndexPath:(NSIndexPath *)indexPath
     - {
     -   static NSString *CellIdentifier = @"Cell";
     5
     -   UITableViewCell *cell = [tableView
                              dequeueReusableCellWithIdentifier:CellIdentifier];
     -   if (cell == nil) {
     -     cell = [[UITableViewCell alloc] initWithStyle:UITableViewCellStyleDefault
    10                            reuseIdentifier:CellIdentifier];
     -   }
     -
     -   cell.textLabel.text = [[self.dataSource recipeAtIndex:indexPath.row] title];
     -   cell.imageView.image = [[self.dataSource recipeAtIndex:indexPath.row] image];
    15   return cell;
     - }
```

On line 14 we get the image from the recipe and place it into the imageView's image property. Now if we run the application again we have thumbnail images on the left side of each cell!

This is pretty cool: with only a one-line change, we got a nice bit of pizzazz added to our application. But we're doing this at a significant cost: we are placing an image that is 280 x 280 into a much smaller area (about 42 x 42 in iOS 6, but always subject to change in future versions), and as was discussed back in *Sizing Images*, on page 91, forcing the image view to down-sample the image can be costly. A better approach would be to add a new property to our PRPRecipes class for a thumbnail image, and then when the recipes are created in our PRPRecipesSource, we'd make sure to set the thumbnail to be a smaller version of the same image. For our current data set, this change is not really necessary, but for more sophisticated applications, making the app down-sample images while fetching new cells can adversely affect the scrolling performance.

We have taken the default cell style about as far as we can. But there's more we want to do with the app. The next step is to include the preparation time for each of the recipes. To do that, add a new property to the PRPRecipe called preparationTime of type NSNumber, use "strong" and "nonatomic" for the property. When the model class is updated, go to the PRPRecipesSource's recipes method and specify a preparation time for each of the recipes created there.

We have new data to display: what do we do with it? There doesn't seem to be any place left in the cell since we already use the textLabel for the name of the recipe. Fortunately, one line of text and an image isn't our only option. We can change the style of our table view cells to UITableViewCellStyleSubtitle: cells with this style have an additional label called detailTextLabel, located just below the main textLabel, and which by default draws its text in light gray and in a smaller font.

To use this style, we edit the PRPRecipesListViewController class and update the tableView:cellForRowAtIndexPath: method to look like this:

TableViews/Recipes_09/Recipes/PRPRecipesListViewController.m
```
Line 1 - (UITableViewCell *)tableView:(UITableView *)tableView
    -          cellForRowAtIndexPath:(NSIndexPath *)indexPath
    - {
    -   static NSString *CellIdentifier = @"Cell";
    5
    -   UITableViewCell *cell = [tableView
    -                           dequeueReusableCellWithIdentifier:CellIdentifier];
    -   if (cell == nil) {
    -     cell = [[UITableViewCell alloc] initWithStyle:UITableViewCellStyleSubtitle
   10                                     reuseIdentifier:CellIdentifier];
    -   }
    -
    -   PRPRecipe *recipe = [self.dataSource recipeAtIndex:indexPath.row];
    -   cell.textLabel.text = [recipe title];
   15   cell.imageView.image = [recipe image];
    -   cell.detailTextLabel.text = [NSString stringWithFormat:@"%@ %@",
    -                               [recipe preparationTime],
    -                               NSLocalizedString(@"minutes", nil)];
    -   return cell;
   20 }
```

On line 9, we now use the subtitle cell style to initialize the cell. Later, on line 18, we set the detailTextLabel's text value to the recipe's preparationTime after turning that into a string.

Let's run the application again. Once it's up and going, it should look like Figure 43, *Images and subtitles*, on page 111.

Figure 43—Images and subtitles

This is much more interesting visually than the title alone! We've come a long way from the beginning of this chapter. Yes, there's one more step to take: when we tap on a recipe, we'd like to see the details. Let's look at how to make that happen in the next section.

5.5 Recipe Details

Now that we have a list of recipes, we want to be able to see the details. In Chapter 4, *View Controllers*, on page 77, we built a view controller to display the details of a recipe. We're going to reuse that view controller in this section.

When the user taps on a row in our table view, it sends the tableView:didSelectRowAtIndexPath method to its delegate. The delegate is an object implementing the UITableViewDelegate protocol, which is responsible for handling user interaction with the table as well as certain appearance-related concerns, like providing the titles of section headers and footers. The table's delegate and dataSource can be different objects, but they are often the same. In our app, we have subclassed UITableViewController, which implements both UITableViewDelegate and UITableViewDataSource, so we handle both protocols in the same place.

In fact, if we go back to PRPRecipesListViewController.m, we'll find the tableView:didSelectRowAtIndexPath method implemented with its body commented out. The commented-out portions have references to a "navigation controller": we will be looking at navigation controllers in Chapter 6, *Storyboards and Container Controllers*, on page 119, so we'll ignore that for now. In this implementation, we are going to handle a tap by presenting our recipe detail view controller *modally*.

On the iPhone, modal UIViewControllers take over the whole screen. A modal view is used when we want to convey a specific meaning to our users. We are interrupting the normal flow of the application to get some specific data, ask a question, or present some completely different set of views.

On the iPad, modal view controllers can be displayed in one of three ways: full screen, as a page, or as a form. When presented full screen, the view controller's view will take over the whole screen, as on iPhone. When presented as a page, the view controller's view will span the entire height of the iPad but will be centered horizontally and will block interaction with the background view. When a view controller is presented as a form on iPad, it will be centered both horizontally and vertically and will continue to block interaction with the background view.

Let's implement all these changes. In the PRPRecipesListViewController.m, import the PRPViewController.h file, delete all the commented-out code from tableView:didSelectRowAtIndexPath, and make it look like this:

TableViews/Recipes_10/Recipes/PRPRecipesListViewController.m
```
- (void)tableView:(UITableView *)tableView
didSelectRowAtIndexPath:(NSIndexPath *)indexPath {
  PRPViewController *detailVC = [[PRPViewController alloc]
                                initWithNibName:@"PRPViewController"
                                bundle:nil];
  detailVC.recipe = [self.dataSource recipeAtIndex:indexPath.row];
  [self presentViewController:detailVC animated:YES completion:nil];
}
```

Here we create an instance of PRPViewController with the initWithNibName:bundle: method. Next we tell the new instance which recipe to display. Finally we present it modally via UIViewController's presentViewController:animated:completion: method.

If we build and run now, the detail view appears but we have two problems to address. We don't display the preparation time of the recipe, and there is no way to dismiss the detail VC once it's onscreen. Let's address the preparation time first.

Add two properties to the PRPViewController for the label to display the preparation time and a number formatter to turn the preparation time into a string, like this:

TableViews/Recipes_10/Recipes/PRPViewController.h
```
@property(nonatomic, strong) IBOutlet UILabel *prepTime;
@property(nonatomic, strong) NSNumberFormatter *formatter;
```

As you can probably guess, the IBOutlet on the prepTime property means we need to connect our view controller to a label on the view. Go to Interface Builder, drag out a new label, and place it between the directions text and the image view. You might have to resize the directions text or the image view to make room. Change its value to "Prep Time:" and change its font from System to System Bold. Drag another label out and place it to the right of the "Prep Time:" label. When done, the view should look like Figure 44, *Prep Time labels placed*, on page 114.

Now connect the VC's prepTimeIBOutlet to the second label, and the interface changes are done. Now to fill in the implementation details.

In the PRPViewController.m, create a number formatter in the viewDidLoad method, like this:

TableViews/Recipes_10/Recipes/PRPViewController.m
```
- (void)viewDidLoad {
  [super viewDidLoad];
  self.formatter = [[NSNumberFormatter alloc] init];
}
```

We use the formatter to convert the preparation time from an NSNumber to an NSString. It's important to use a formatter rather than other approaches because NSNumberFormatter understands internationalization and the user's preferences. The formatter understands that in some languages a "," is the decimal separator, instead of a ".".

In the viewWillAppear: we use the stringFromNumber: method to do the conversion, like this:

TableViews/Recipes_10/Recipes/PRPViewController.m
```
self.prepTime.text = [self.formatter stringFromNumber:self.recipe.preparationTime];
```

Figure 44—Prep Time labels placed

We need a control that the user can tap to dismiss the detail view. We'll use a UIButton. A tap on the button will invoke a method on our view controller, and in that method we'll dismiss the view controller.

Back in the interface for PRPViewController, add a single method description, like this:

TableViews/Recipes_10/Recipes/PRPViewController.h
```
- (IBAction)dismiss:(id)sender;
```

We'll add the implementation in just a moment. Let's set up the UI first. Open the PRPViewController.xib. Place a UIButton in the top right and change its label to be Done. Next we need to connect the button to the dismiss: method. Hold down the Control key (^) and drag from the button to File's Owner. Once there, a pop-up should appear that looks like Figure 45, *Connect Dismiss action*, on page 115. Select dismiss: and release the mouse button.

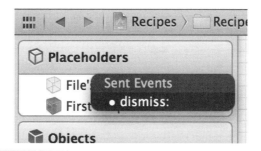

Figure 45—Connect Dismiss action

Open the PRPViewController.m and scroll down to the bottom of the file. We only need to add one line of code here, like this:

```
TableViews/Recipes_10/Recipes/PRPViewController.m
- (IBAction)dismiss:(id)sender {
  [self dismissViewControllerAnimated:YES completion:nil];
}
```

We are now ready to run our app. Once it's running, tap on a recipe to see its details slide into view, and then tap on the Done button to dismiss it. Now we are displaying details of our recipes, and we are able to go back to the list. Figure 46, *Recipe details*, on page 116, is a screenshot of our updated recipe details view with the Done button.

As a refresher on what we learned in Chapter 4, *View Controllers*, on page 77, recall that as the detail view controller is coming onscreen, it is sent the viewWillAppear: method. That's where we placed all the code to take the details from the recipes and place them into various subviews (the label, image view, and so on). Since we did that work up front in the earlier chapter, we were able to drop in and reuse this view controller. Drop-in reusability is an important trait we always want to strive for with our view controllers. In the next chapter (Chapter 6, *Storyboards and Container Controllers*, on page 119), we are going to reuse both view controllers we built in this chapter in container controllers.

5.6 Wrap-Up

We have come a long way since we first started this little Recipes app. We now have two view controllers: one to manage the list of recipes and a second to manage the details of a particular recipe. You've seen how table views work with their data source to get lists of data onto the screen and how the delegate of the table view is responsible for responding to user actions, like tapping on a row. We also explored editing a table view by deleting rows. Next, let's

Figure 46—Recipe details

dive into view controller containment and see how multiple view controllers work together.

For Further Thought

Here are a few things to think about or try out to expand your understanding of the stuff we've covered in this chapter. The questions don't necessarily have "correct" answers. Please join us on the forums at http://forums.pragprog.com/ to discuss your ideas about them.

1. When we were deleting table view rows in tableView:commitEditingStyle:forRowAtIndexPath:, we used the fade animation style. There are several other styles listed in the documentation. Take a minute to try them out. Which ones work for which positions? Delete the first and last rows specifically to see how the various animation styles look. Next, try setting the animation style to UITableViewRowAnimationAutomatic and see what transitions you get.

2. In tableView:didSelectRowAtIndexPath:, we used the default (slide in from the bottom) animation mode for presenting our detailed view controller. Try setting the modalTransitionStyle on the detailVC to some of the other available styles. Which ones do you like? Which ones don't work?

3. Add a thumbnailImage property to the recipe class and display that in the table view cells rather than the full size image. Don't forget to create new, smaller images, which you can do with the Preview application built into OS X and the Tools->Adjust Size... menu.

4. Spend a couple of minutes looking over the UITableViewDataSource and the UITableViewDelegate protocols in the documentation. Does the location of the methods in each of the protocols make sense to you? Are there methods in one that you think belong in the other?

CHAPTER 6

Storyboards and Container Controllers

Every great application tells a story and creates an experience for the user. From the humble Weather app to the all-business Mail app, it's all about telling the story. The Weather app makes it easy to prepare for the day or for a trip to another city. Mail makes it easy to keep in touch with friends and family and even conduct business while on the go.

When people in the entertainment industry create a story, they start with storyboards. Each scene in the story is planned out visually on the boards; each transition from one scene to another is meticulously thought through. All the equipment, staff, actors, and dialogue are fleshed out. The storyboard becomes the guide by which the narrative unfolds. In iOS 5, Apple incorporated this concept into building iOS applications. As we progress through this chapter, we will convert our recipes example into a storyboard-based application that has all the features of the previous recipes app and several more. Let's get started.

6.1 Laying Out Storyboards

iOS storyboards are not about actors, equipment, and dialogue; instead, they help us plan out and provide the experience we want to give users. A storyboard is made up of scenes that are connected with segues. Each scene contains a view controller and a view. Segues specify how the view from the destination view controller will animate over the view from the current view controller. Segues give us control over conveying contextual shifts and switches. Figure 47, *Complete storyboard*, on page 120, shows the storyboard for our Recipes application as it will look at the end of this chapter.

This storyboard consists of seven scenes. The initial view controller is the leftmost navigation controller. It has an arrow that fades as it extends to the left, not connected to anything, which is the visual cue that this view controller

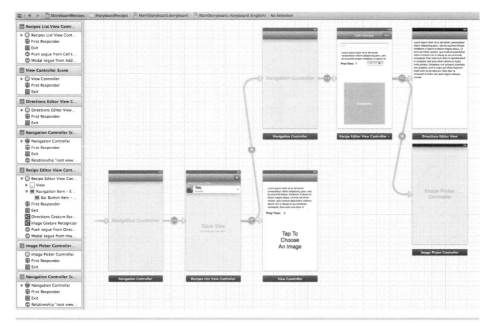

Figure 47—Complete storyboard

is the beginning of the storyboard. We can add as many view controllers to a storyboard as needed to fully describe our application. Fortunately, all the knowledge about view controllers and how they work continues to apply. View controllers still lazily load their views. They still get the view appearance callbacks (that is, viewWillAppear:, viewDidAppear:, and so on). A storyboard can be thought of as a collection of view controllers and their nib files. With a storyboard, we can easily see and edit the whole flow of our application. Behind the scenes, UIKit does all the heavy lifting of splitting the storyboard into small files that are loaded on demand by their view controller.

As users traverse through an application, the storyboard specifies which view controllers become active. We describe the possible paths via segues. In Figure 48, *Selected view controller with segue*, on page 121, the right-side view controller is selected. This view controller is the destination of the push segue from the Recipes table view controller on the left. As recipes are selected, this view controller will be pushed over the recipes list view controller.

Notice the tray under the view of the selected view controller. This tray holds all the "top level objects" in this scene, most notably the view controller. This is the point to which you will connect controls in the view and the point from which you will connect IBOutlets to views.

Figure 48—Selected view controller with segue

Prior to iOS 5, view controllers existed as "islands" of functionality strung together manually. Our recipes application, to this point, has been built with this pre-iOS 5 mindset. Each view controller has its own nib file where its view is specified. The navigation between the view controllers is coded by hand either in action methods (the Done button) or delegate callbacks (the cell was selected callback). This approach works—all the hundreds of thousands of applications submitted to the App Store prior to iOS 5 used it—but writing the navigation code can be tedious. With the arrival of storyboards, we can eliminate that code and replace it with connections, visually drawn in Interface Builder.

With a storyboard, we can define a complete application from the initial view controller to the deepest detail view controller and all the interactions between them. The entire flow of our application can be specified in one storyboard. And the best part is that we just specify the view controllers and their relationships, while UIKit maintains the code to do the actual navigation.

Rebuild Recipes with Storyboards

To begin our storyboard-based recipes app, create a new single view-based application called StoryboardRecipes in Xcode. Make sure to choose the Use Storyboard option in the new project dialog, and don't forget to specify the Class Prefix as PRP.

Click Next and save the project. This first step seems like starting over, but it's really not. We are going to reuse all the view controllers that we have built thus far and just replace the navigation code with connections in Interface Builder. Before we can copy the view controller files over though, we need to delete the ones created for us in the template. Select PRPViewController.h and PRPViewController.m and delete them.

Now, with the Recipes project open in Xcode, select the following files:

- PRPRecipesListViewController, header, and implementation
- PRPRecipesSource, header, and implementation
- PRPRecipesListDataSource header
- PRPRecipe, header, and implementation
- PRPViewController, header, and implementation
- Any image files you made for the recipes

Drag these files to our new StoryboardRecipes project and specify both that you want to copy the files and that you want the source files added to the StoryboardRecipes target. The import dialogue should look like Figure 49, *Import dialogue*, on page 122.

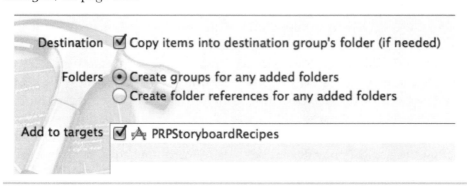

Figure 49—Import dialogue

Now that we have our view controllers copied over, it's time to build our storyboard. Select the MainStoryboard.storyboard in Xcode.

Building the Recipes Storyboard

The single view controller in the default storyboard is called the *initial view controller*, which as the name suggests, is the first view controller for our storyboard. In the previous version of the application, this was the list of recipes. To reproduce the list of recipes, we need to change the class of the view controller and convert the view into a table view.

Select the initial view controller. In the Identity inspector (⌥⌘3), change the class to PRPRecipesListViewController. Now, change the view to a table view by selecting the view and deleting it. From the Object library (^⌥⌘3), select a table view and drag it out onto the view controller. Now connect the table view's delegate and dataSource outlets to the view controller and connect the view controller's view outlet to the table view. Next, go to the Table View's Attributes inspector and specify that there is one prototype cell.

Now, assign an identifier to the table view cells, select the prototype cell, and open the Attributes inspector (⌥⌘4). Change the identifier to Cell. And while we are on the Attributes inspector, also change the style to Subtitle and set a default image. When done, the inspector should look like Figure 50, *Table view cell attributes*, on page 123.

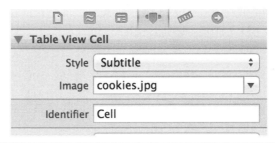

Figure 50—Table view cell attributes

Now we have a table view controller and its view, but we need to set the dataSource for it to work properly. In the previous version of this application, we set the data source for our list view controller during application startup. Let's do the same here, but our code will have to be different since we are using a storyboard. We don't need to create the list view controller in the application:didFinishLaunchingWithOptions: method; it will be created for us as objects are read from the storyboard. When the storyboard is loaded, the initial view controller becomes the window's rootViewController. Since our recipe list view controller is the initial view controller, we can get to it via the rootViewController. Change the application:didFinishLaunchingWithOptions: method to look like this:

Storyboard/SBRecipes_01/StoryboardRecipes/PRPAppDelegate.m
```
- (BOOL)application:(UIApplication *)application
didFinishLaunchingWithOptions:(NSDictionary *)launchOptions {
  PRPRecipesListViewController *controller =
  (PRPRecipesListViewController *)self.window.rootViewController;
  controller.dataSource = [[PRPRecipesSource alloc] init];
  return YES;
}
```

Our app still contains the old navigation code, which will not work with the storyboard. Instead, the navigation is replaced by a segue, so we can delete the tableView:didSelectRowAtIndexPath: method in the PRPRecipesListViewController. Now we can run our application and navigate as we did before.

Segue to Recipe Detail

Segues define the connections and transitions between view controllers in a storyboard. They give us the ability to visually specify "when the user taps here, transition to this other view controller," allowing us to delete our navigation code. Let's add our recipes detail view controller to the mix and use a storyboard segue to navigate to it.

Go back to MainStoryboard.storyboard. From the Object library (^⌥⌘3), select a view controller and drag it out into the storyboard. While this new view controller is selected, go to the Identity inspector (⌥⌘3) and change its class name to PRPViewController.

We have the view controller; now we need to re-create the interface. We could copy and paste from the old view hierarchy, but re-creating it will provide more practice in using Interface Builder and making connections between objects. We need to put all six of the views onscreen and make the various connections.

First, place the Done button in the top right, click control and drag to the view controller, and connect the button to the dismiss: method. Now place a UILabel in the top left, control-drag from the view controller to the label, and connect to the recipeTitle outlet. The view controller will populate this label with the title of the recipe when the view is displayed.

Next, place a UITextView to the interface. Size it to 169 points high and have it span the scene. We also need a connection from the view controller to the text view, so control-drag from the view controller to the text view and connect it to the directionsView property. When the view is displayed onscreen, the view controller will fill this text view with the directions for the recipe.

The next pair of views displays the preparation time. On the left place a label, change its font to bold, and set "Prep Time:" to be the value. Next, place a label to the right and expand it to take the remainder of the width. Control-drag from the view controller to the second label and connect to the prepTime outlet.

Finally, we need to add an image view and connect to it. Drag an instance from the Object library, size it to fit the remainder of the area, center it horizontally, and drag it down to the bottom until the blue guidelines appear. Now connect the view controller's imageView outlet to this new image view.

Now we've completely re-created our recipe detail view and controller. It should look like Figure 51, *Recipe Detail view controller*, on page 126, when finished.

Why Delete Code?

Deleting code from an application might feel like a step backward. A common question is this: "We've just spent all this time putting this code in here; why delete it?" If you're asking that question, you're in good company. The biggest advantage to deleting code comes later in the life cycle of the app, while we are maintaining it. Every line of code that we can delete now is one less line to worry about in the future. Almost without exception it's better to delete code than to leave it in.

Now let's connect the two scenes with a segue. We create segues just like we create connections. Control-drag from the table view cell in our first scene to the recipes detail scene. When you mouse up, select Modal as the style from the pop-up. As a result, Interface Builder creates a new segue and the storyboard looks like Figure 52, *Segue connection*, on page 127.

Now we have two view controllers in our storyboard and a segue between them. The segue defines the navigation between the view controllers. Select the segue and open the Attributes inspector (⌥⌘4). Notice that Style is set to Modal and Transition is set to Default. While we are here, let's specify the segue's identifier to "presentRecipeDetail." We will be using this identifier value in just a moment. With a segue to our recipe detail in place, we need to pass along the recipe and display it.

Display Recipe Detail

When a segue is activated, the source view controller is sent the prepareForSegue:sender: method. We can override this method to provide the segue's destinationViewController any information it needs. In our example, PRPRecipesListViewController is sent the prepareForSegue:sender: method and PRPViewController is the

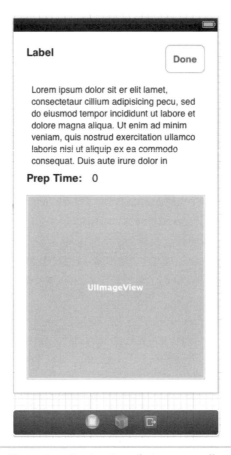

Figure 51—Recipe Detail view controller

destination view controller. In other words, the list view controller needs to tell the recipes detail view controller which recipe was selected, like this:

Storyboard/SBRecipes_01/StoryboardRecipes/PRPRecipesListViewController.m
```
Line 1 - (void)prepareForSegue:(UIStoryboardSegue *)segue sender:(id)sender {
     2   if([@"presentRecipeDetail" isEqualToString:segue.identifier]) {
     3     NSIndexPath *index = [self.tableView indexPathForCell:sender];
     4     PRPRecipe *recipe = [self.dataSource recipeAtIndex:index.row];
     5     [[segue destinationViewController] setRecipe:recipe];
     6   }
     7 }
```

On line 2, we compare the segue's name with the identifier specified in IB. It's important to make sure that the segue is the one we expect. We use the segue's identifier to distinguish between segues. Our current implementation only has one segue, but we will shortly add another.

Figure 52—Segue connection

On the next two lines we figure out which index path was tapped and use that to get the selected recipe. Then on line 5, we pass along the recipe to the detail view controller.

Our app is back to where it was before. When users tap on a recipe, they see the details; when done, they tap the Done button and they are brought back to the list. And as promised, we were able to delete our navigation code in the process. Now all we do is prepare for the segue by passing along the appropriate details to the view controller that's about to appear.

Dismiss Recipe Detail

Recall that the detail view controller is removed from the screen when the user taps the Done button. We added this functionality back in Section 5.5, *Recipe Details*, on page 111. We did not discuss the dismiss: method in this chapter, nor did we change it. Here is the code for reference:

Storyboard/SBRecipes_01/StoryboardRecipes/PRPViewController.m

```
- (IBAction)dismiss:(id)sender {
    [self dismissViewControllerAnimated:YES completion:nil];
}
```

We still need this code to remove the detail view from the screen. It seems a bit odd to have to keep this code since we've been working so hard to delete our navigation code in favor of segues. That is exactly what we are going to do in the next section, but we'll have to learn about container controllers first.

6.2 Using Container Controllers

Until now we have been looking at view controllers that manage content. We now know enough about view controllers to dig into container view controllers. A container controller manages content controllers in a particular way; it defines how the content controllers it contains interact with each other.

You are already familiar with many of these container controllers from use if not from their API. The tab bar controller is used in the Music application to switch between the Artist view and the Album view. Tab controllers replace the current view controller with a new one every time a different tab is tapped, without animation. When you have the Artist tab selected, the Artist content controller is visible. When you tap on the Album tab, that view is visible.

Another container controller, the navigation controller, is used in the Mail application. A table view controller lists email messages in a mailbox. When a message is tapped, the detailed content of the message is displayed in a new view controller that is animated in from the right side.

Both of these container controllers define the interaction model of the content controllers they manage. One switches immediately between the current view controller and the new one. The other does a push animation from the current view controller to the new one.

Container controllers define this interaction model between the content controllers they contain. iOS provides several container controllers for us to use. When designing the user interface for an application, it's wise to look at these container view controllers because they give us a well-defined and well-understood interaction model. All iPhone users expect certain behavior from a tab bar controller or a navigation controller. iPad users know and understand what a pop-over controller is and how it works. Consistency is important in every application so that users know what to expect.

For those cases when a custom interaction model makes sense for an application, iOS formally defines the relationship between a view controller and the container controller that manages it so that we can write our own. Still, we are going to focus on the provided container controllers in this chapter.

Storyboards give us a way to organize our view controllers into the container controllers that define the flow of our applications.

6.3 Moving Around with Navigation Controllers

The navigation controller is a great interaction model for our recipes application, so our next task is to embed our recipes table view into a navigation controller and then use the navigation interaction model to animate over to our detail view.

Recipe Navigation

To embed the list controller into a navigation controller, select the recipes table view controller in the interface editor and invoke the "Embed in Navigation Controller" tool from the Editor → Embed In → Navigation Controller menu item. When Xcode finishes, your storyboard should look like Figure 53, *Navigation controller added*, on page 130.

One simple menu item click changed our application in many ways. The recipes list view controller is no longer the initial view controller of our storyboard. Instead the new navigation controller has taken that role. When our application starts, that navigation controller will become the window's rootViewController. This change adds some interesting twists to the way the recipes list view controller's view gets onscreen.

Remember from Chapter 4, *View Controllers*, on page 77, that the window asks its rootViewController for a view to display. But a navigation controller does not have anything of its own to display. That's where our recipes view controller comes into the picture. We need to fix up our PRPAppDelegate's implementation of the application:didFinishLaunchingWithOptions: method to take into account the new root view controller by changing our code to look like this:

Storyboard/SBRecipes_02/StoryboardRecipes/PRPAppDelegate.m

```
- (BOOL)application:(UIApplication *)application
didFinishLaunchingWithOptions:(NSDictionary *)launchOptions {
  UINavigationController *navigationController =
  (UINavigationController *)self.window.rootViewController;
  PRPRecipesListViewController *controller =
  (PRPRecipesListViewController *)navigationController.topViewController;
  controller.dataSource = [[PRPRecipesSource alloc] init];
  return YES;
}
```

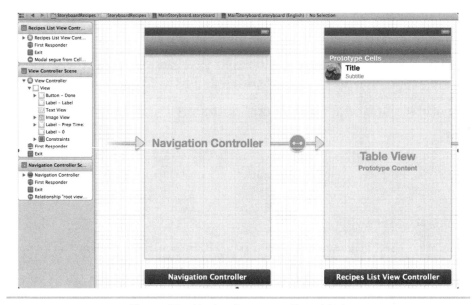

Figure 53—Navigation controller added

The structure of the code is the same, but our PRPRecipesListViewController is now the topViewController of the navigation controller rather than the rootViewController of the window.

When the window asks the navigation controller for its view, the navigation controller retrieves the view from its topViewController. All container controllers, including the navigation controller, forward the life cycle and rotation methods to the contained view controllers, so all the knowledge we've gained thus far still applies even when our content controllers are contained in another view controller.

Container view controllers typically have some space on the view reserved for their use, such as the navigation controller's nav bar. When a content controller is pushed into a nav controller, its content is typically resized. However, if the "Resize View From NIB" check box in the Attributes inspector is unchecked, the content controller won't resize its view. If a view is strangely placed or showing some of the window behind it (usually a white stripe on the top or bottom), it's usually because some resizing has been neglected. So look in Interface Builder and make sure that box is checked.

Now that we have our recipe list embedded in a navigation controller, let's rework the segue to get the sideways navigation transition instead of the modal transition we currently have.

Navigation Segue

What we have now works, but it's not very iPhone-like. Users expect that when they tap on a row in a table view, the detailed information related to that row will animate in from the right side. Go ahead and run the app again and tap on any of those rows. Doesn't it feel *wrong* somehow that the details come up from the bottom? That feeling of wrongness will be shared by our users. Making our user interface behave as the user expects is an important part of building applications that are intuitive and easy to use.

We'll use a navigation segue to correct our interface. In the storyboard, select the segue between the list and the details, and then open the Attributes inspector (⌥⌘4). In the Style pull-down, change the type from Modal to Push. Now the transition between the list and the details will use the slide-in animation. That is much better. We are very close, but if you run the app now you'd notice that the navigation bar does not have a title for either the recipe list or the details.

6.4 Managing View Controllers in Navigation Controllers

Title the View Controllers

When a navigation bar is present onscreen, it asks the top view controller for its title and displays that. If the view controller does not have a title set, then the navigation bar uses the title that was set in Interface Builder. Since we are currently neither setting the navigation bar title nor the recipes list title, our navigation bar ends up without a title. With the storyboard open, double-click the navigation bar above the recipes list view controller. Type "Recipes" in the text box. Now our first title is set; let's set the second.

The recipes detail should be titled after the recipe we are displaying in the detail view. In the PRPViewController.m file, navigate to the viewWillAppear: method. Add a new line of code to set the title of the details view controller, like this:

Storyboard/SBRecipes_02/StoryboardRecipes/PRPViewController.m
```
Line 1  - (void)viewWillAppear:(BOOL)animated {
     -     [super viewWillAppear:animated];
     -     self.title = self.recipe.title;
     -     self.recipeTitle.text = self.recipe.title;
     5     self.directionsView.text = self.recipe.directions;
     -     if(nil != self.recipe.image) {
     -         self.imageView.image = self.recipe.image;
     -     }
     -     self.prepTime.text =
     10        [self.formatter stringFromNumber:self.recipe.preparationTime];
     - }
```

Notice on line 3 that we are setting the view controller's title. The navigation bar displays the current view controller's title when it navigates onto the screen.

Run the application in the Simulator. The list has *Recipes* in the title as we'd expect. Now tap on a recipe and notice that the navigation bar title is set to the recipe's title. Also, the back button now has *Recipes* as its label instead of *Back*. The navigation controller sets the back button's title to the previous navigation bar's title. This subtle hint helps our users keep context.

UI Refinement

Since we have the title of the recipe in the navigation bar, we no longer need the text field we were using to display that information. So let's delete it. When we delete an object from Interface Builder, it will automatically delete any connections to or from that object. We still want to delete the property from the view controller, so open the PRPViewController.h and delete the recipeTitle property. We used recipeTitle in the viewWillAppear: so delete those lines as well.

The Done button is also out of place in our new and improved user interface. Delete the button and expand the directions text to take up the unused space. With the button gone, we don't need the dismiss: method anymore either, so its declaration can be deleted from the PRPViewController.h header file and the method implementation can be deleted from the implementation file.

When these changes have been made the header file should look like this:

Storyboard/SBRecipes_03/StoryboardRecipes/PRPViewController.h
```
#import <UIKit/UIKit.h>
#import "PRPRecipe.h"

@interface PRPViewController : UIViewController

@property(nonatomic, strong) PRPRecipe *recipe;

@property(nonatomic, strong) IBOutlet UITextView *directionsView;
@property(nonatomic, strong) IBOutlet UIImageView *imageView;

@property(nonatomic, strong) IBOutlet UILabel *prepTime;
@property(nonatomic, strong) NSNumberFormatter *formatter;

@end
```

The interface should be modified to look like Figure 54, *Cleaned up UI*, on page 133

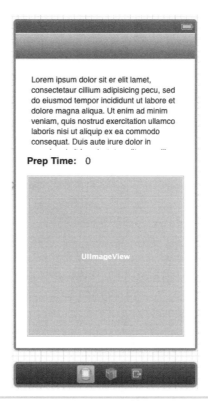

Figure 54—Cleaned up UI

And the implementation of the PRPViewController should now look like this:

Storyboard/SBRecipes_03/StoryboardRecipes/PRPViewController.m

```objc
@implementation PRPViewController

- (void)viewDidLoad {
  [super viewDidLoad];
  self.formatter = [[NSNumberFormatter alloc] init];
}

- (void)viewWillAppear:(BOOL)animated {
  [super viewWillAppear:animated];
  self.title = self.recipe.title;
  self.directionsView.text = self.recipe.directions;
  if(nil != self.recipe.image) {
    self.imageView.image = self.recipe.image;
  }
  self.prepTime.text = [self.formatter
                        stringFromNumber:self.recipe.preparationTime];
}
@end
```

We've made major changes to our humble recipes application in this section. Along the way we have made it look much more consistent by using the navigation interaction model. Our users will appreciate the consistent experience the Recipes app now provides. However, we still don't have any means of creating a new recipe. Let's go fix that now.

6.5 Transferring App Control and Data

Adding a recipe will require a few changes to our application. We need to create a view controller for editing the recipes, update the current application to segue to this new view controller, and add a way to dismiss the new view controller when we're done editing. Finally, we need to update the list to reflect the new recipe. Let's get started with the new view controller.

Recipe Editor View Controller

Start in the storyboard by dragging out a new view controller instance from the Object library (^⌥⌘3). To quickly get most of the UI in place, copy all the items from the details view controller to this new view. That will get us most of the way, but we also need a text field for the recipe's title and a UIStepper for the preparation time. Drag a text field from the Object library and place it at the top of the view. Grab a stepper and place it to the right of the preparation time label.

The view controller needs to be embedded in a navigation controller. Editing the directions text here would be a poor user experience, so we want to tap on the directions text and navigate to a screen dedicated to editing the directions. In the storyboard, select the editing view controller and choose Editor → Embed In - Navigation Controller. Now our view has a navigation bar at the top, so we need to rearrange the UI elements. Also, double-click the navigation bar and change its title to Edit Recipe. When done, the UI should look similar to Figure 55, *Editing UI*, on page 135.

We've got our view, so let's create a controller. Select the StoryboardRecipes group in the project navigator in Xcode and hit ⌘N to bring up the new file dialogue. Select the UIViewController subclass and click Next. Name the view controller PRPRecipeEditorViewController and make sure that UIViewController is set in the Subclass of field. Make sure the "With XIB for user interface" item is not checked, and click Next and then Create.

As this view controller's view comes onscreen, values from the selected recipe need to be placed into the various UI elements. We need to add an IBOutlet for each of the items to our header file and a property for the recipe we will

Figure 55—Editing UI

display. Also add a property for an NSNumberFormatter: we'll create an instance and use it to convert the preparation time to a string.

We also need an action to invoke when the stepper is tapped that will update the recipe's preparation time. Let's call the changePreparationTime: action method. When done, the header file should look like this:

Storyboard/SBRecipes_04/StoryboardRecipes/PRPRecipeEditorViewController.h
```
@class PRPRecipe;
@interface PRPRecipeEditorViewController : UIViewController
@property(nonatomic, strong) PRPRecipe *recipe;
@property(nonatomic, strong) NSNumberFormatter *formatter;
@property(nonatomic, strong) IBOutlet UITextField *titleField;
@property(nonatomic, strong) IBOutlet UITextView *directionsText;
@property(nonatomic, strong) IBOutlet UILabel *prepTimeLabel;
@property(nonatomic, strong) IBOutlet UIImageView *recipeImage;
@property(nonatomic, strong) IBOutlet UIStepper *prepTimeStepper;

- (IBAction)changePreparationTime:(UIStepper *)sender;
@end
```

Make sure you create the number formatter in the viewDidLoad method.

Get the current value from the stepper and update the recipe with the new value in the changePreparationTime: method. To keep the label in sync, convert the new value to a string and place it into the prepTime label. We will look at this method in more detail shortly.

In the viewWillAppear: method, update the UI elements with values from the selected recipe. The formatter is used to convert the preparation time to a string. Make sure to conditionally set the image view's image; later we'll place a default image that we don't want to be overwritten with nil. When the changes are made, viewWillAppear will look like this:

```
Storyboard/SBRecipes_04/StoryboardRecipes/PRPRecipeEditorViewController.m
#import "PRPRecipe.h"
@implementation PRPRecipeEditorViewController
- (IBAction)changePreparationTime:(UIStepper *)sender {
  NSInteger value = (NSInteger)[sender value];
  self.recipe.preparationTime = [NSNumber numberWithInteger:value];
  self.prepTimeLabel.text =
  [self.formatter stringFromNumber:self.recipe.preparationTime];
}

#pragma mark - View lifecycle
- (void)viewDidLoad {
  [super viewDidLoad];
  self.formatter = [[NSNumberFormatter alloc] init];
}
- (void)viewWillAppear:(BOOL)animated {
  [super viewWillAppear:animated];
  self.titleField.text = self.recipe.title;
  self.directionsText.text = self.recipe.directions;
  self.prepTimeLabel.text = [self.formatter
                             stringFromNumber:self.recipe.preparationTime];
  self.prepTimeStepper.value = [self.recipe.preparationTime doubleValue];
  if(nil != self.recipe.image) {
    self.recipeImage.image = self.recipe.image;
  }
}
@end
```

Now that we have completed the code for our new view controller, it's time to make the connections in the storyboard editor. Select the view controller in the storyboard editor and change its class to PRPRecipeEditorViewController with the Identity inspector (^⌘3). Each of the outlets we defined in the interface should be connected to the proper UI element. Also, connect the stepper to the changePreparationTime: method. To get to the editor, we'll add a segue from the recipe list to the editor navigation controller.

Segue to Editing

Let's place the new control in the navigation bar at the top of the list of recipes. We want to follow the pattern of apps like Contacts and place a + button in the top right side of the screen. Place a UIBarButtonItem from the Object library on the navigation bar above the list of recipes. Change its identifier to Add in the Attributes inspector (⌥⌘4).

Now connect the control to the segue. Control-drag from the Add button to the new navigation controller. Choose Modal as the transition type when prompted. Once the connection is made, the storyboard should look something like Figure 56, *New recipe transition*, on page 137.

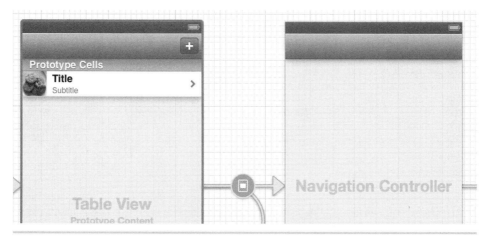

Figure 56—New recipe transition

With the segue selected, go to the Attributes inspector and change its identifier to addNewRecipe. Now if we build and run our application, we are able to get to the editor view. However, nothing is displayed. We've not created a new recipe or told the editor about it; let's fix that now.

Create a New Recipe

Creating a new recipe to pass to our editor is easy; we could just alloc and init a new instance and pass that along. However, that would break the encapsulation we so carefully built into the PRPRecipesListDataSource protocol. So instead of creating a recipe in the view controller, we are going to add a method to the protocol that will take on that responsibility. In the PRPRecipesListDataSource.h, add a single method, like this:

```
- (PRPRecipe *)createNewRecipe;
```

Saving that change and doing a build (⌘B) should result in a warning that we've not implemented the method in PRPRecipesSource. Add the implementation to PRPRecipesSource.m, like this:

Storyboard/SBRecipes_04/StoryboardRecipes/PRPRecipesSource.m
```
- (PRPRecipe *)createNewRecipe {
  PRPRecipe *recipe = [[PRPRecipe alloc] init];
  [self.recipes addObject:recipe];
  return recipe;
}
```

Now our data source can provide the services we need. Next, use the data source to create a new recipe and show it in the editing view controller's view. We need to go back to our recipes list view controller and update the prepare-ForSegue:sender: method to call the data source and then pass the new recipe onto the editor. Here is the code:

Storyboard/SBRecipes_04/StoryboardRecipes/PRPRecipesListViewController.m
```
Line 1 if([@"addNewRecipe" isEqualToString:segue.identifier]) {
2    PRPRecipe *recipe = [self.dataSource createNewRecipe];
3    UIViewController *topVC = [[segue destinationViewController]
4                                topViewController];
5    PRPRecipeEditorViewController *editor =
6    (PRPRecipeEditorViewController *)topVC;
7    editor.recipe = recipe;
8 }
```

Notice that the segue's destinationViewController is not the editor view controller, but instead it's a navigation controller. As we saw earlier, the editor view controller is embedded in the navigation controller. The navigation controller's topViewController is our editor view controller. Once we get that, we can then set its recipe as we do on line 7.

With the segue in place, we can navigate between our list and the new recipe editor. Go ahead and build and run the application. Once it's started, hit the plus (+) button. The editor view should slide into place and look like Figure 57, *First editing UI*, on page 139.

Our app is in good shape. However, if we spend a few minutes poking around, we'll notice a few items that need to be addressed. The keyboard won't go away if we tap on the text field, we can edit the directions text on this view, and we cannot set the image for the recipe or dismiss the editor view. We need to fix all four of these things. Let's start with the text field.

Figure 57—First editing UI

Editing the Recipe Title

When users tap in the recipe title field, we want to allow them to enter the new title. Then, when they tap the return button on the keyboard, we want to place the new title into the recipe's title field and dismiss the keyboard. To accomplish that we'll implement the relevant methods from the UITextFieldDelegate protocol. Then we'll place the newly entered string into the recipe's titleproperty.

We need to declare that our editing view controller is a text field delegate. To do that we add the UITextFieldDelegate protocol to our interface declaration, like this:

Storyboard/SBRecipes_05/StoryboardRecipes/PRPRecipeEditorViewController.h
```
@interface PRPRecipeEditorViewController : UIViewController
<UITextFieldDelegate>
```

Once we claim to implement this protocol, we need to implement the appropriate methods in our implementation. In our case we want to implement textFieldShouldReturn: to invoke resignFirstResponder and then return YES. Then we need to implement textFieldDidEndEditing: to take the new text and place it into the title of the recipe we are editing. The code should look like this:

Storyboard/SBRecipes_05/StoryboardRecipes/PRPRecipeEditorViewController.m
```
#pragma mark - Text Field Delegate Methods
- (BOOL)textFieldShouldReturn:(UITextField *)textField {
  [textField resignFirstResponder];
  return YES;
}

- (void)textFieldDidEndEditing:(UITextField *)textField {
  self.recipe.title = textField.text;
}
```

With these code changes in place, we can connect the text field's delegate to the editor view controller. To do that, go back to Interface Builder, select the text field, and control-drag from the text field to the view controller in this scene. Once over the view controller, mouse up and then choose delegate from the list in the pop-up window.

Build and run the app again. Now we can edit the title text field and tap the return key, and the keyboard should slide off the screen. First problem solved.

Edit Directions

When we tap the directions text, it becomes the first responder: the keyboard appears and we can edit the text, but there is no way to finish editing the text. A better user experience would be to navigate to a new view controller that manages a whole screen, one dedicated to editing the directions text. Let's make that new view controller. We will follow the same approach we have seen several times: build the user interface in IB, move to the code editor and add some code, and then return to Interface Builder to make connections.

Joe asks:
What Is a First Responder?

First responder is another of those time-tested concepts that was migrated from Mac OS X to iOS. The idea is that on any given screen an application might have many different types of objects that could receive input from the keyboard. For example, we might have an instance of UITextView to capture the directions for a recipe and a UITextField to capture the title of the recipe. The first responder is where UIKit keeps track of the object that currently has focus, regardless of its type. All keyboard events get sent to the first responder.

The first responder is only the first in a chain of responders that get a chance to respond to an event. In fact the documentation for nextResponder on UIResponder teaches us about the *responder chain* and explains the path events take from a view object to the application object.

In Interface Builder, drag out a new view controller, add a text view to its view, and make it full screen.

Now we need the code to back up this new view. Select the Storyboard Recipes group in the navigator and hit ⌘N. Choose Objective-C class and hit Next. Name the new class PRPDirectionsEditorViewController and choose UIViewController as its super class. Make sure the check box to create an XIB is unchecked and save it. This view controller needs to implement the UITextViewDelegate protocol.

Also add an outlet to point to the UITextView and a property to hold onto the recipe. Let's add all of that to the header file. When done, it should look like:

Storyboard/SBRecipes_05/StoryboardRecipes/PRPDirectionsEditorViewController.h
```
@class PRPRecipe;

@interface PRPDirectionsEditorViewController : UIViewController <UITextViewDelegate>

@property(nonatomic, strong) PRPRecipe *recipe;
@property(nonatomic, strong) IBOutlet UITextView *textView;
@end
```

With our edits to the view controller's interface done, we need to go wire everything together in Interface Builder. Open the storyboard and select the new view controller. In the object bar at the bottom, select the view controller. Open the Identity inspector (⌘⌥3) and change the class to PRPDirectionsEditorView-Controller. Now control-drag from the view controller in the object bar to the text view and connect the textView outlet to the text view in the interface. Then connect the text view's delegate to the view controller by control-clicking from the text view to the view controller.

Implement the Editor View Controller

The UITextViewDelegate protocol defines methods that we can implement to learn about the state of the text view. When it finishes editing is the ideal time to take the text and place it into the directions property on the recipe. The text view ends editing when it resigns firstResponder status. Resigning first responder happens under two conditions: if we tell it to via the resignFirstResponder method or when the text view leaves the screen. When the text view resigns first responder status, the textViewDidEndEditing: method is called. We implement that method to transfer the text into the recipe, like this:

Storyboard/SBRecipes_05/StoryboardRecipes/PRPDirectionsEditorViewController.m
```
- (void)textViewDidEndEditing:(UITextView *)textView {
  self.recipe.directions = self.textView.text;
}
```

Since our text view will be in a navigation controller, it will leave the screen when the user taps on the back button. As the view leaves the screen, we'll get the textViewDidEndEditing: method call and our recipe will get the new directions text.

Next let's implement the viewWillAppear: method to do three things: set the directions editor's title to be Edit Directions, make the text view the firstResponder by sending it the becomeFirstResponder method, and set the text view's text to be the recipe's directions. The code should look like this:

Storyboard/SBRecipes_05/StoryboardRecipes/PRPDirectionsEditorViewController.m

```
- (void)viewWillAppear:(BOOL)animated {
  [super viewWillAppear:animated];
  self.title = @"Edit Directions";
  [self.textView becomeFirstResponder];
  self.textView.text = self.recipe.directions;
}
```

The recipe's directions text needs to be set before the recipe editor is back onscreen so that it will display the new directions. So as the directions editor leaves the scene, we need to call resignFirstResponder on the text view to ensure that textViewDidEndEditing: method is called before the recipe editor displayed. The viewWillDisappear: method is the ideal spot to do that. The viewWillDisappear: method is called before a view leaves the screen, so we will get this message well before our recipe editor view controller is sent viewWillAppear:. That code should look like this:

Storyboard/SBRecipes_05/StoryboardRecipes/PRPDirectionsEditorViewController.m

```
- (void)viewWillDisappear:(BOOL)animated {
  [super viewWillDisappear:animated];
  [self.textView resignFirstResponder];
}
```

Now that we have our directions editor view controller we need to return to the recipe editor and set up a new segue from the recipe editor to the directions editor.

Segue to Directions

As we discussed back in *Edit Directions*, on page 140, recall that text views become the first responder when tapped. When a text view is first responder, it brings up the keyboard, and in our case, the user is left with no way to dismiss the keyboard. We are going to fix that by making the text view in our directions editor uneditable. Select the text view, bring up the Attributes inspector (⌘⌥4), and switch the Editable check box to off.

Now our users won't be stuck with a keyboard that won't go away, but they have no way to edit the text. We need to add a segue from our recipe editor view to the directions editor view. Text views don't support being the source of a segue. Fortunately we have another option—a tap gesture recognizer. From the Object library (^⌥⌘3), search for "tap gesture recognizer" using the search field at the bottom of the Object library. The Object library should look like Figure 58, *Tap gesture recognizer*, on page 143.

Drag the gesture recognizer out and drop it onto the text view. Once done, the gesture recognizer will be placed in the object tray under the recipe view

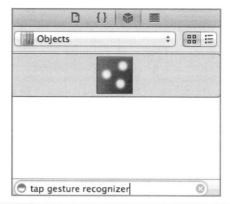

Figure 58—Tap gesture recognizer

controller. We will discuss gesture recognizers in detail in Chapter 8, *Drawing and Animating*, on page 189; for now we are just going to use a very simple one.

Select the gesture recognizer and change its label to Directions Gesture Recognizer in the Identity inspector (via ⌥⌘3). While not necessary, this simplifies distinguishing multiple gesture recognizers in this scene.

Let's make our new gesture recognizer instigate a segue to the directions view controller. Control-drag from the gesture recognizer to the directions view controller. When you mouse up, choose the Push style from the pop-up window, which should look like Figure 59, *Choosing the Push segue style*, on page 144. Name the segue "editDirections" in the segue's Attributes inspector Identifier field. When our text view is tapped, it will instigate this segue from our recipe editor to the directions editor.

We still need to pass along the recipe from our recipe editor to the directions editor. Let's add prepareForSegue:sender: to our recipes editor to pass along the recipe.

Storyboard/SBRecipes_05/StoryboardRecipes/PRPRecipeEditorViewController.m
```
- (void)prepareForSegue:(UIStoryboardSegue *)segue sender:(id)sender {
  if([@"editDirections" isEqualToString:segue.identifier]) {
    [[segue destinationViewController] setRecipe:self.recipe];
  }
}
```

Build and run the application. Once the app is running, hit the + button to add a new recipe. You should be able to set the title, and if you tap on the directions, the new view controller should slide into place with the keyboard

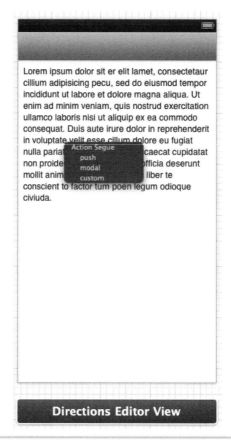

Figure 59—Choosing the Push segue style

visible, ready for users to enter text. Two of our four recipe properties are now editable. Next up, let's tackle the stepper and the preparation time.

Preparation Time Stepper

Controls use the target/action paradigm to communicate changes. Our stepper is no different. As it's tapped on, our action method is invoked. We saw the implementation for this method earlier in *Recipe Editor View Controller*, on page 134. Here it is again for reference:

Storyboard/SBRecipes_05/StoryboardRecipes/PRPRecipeEditorViewController.m
```
- (IBAction)changePreparationTime:(UIStepper *)sender {
  NSInteger value = (NSInteger)[sender value];
  self.recipe.preparationTime = [NSNumber numberWithInteger:value];
  self.prepTimeLabel.text =
  [self.formatter stringFromNumber:self.recipe.preparationTime];
}
```

This method is invoked each time the stepper is tapped. For each invocation we grab the value from the stepper and place that value (as an NSNumber) into the recipe and (as an NSString) into the text field.

The final step to editing our recipe is to set an image. To do that we are going to use the image library and along the way learn about a view controller provided by UIKit.

Getting an Image

We need to get a photo into the photo library so we can add it to a new recipe. We'll use Safari's Save Image feature to grab a picture off the 'Net. Launch the Simulator if it's not already running. Stop any of our code that might be running by hitting the Stop button in Xcode and launch Safari back in the Simulator. Search for an image by typing "chocolate chip cookies." Once you have found an image, tap and hold the image. Choose Save Image from the action sheet that pops up. Now that we have saved this image (to the photo library), we will be able to use it in this next step. Quit the Simulator with ⌘Q.

Now we need a way to attach our new image to a recipe. We'll use the UIKit UIImagePickerController class. The image picker is used to present a standard or customized UI for our users to choose images from their photo library or to present UI to take a photo or video. The image picker controller is a subclass of UIViewController, so we can present it the same way we have been presenting other view controllers.

The image picker controller uses the delegation pattern. It knows how to show the user's image library and how to interact with the camera. Once the user has chosen an image from either source, the image picker controller tells us about that via delegate callback methods.

So that we know which image was chosen, we need to implement the UIImagePickerControllerDelegate protocol, which has two interesting methods for us to implement. The first is imagePickerController:didFinishPickingMediaWithInfo:. And as we can tell from this descriptive method name, the image picker calls its delegate with this method when the user has chosen an image. The second method, imagePickerControllerDidCancel:, is called when the user cancels. With these two methods implemented, we'll be able to correctly interact with the image picker and allow our users to choose an image for a new recipe.

Now we need to choose the object to be the image picker's delegate. The delegate will be responsible for taking the image the user chose and placing it into the recipe. Since our PRPRecipesEditorViewController is in charge of editing the new recipe, it makes sense that this object be the delegate. We need to go to the PRPRecipesEditorViewController.h header file and declare that the PRPRecipesEditorViewController will implement this protocol. Change the class declaration to look like this:

Storyboard/SBRecipes_06/StoryboardRecipes/PRPRecipeEditorViewController.h
```
@interface PRPRecipeEditorViewController : UIViewController
<UITextFieldDelegate, UIImagePickerControllerDelegate>
```

Since we have declared this protocol, we need to write the two methods in the implementation file. We can jump quickly to the implementation file with ^⌘Up Arrow or bring up the Assistant editor with ⌥⌘↩. Add the two methods so the code looks like this:

Storyboard/SBRecipes_06/StoryboardRecipes/PRPRecipeEditorViewController.m
```
Line 1 #pragma mark - Image Picker Delegate Methods

    - (void)imagePickerController:(UIImagePickerController *)picker
    didFinishPickingMediaWithInfo:(NSDictionary *)info {
5     self.recipe.image = [info valueForKey:UIImagePickerControllerOriginalImage];
      [picker dismissViewControllerAnimated:YES completion:NULL];
    }

    - (void)imagePickerControllerDidCancel:(UIImagePickerController *)picker {
10    [picker dismissViewControllerAnimated:YES completion:NULL];
    }
```

On line 5 we grab the original image from the info dictionary passed back by the image picker, and then we place that image into our recipe. On line 6 we tell the image picker to dismiss. When the user taps Cancel, the imagePickerControllerDidCancel: method is called; on line 10 we call dismiss as well. The image picker is a sophisticated component of UIKit and has many options, and we are only barely scratching the surface of what it provides. The documentation is quite good and provides all the details about the various ways the image picker can be used.

With our coding done, it's time to jump back into Interface Builder and connect things so we get the image picker. We have to make it obvious how users can select a photo. The code download bundle has an image called TapToChoose.png that we will place into the image view on our editing screen, which will be a clear sign to our users. In an application for the App Store, we'd get an artist to provide this graphic. We would not want to ship with this "programmer art" in our app. Add the TapToChoose.png image to your project by dragging it from Finder into the project navigator in Xcode.

Open the storyboard and select the UIImageView in the recipe editor scene. Open the Attributes inspector (via ⌥⌘4) and choose the TapToChoose.png file for the image. We also need to turn on user interaction since we want this image view to present the image picker controller. When the changes are done, the Attributes inspector should look like Figure 60, *Modified image view*, on page 147

Figure 60—Modified image view

Next, add an instance of UIViewController to the storyboard. From the Object library (via ⌃⌥⌘3), grab a view controller and drag it out onto the storyboard. Once it's added, select it, and in the Identity inspector (via ⌥⌘3), change its class to UIImagePickerController.

With our image view set up let's add a tap gesture recognizer and then have that kick off the segue. In the Object library (via ⌃⌥⌘3), select a tap gesture recognizer and drag and drop it onto the image view. Change its label to Image Gesture Recognizer in the Identity inspector. Control-drag from the Image Gesture Recognizer to the image picker view controller and choose Modal from the pop-up. Name the segue "choosePhoto." When done, the view controller should look like Figure 61, *Recipes editor scene*, on page 148, in Interface Builder.

Our Interface Builder work is done, so now we need to go back into the PRPRecipeEditorViewController to do the setup work for image picker. Modify the prepForSegue:sender: method to set the image picker's delegate before it is displayed. Here is the modified code.

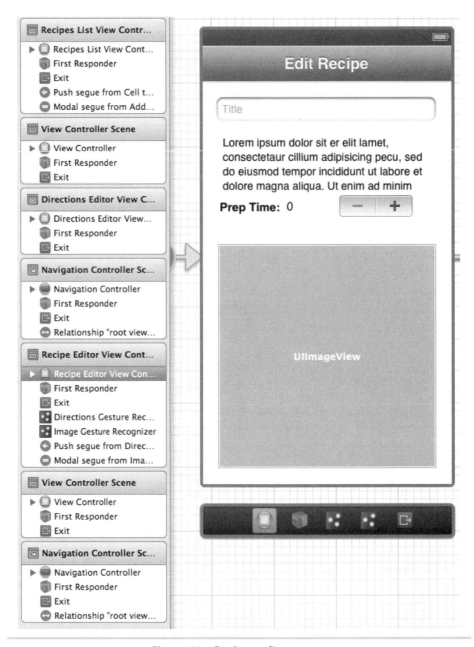

Figure 61—Recipes editor scene

Storyboard/SBRecipes_06/StoryboardRecipes/PRPRecipeEditorViewController.m

```
- (void)prepareForSegue:(UIStoryboardSegue *)segue sender:(id)sender {
  if([@"editDirections" isEqualToString:segue.identifier]) {
    [[segue destinationViewController] setRecipe:self.recipe];
  }
  if([@"choosePhoto" isEqualToString:segue.identifier]) {
    [[segue destinationViewController] setDelegate:self];
  }
}
```

Run and test the application. Click the Add button in the list of recipes and change the title, directions, preparation time, and image. When done, the edited recipe should look like Figure 62, *Recipe editor view*, on page 150. Pretty cool that we are able to do all this now, isn't it?

All the fields we have in our recipe model object are now editable. It's time to let our users indicate they are done editing.

6.6 Returning App Control and Data

We've completed three of the four steps spelled out in Section 6.5, *Transferring App Control and Data*, on page 134. The final step is to allow our users to return to the list of recipes. We need the list to reflect the new recipe along with its updated values. In essence, our editing view controller needs to transfer control back up the controller hierarchy so the list view controller can take over again.

Finishing Up

Our users will want to indicate that they are done editing the recipe. We need a Done button in the navigation bar for the editor, and we need to transfer control and new data back to the list.

Three classes and the storyboard are involved in this transfer.

The PRPRecipeEditorViewController has to inform the PRPRecipesListViewController when editing is finished. The PRPRecipesListViewController has to update the table view and the cell that's been edited. The list controller will ask its data source for the index of the edited recipe. We will modify the PRPRecipesListDataSource protocol and our implementation in PRPRecipesSource to make that possible. Let's get started in the storyboard.

Back in Interface Builder, select a UIBarButtonItem from the Object library (^⌥⌘3) and drag it into the navigation bar for the recipe editor. Change its identifier to Done. With the bar button selected, open the Attributes inspector (⌥⌘4) and change the Identifier pull-down to use the Done button type. Now that

Figure 62—Recipe editor view

we have a control, we need an IBAction in our view controller. Open the PRPRecipeEditorViewController.h file and add an action called done:, like this:

Storyboard/SBRecipes_06/StoryboardRecipes/PRPRecipeEditorViewController.h
```
- (IBAction)done:(UIBarButtonItem *)sender;
```

Now we need to connect the Done button: control-drag from the button to the view controller and connect it to the done: action method.

To implement the done: method, let's enhance our old implementation to tell the recipe list view controller that we have finished editing. We need a property that can point to the recipe list view controller and a method we can call to inform the recipe list view controller that editing has finished.

Let's set up the property first. Add a property called recipeListVC to the header file, like this:

Storyboard/SBRecipes_06/StoryboardRecipes/PRPRecipeEditorViewController.h

```
@property(nonatomic, weak) PRPRecipesListViewController *recipeListVC;
```

In the implementation file, we need to import PRPRecipesListViewController.h.

Next we need to add the method in PRPRecipesListViewController.h so we can tell it editing has finished. Add that method like this:

Storyboard/SBRecipes_06/StoryboardRecipes/PRPRecipesListViewController.h

```
- (void)finishedEditingRecipe:(PRPRecipe *)recipe;
```

Now we need to implement this method. It needs to update the table view with the newly edited recipe. We need to know the index of the edited recipe, but we don't have an easy way to do that. Our data source should be able to answer that question since its main role is to understand everything about our recipes. Let's change the PRPRecipesListDataSource protocol and add this method:

Storyboard/SBRecipes_06/StoryboardRecipes/PRPRecipesListDataSource.h

```
- (NSUInteger)indexOfRecipe:(PRPRecipe *)recipe;
```

With the method declared, we need to go to our PRPRecipesSouce and implement it. All we need to do here is ask the array of recipes for the index of the passed-in recipe object, like this:

Storyboard/SBRecipes_06/StoryboardRecipes/PRPRecipesSource.m

```
- (NSUInteger)indexOfRecipe:(PRPRecipe *)recipe {
  return [self.recipes indexOfObject:recipe];
}
```

Now that our data source can tell us the index, we can implement the finishedEditingRecipe: method. Back in the PRPRecipesListViewController.m file, add the method implementation, like this:

Storyboard/SBRecipes_06/StoryboardRecipes/PRPRecipesListViewController.m

```
Line 1  - (void)finishedEditingRecipe:(PRPRecipe *)recipe {
     2    NSUInteger row = [self.dataSource indexOfRecipe:recipe];
     3    NSIndexPath *path = [NSIndexPath indexPathForRow:row inSection:0];
     4    [self.tableView insertRowsAtIndexPaths:[NSArray arrayWithObject:path]
     5                           withRowAnimation:UITableViewRowAnimationLeft];
     6  }
```

First we ask our data source for the row of the freshly edited recipe, and then we create an index path with that row for section zero (the only section we have). On line 4, we tell the table view to insert a new row. This approach of incrementally updating the table view is almost always faster than using the reloadData method. The other thing to notice here is that we have to place the indexPath we made into an array. The table view API requires an array of index paths, so we provide that with the arrayWithObject: method.

Next we need to set the recipeListVC on the recipe editor in the prepareForSegue:sender: method, like this:

Storyboard/SBRecipes_06/StoryboardRecipes/PRPRecipesListViewController.m
```
if([@"addNewRecipe" isEqualToString:segue.identifier]) {
  PRPRecipe *recipe = [self.dataSource createNewRecipe];
  UIViewController *topVC = [[segue destinationViewController]
                             topViewController];
  PRPRecipeEditorViewController *editor =
  (PRPRecipeEditorViewController *)topVC;
  editor.recipeListVC = self;
  editor.recipe = recipe;
}
```

And now we can go back to our done: method and add the call to the recipeListVC to inform it editing is done, like this:

Storyboard/SBRecipes_06/StoryboardRecipes/PRPRecipeEditorViewController.m
```
- (IBAction)done:(UIBarButtonItem *)sender {
  [self dismissViewControllerAnimated:YES
                           completion:NULL];
  [self.recipeListVC finishedEditingRecipe:self.recipe];
}
```

We purposefully flew through adding this callback because building this type of strong relationship between two view controllers is often brittle and resists change. Fortunately, we will be exploring ways to make this relationship loosely coupled later in *Inform the Document of Changes*, on page 165. We'll see how to use delegation to break apart this strong coupling.

6.7 Wrap-Up

We learned a lot in this chapter. First we saw how easy it is to wire together existing view controllers via a storyboard. We are able to visually lay out the way the view controllers transition to and from each other. We also learned how to set up our own delegate protocol so we could have one view controller communicate back up the controller hierarchy when changes are complete. The delegation approach is crucial for maintaining loose coupling between the various elements of the controller hierarchy.

Since we built a new app that reused existing view controllers, we were able to do more bouncing back and forth between Interface Builder and our source code. You will find as you become more proficient at iOS development that this flow of jumping back and forth will become second nature.

The Recipes app has come a long way in this chapter, but it still has a fatal flaw: none of our changes persist beyond the app running. With every fresh start all our changes are lost and we are back to the default set of recipes.

Next, in Chapter 7, *Documents and iCloud*, on page 155, we will fix that and learn about UIDocument along the way.

For Further Thought

Here are a few things to think about or try out to expand your understanding of what we've covered in this chapter. The questions here don't necessarily have "correct" answers. Please join us on the forums at http://forums.pragprog.com/ to discuss your ideas about them.

1. Change the table view of recipes to add an Edit button to the top left side. When the table view is in edit mode, invoke a different segue and go to the recipe editor instead of the detail view controller. To solve this, you'll have to reimplement the tableView:didSelectRowAtIndexPath: and test if the table view is in editing mode or not and then invoke the correct segue.

2. Add a course property to the PRPRecipe class and then modify the editor to allow you to specify the course. For extra credit; make the course an enumerated type {Appetizer, Drink, Entrée, Dessert}. Then use a static table view to choose from the enumerated list. As a hint, on the new table view you add for the course, change its Content field in the Attributes inspector to Static Cells.

3. Change the editor view to be a table view. Place each of the items we are editing into its own cell. Make these cells transition to a new view controller that allows us to edit the field that was selected.

4. In the segue between the list view and the detail view, we set the transition style to Default. Try out the other styles to get a feel for what else might be possible.

CHAPTER 7

Documents and iCloud

Documents and the work related to keeping track of them is a major part of the modern innovations found in desktop computing. The Mac has the Quick Look feature to reveal the contents of our documents and Spotlight to assist in finding them. Finder has evolved to help us organize and locate our documents. But as soon as technology changes to help manage documents, storage space increases. With more space comes more documents and more management.

iOS has taken a very different approach to managing users' information. An iOS device becomes the application. Rather than the documents being the focus of iOS, the apps are the focus. Every application is self-contained: it can only access the information stored in its space. Users rarely think about or notice documents. Instead, users think about apps, and the apps do all the document management tasks.

The current version of the recipes application has come a long way, but we have a major flaw. None of the changes we make to the recipes persist beyond a single run of the application. On a fresh start, the original list of recipes is restored. We are going to fix that by storing our recipes in a document.

To turn Recipes into a document-aware app, we need to be able to persist the data and let users open and share documents. Eventually, we also want to integrate with iCloud, but we will wait to do that in Section 7.5, *Storing Documents in iCloud*, on page 182. Let's get started.

7.1 Making Recipes Persist

We will pick up where we left off in Chapter 6, *Storyboards and Container Controllers*, on page 119. If you did not complete the StoryboardRecipes app, use DocumentRecipes_start from the code download bundle. The references in this chapter to groups and file names assume you are using the DocumentRecipes_start project. If you are following along, replace the references to DocumentRecipes with StoryboardRecipes appropriately.

Now that we have a project to work with, let's add persistence to the PRPRecipe class by streaming our objects into an archive and writing that archive to disk. An archive is a binary representation of an object graph. Objects are "archived" into the stream of bytes by implementing the NSCoding protocol's archiving methods, creating a coder, and archiving the object. Open the PRPRecipe.h file and add the protocol declaration, like this:

Documents/DocumentRecipes_01/DocumentRecipes/PRPRecipe.h
```
@interface PRPRecipe : NSObject <NSCoding>
```

The NSCoding protocol requires us to write the objects' properties to an instance of NSCoder, read those properties from an NSCoder, and place them into the object. Let's look at writing the objects' properties to a coder first. Here is the PRPRecipe implementation of encodeWithCoder:. For each property in our recipe object, we write out the value associated with a key.

Documents/DocumentRecipes_01/DocumentRecipes/PRPRecipe.m
```
Line 1  - (void)encodeWithCoder:(NSCoder *)coder {
     2      [coder encodeObject:self.title forKey:@"title"];
     3      [coder encodeObject:self.directions forKey:@"directions"];
     4      [coder encodeObject:self.preparationTime forKey:@"preparationTime"];
     5      [coder encodeObject:self.image forKey:@"image"];
     6  }
```

The implementation of initWithCoder: then looks like this:

Documents/DocumentRecipes_01/DocumentRecipes/PRPRecipe.m
```
Line 1  - (id)initWithCoder:(NSCoder *)coder {
     2      self = [super init];
     3      if (self) {
     4          self.title = [coder decodeObjectForKey:@"title"];
     5          self.directions = [coder decodeObjectForKey:@"directions"];
     6          self.preparationTime = [coder decodeObjectForKey:@"preparationTime"];
     7          self.image = [coder decodeObjectForKey:@"image"];
     8      }
     9      return self;
    10  }
```

Notice on line 2 that we call superinit rather than the designated initializer. Presumably, the designated initializer will do some interesting work, which will be overwritten by the properties we read out of the coder. In our case, the only thing wasted would be setting the title property. We still care about it, because any wasted work is more electrons turned into heat and fewer remaining in the battery.

NSCoder has a deep and wide feature set. Writing properties as we did here with the encodeObject:forKey: allows us to read values from the coder in any order we want to, or not at all. The data is also architecture independent, so despite the endian differences in Macs and iOS devices, objects can be encoded on one and decoded on the other, or vice versa. More information is available in the Apple docs.[1]

Now that our recipes can persist, we need a container in which to write them. We will subclass UIDocument to take advantage of its rich document support.

Build Recipes Document

PRPRecipesSource managed the list of recipes in the previous version of our app, but it cannot currently persist our recipes. It could be coded to do that, but we would end up reimplementing much of UIDocument. There is a lot of complexity in ensuring documents read and write properly. The read and write operations are multithreaded and must be coordinated with the rest of the system. As good programmers, we are lazy and would rather just reuse UIDocument.

Our document subclass needs to take care of all the reading and writing, and it needs to act as a PRPRecipesListDataSource. The first part is almost entirely taken care of by UIDocument, while the second part is our responsibility. Let's head back to Xcode and build our new document class. To create the new PRPRecipesDocument, do the following:

1. Select the DocumentRecipes group.
2. Control-click and choose "New File…" or ⌘N.
3. Choose Cocoa Touch and "Objective-C class."
4. Click Next.
5. Name the class PRPRecipesDocument.
6. Specify UIDocument as the superclass.
7. Click the Next and Create buttons.

Let's flesh out this new skeleton of a class. Our document needs to manage the recipes just as the PRPRecipesSource did. We defined the PRPRecipesListDataSource protocol to formally specify the interaction between the table view and the list of recipes. Our new document class must implement that protocol too. With that change in place we won't have to modify the PRPRecipesListViewController to work with the new document. The protocol protects the view controller from changes to the underlying implementation.

---

1. http://developer.apple.com/library/ios/#DOCUMENTATION/Cocoa/Conceptual/Archiving/Archiving.html

Specify that the PRPRecipesDocument class will implement the protocol, like this:

Documents/DocumentRecipes_01/DocumentRecipes/PRPRecipesDocument.h
```
#import "PRPRecipesListDataSource.h"
@interface PRPRecipesDocument : UIDocument <PRPRecipesListDataSource>
```

We need an array to keep track of the recipes before we can implement the protocol. Add a property in a class extension as shown in the code below.

Documents/DocumentRecipes_01/DocumentRecipes/PRPRecipesDocument.m
```
@interface PRPRecipesDocument()

@property(nonatomic, strong) NSMutableArray *recipes;

@end
```

Now on to implement the protocol. The first three methods are straightforward and similar to the implementation of PRPRecipesSource. Since they do not alter anything, no further interaction with the document is required. The code should look like this:

Documents/DocumentRecipes_01/DocumentRecipes/PRPRecipesDocument.m
```
- (NSInteger)recipeCount {
  return [self.recipes count];
}

- (NSUInteger)indexOfRecipe:(PRPRecipe *)recipe {
  return [self.recipes indexOfObject:recipe];
}

- (PRPRecipe *)recipeAtIndex:(NSInteger)index {
  return [self.recipes objectAtIndex:index];
}
```

The next two methods change the contents of the document, so we need to inform the document of the change. The document handles the complexity of writing the new state to disk. All we have to do is call the updateChangeCount: and the document takes care of the rest. The deleteRecipeAtIndex: method should look like this:

Documents/DocumentRecipes_01/DocumentRecipes/PRPRecipesDocument.m
```
Line 1 - (void)deleteRecipeAtIndex:(NSInteger)index {
  2    [self.recipes removeObjectAtIndex:index];
  3    [self updateChangeCount:UIDocumentChangeDone];
  4 }
```

On line 3 we tell our document about the change. Now our document can take the appropriate steps to persist the changes.

We also change the contents of the document when we create a new recipe, so we need to tell the document about this change in the same way. Here is the code:

```
- (PRPRecipe *)createNewRecipe {
  PRPRecipe *recipe = [[PRPRecipe alloc] init];
  [self.recipes addObject:recipe];
  [self updateChangeCount:UIDocumentChangeDone];
  return recipe;
}
```

Now that our document handles the list of recipes properly, we will teach it how to persist the recipes. Again, UIDocument makes it easy. For this case, we need to implement one method that produces the documents' content and a second method that turns data passed to us into a list of recipes. Override the contentsForType:error: method to convert our recipes to data using the following implementation:

```
Line 1  - (id)contentsForType:(NSString *)typeName error:(NSError **)outError {
     2      return [NSKeyedArchiver archivedDataWithRootObject:self.recipes];
     3  }
```

On line 2 we ask the NSKeyedArchiver to archive our recipes list into an NSData. The keyed archiver, a subclass of NSCoder, takes the object we pass in as the root object and sends it encodeWithCoder:. Since our root object is an NSMutableArray, it sends encodeWithCoder: to each of its objects, which is how each of our recipes receives encodeWithCoder:. Once the encoding is complete, we return an instance of NSData and that object is written out to disk for us by UIDocument.

With a way to produce data from our recipes, it's time to turn data into recipes. We do that by overriding the loadFromContents:ofType:error: method and using an NSKeyedUnarchiver, like this:

```
Line 1  - (BOOL)loadFromContents:(id)contents
     -                   ofType:(NSString *)typeName
     -                    error:(NSError **)outError {
     -      BOOL success = NO;
     5      if([contents isKindOfClass:[NSData class]] && [contents length] > 0) {
     -          NSData *data = (NSData *)contents;
     -          self.recipes = [NSKeyedUnarchiver unarchiveObjectWithData:data];
     -          success = YES;
     -      }
    10      return success;
     -  }
```

On line 5 we get defensive and make sure that the object passed in is an instance of NSData. In our current code this approach is a bit of overkill, but documents can also be stored in NSFileWrappers. When our documents are stored in iCloud, the content can be either of these types and we will want to work with them separately. On line 7 we ask the keyed unarchiver to take the data and turn it into an object. Since we wrote out our recipes array as the root object in the contentsForType:error:, the root object returned from the unarchiveObjectWithData: will be an array. To finish, we set the recipes property to this newly unarchived array.

Our document class is now the container of our recipes. It is able to read and write an array of recipes to and from a data object. Since we subclassed from UIDocument, we don't have to worry about how that NSData instance gets onto disk; our superclass takes care of that for us. We need to ensure that we have an array ready in which to store recipes when the document is created, so let's override the initWithFileURL: method. Add the method to the top of the implementation block, like this:

Documents/DocumentRecipes_01/DocumentRecipes/PRPRecipesDocument.m
```
Line 1  - (id)initWithFileURL:(NSURL *)url {
      -     self = [super initWithFileURL:url];
      -     if (self) {
      -         id value = nil;
     5         NSError *error = nil;
      -         if(![url getResourceValue:&value
      -                            forKey:NSURLAttributeModificationDateKey
      -                             error:&error]) {
      -           [self saveToURL:url
    10         forSaveOperation:UIDocumentSaveForCreating
      -         completionHandler:^(BOOL success) {
      -             if(!success) {
      -               NSLog(@"Failed to create file");
      -             }
    15         }];
      -       }
      -     }
      -     return self;
      - }
```

Now each time a PRPRecipesDocument is initialized, it will also have an array to store the recipes.

Our document is now ready to use as the dataSource for the PRPRecipesListViewController, so we can delete the PRPRecipesSource class from our Xcode project. Now that we've implemented the document, let's use it.

Use the Document Class

Change the app delegate from using the PRPRecipesSource class to our document class. Open PRPAppDelegate.m and switch the import from PRPRecipesSource to PRPRecipesDocument. Next, find application:didFinishLaunchingWithOptions:. We need to swap out our nonpersistent PRPRecipesSource for an instance of PRPRecipesDocument. Change the code to look like this:

```
Documents/DocumentRecipes_01/DocumentRecipes/PRPAppDelegate.m
Line 1 - (BOOL)application:(UIApplication *)application
     - didFinishLaunchingWithOptions:(NSDictionary *)launchOptions {
     -   UINavigationController *navigationController =
     -   (UINavigationController *)self.window.rootViewController;
     5   PRPRecipesListViewController *controller =
     -   (PRPRecipesListViewController *)navigationController.topViewController;
     -   NSURL *docDir = [[[NSFileManager defaultManager]
     -                     URLsForDirectory:NSDocumentDirectory
     -                     inDomains:NSUserDomainMask] lastObject];
     10  NSURL *docURL = [docDir URLByAppendingPathComponent:@"Recipes.recipes"];
     -   PRPRecipesDocument *doc = [[PRPRecipesDocument alloc] initWithFileURL:docURL];
     -   controller.dataSource = doc;
     -   [doc openWithCompletionHandler:^(BOOL success) {
     -     if(success) {
     15      [controller.tableView reloadData];
     -     } else {
     -       NSLog(@"Failed to open document");
     -     }
     -   }];
     20  return YES;
     - }
```

Since UIDocument needs a URL to function properly, we grab the documents directory on line 8 and add Recipes.recipes. On lines 11 and 12, we create the document and set it to be the dataSource for the view controller.

Next, we open the document on line 13. Remember all the complexity that UIDocument handles for us? Some of that becomes evident when we open a document. Reading and writing happen on a background thread to prevent blocking the event loop while the document is loaded from the filesystem. When we request a document be opened, the read is performed in the background. When it's done, the block we pass in here is invoked on the main thread. If anything goes wrong, success will be NO; otherwise it will be YES. We have to wait until the document is successfully opened before telling the table view to reload to ensure that the recipes will be there when the table view asks.

Build and run the app now and experiment with adding and removing recipes. Stop the app and then rerun to make sure that things are actually persisting as expected. Adding log statements to contentsForType:error: and encodeWithCoder: might help solidify the flow of method calls as our recipes are persisted.

Refine the Document

If you delete the app from the Simulator and then rerun it from Xcode, you'll notice in the console that our document fails to open. The problem is that the file does not exist. When we ask it to open, the document can't find the file, so it fails. Fortunately we can easily fix this problem by overriding the handleError:userInteractionPermitted: method on our document subclass. As the name suggests, this method is called when the document encounters an error. In this case, we only care about the NSFileReadNoSuchFileError error, since for all other errors we'll invoke the superclass implementation. Here is the code:

Documents/DocumentRecipes_01/DocumentRecipes/PRPRecipesDocument.m
```objc
- (void)handleError:(NSError *)error
userInteractionPermitted:(BOOL)userInteractionPermitted {
  if([[error domain] isEqualToString:NSCocoaErrorDomain] &&
     [error code] == NSFileReadNoSuchFileError) {
    [self saveToURL:[self fileURL]
   forSaveOperation:UIDocumentSaveForCreating
  completionHandler:^(BOOL success) {
    // ignore it here, we just wanted to make sure the document is created
    NSLog(@"handled open error with a new doc");
  }];
  } else {
    // if it's not a NSFileReadNoSuchFileError just call super
    [super handleError:error
userInteractionPermitted:userInteractionPermitted];
  }
}
```

We first check to see if the error is NSFileReadNoSuchFileError, and if so we open the document for creating. We don't need to do anything in the completion block, so we just log a message.

In an application that exposed multiple documents, this approach would not work. If the user were to tap on a document and it failed to open, we'd want to understand why that document was shown to the user in the first place rather than creating a new one. But for our application this approach works well.

7.2 Telling the Recipe Document About Edits

We can add and delete recipes, and now whatever state the recipe list is in when we leave the app is the same state we find it in when we return. If you hit stop in Xcode, though, only part of the state of the last recipe added is persisted. To understand why this happens, we need to understand more of how UIDocument works.

When we send updateChangeCount:, the document is marked as "dirty." A dirty document wants to save its contents to disk and will do so as soon as it can. If we don't send updateChangeCount:, the document thinks its contents are already on disk. The document won't write to disk again until we tell it about a change via the updateChangeCount: method or until the UIApplicationWillResignActiveNotification notification is received. In most cases, that notification will be received and the final changes to our recipe will make it to disk. But if we hit the stop button in Xcode or if our app crashes, the notification won't be received and unsaved changes will be lost.

Losing data is unacceptable and needs to be fixed. We'll fix the bug in the context of editing existing recipes. We need a couple of changes to enable editing existing recipes:

- We have to fix the bug we've just discussed, so we need to ensure the document knows when each edit happens. To do that we will define a protocol for the editor to interact with as each property is changed.

- The table view cell needs to use the detail disclosure indicator instead of the disclosure indicator we have been using. The detail disclosure button allows users to access additional functionality or more specific functionality. Tapping on the row will continue to take our users to the recipe view, but tapping on the detail disclosure will take them to the editor.

To accomplish these two tasks we will need to edit the editor view controller, the list view controller, and the interface in our storyboard, as well as add a new protocol. Let's get started in Interface Builder.

Edit Existing Recipes

Open the MainStoryboard.storyboard and select the recipe table view cell. Modify the cell to use the "Detail Disclosure" accessory view. Make the modifications in the Attributes inspector (⌥⌘4) and change the Accessory pull-down to Detail Disclosure. Changing the value causes the table view cell to use the blue circle with the chevron in it, like in Figure 63, *Detail disclosure table view cell*, on page 164.

Figure 63—Detail disclosure table view cell

The UI is now updated; next we need to add a modal segue that will take us from the recipes list to the editing view controller. Since we can't make a segue from the detail disclosure button, we'll make it from the recipes list view controller to the editing view controller. Select the Recipes List View Controller, control-drag to the editor view controller's navigation controller, and choose Modal from the pop-up. Next, identify the segue, select it, and change its identifier to "editExistingRecipe."

To invoke the editExistingRecipe segue, implement the tableView:accessoryButton-TappedForRowWithIndexPath: method in PRPRecipesListViewController so that it calls the performSegueWithIdentifier:sender: method, passing the identifier "editExistingRecipe." The tableView:accessoryButtonTappedForRowWithIndexPath: method is called when the user taps on the accessory button, which is precisely when we want to invoke the new segue. The implementation should look like this:

Documents/DocumentRecipes_02/DocumentRecipes/PRPRecipesListViewController.m
```
- (void)tableView:(UITableView *)tableView

accessoryButtonTappedForRowWithIndexPath:(NSIndexPath *)indexPath {
  UITableViewCell *cell = [tableView cellForRowAtIndexPath:indexPath];
  [self performSegueWithIdentifier:@"editExistingRecipe"
                            sender:cell];
}
```

The segue is invoked, but we need to tell the editing view controller which recipe to edit. To do that we need to extend the prepareForSegue:sender: method to understand "editExistingRecipe." This new code needs to get the indicated recipe and then pass that along to the editor. This code should more or less be the same code that we wrote to handle the "addNewRecipe" segue with the addition of finding the recipe. The additional code looks like this:

Documents/DocumentRecipes_02/DocumentRecipes/PRPRecipesListViewController.m
```
if([@"editExistingRecipe" isEqualToString:segue.identifier]) {
  NSIndexPath *index = [self.tableView indexPathForCell:sender];
  PRPRecipe *recipe = [self.dataSource recipeAtIndex:index.row];
  UINavigationController *nav = [segue destinationViewController];
  PRPRecipeEditorViewController *editor =
```

```
     (PRPRecipeEditorViewController *)[nav topViewController];
     editor.recipeListVC = self;
     editor.recipe = recipe;
}
```

Change the finishedEditingRecipe: method next, which is called when editing finishes. Currently it assumes that when we return from editing a recipe we want to insert a new row. Since we have changed the way that editing works, we need to change this method. We only want to insert a new row if we've created a new row; otherwise we want to update the row we were editing, like this:

Documents/DocumentRecipes_02/DocumentRecipes/PRPRecipesListViewController.m

```
- (void)finishedEditingRecipe:(PRPRecipe *)recipe {
  NSUInteger row = [self.dataSource indexOfRecipe:recipe];
  NSIndexPath *path = [NSIndexPath indexPathForRow:row inSection:0];
  UITableViewCell *cell = [self.tableView cellForRowAtIndexPath:path];

  if(nil == cell) {
    [self.tableView insertRowsAtIndexPaths:[NSArray arrayWithObject:path]
                         withRowAnimation:UITableViewRowAnimationLeft];
  } else {
    [self.tableView reloadRowsAtIndexPaths:[NSArray arrayWithObject:path]
                         withRowAnimation:UITableViewRowAnimationFade];
  }
}
```

Build and run the app and notice existing recipes can be edited.

Inform the Document of Changes

We are close, but the document still needs to be told about edits, which requires several changes. First, let's add a method to the PRPRecipesListDataSource protocol called - (void)recipesChanged;. This method lets the document know that something has changed. Now that we've updated the protocol, we need to add an implementation to PRPRecipesDocument. The method needs to call updateChangeCount:, like this:

Documents/DocumentRecipes_03/DocumentRecipes/PRPRecipesDocument.m

```
- (void)recipesChanged {
  [self updateChangeCount:UIDocumentChangeDone];
}
```

With the method defined on the protocol and implemented in our document subclass, we can update finishedEditingRecipe: to call this new method and thus inform the document that it needs to save its contents. Update the code by adding a call to recipesChanged as shown on line 13:

Documents/DocumentRecipes_03/DocumentRecipes/PRPRecipesListViewController.m

```
Line 1 - (void)finishedEditingRecipe:(PRPRecipe *)recipe {
       -   NSUInteger row = [self.dataSource indexOfRecipe:recipe];
       -   NSIndexPath *path = [NSIndexPath indexPathForRow:row inSection:0];
       -   UITableViewCell *cell = [self.tableView cellForRowAtIndexPath:path];
       5   if(nil == cell) {
       -     [self.tableView insertRowsAtIndexPaths:[NSArray arrayWithObject:path]
       -                          withRowAnimation:UITableViewRowAnimationLeft];
       -   } else {
       -     [self.tableView reloadRowsAtIndexPaths:[NSArray arrayWithObject:path]
       10                          withRowAnimation:UITableViewRowAnimationFade];
       -   }
       -
       -   [self.dataSource recipesChanged];
       - }
```

Even with that change in place, the document is still unaware of changes to the recipe's title or other properties. We need a way for the editor to let the document know of every property change.

We could pass the dataSource along to the editor view controller. With that change, the editor VC would be able to call recipesChanged each time an edit is made and the document would be able to save that changed state. We could do that, but that would be completely wrong for the design of our application. This solution works in the short term, but it is terrible for the design of our application. One of the major features of object-oriented programs is the ability to segment responsibility into easy-to-understand pieces. If we pass the dataSource into the editor, we are saying that we want the editor to know the detail of the PRPRecipesListDataSource. Spreading the detailed knowledge of that protocol provides too much information to the editor. Sure, right now we have the best intentions, and we'd never call createNewRecipe from within the editor. But over time we forget, and eventually a change to the protocol would be in order. We'd have to dig into the way it's used inside the editor before we would know if the change would be more trouble than it's worth. This solution is popular and wrong. Let's move on to the right answer.

The proper way to allow the editor to inform the document about edits is to define the interaction model and then build a protocol to formalize that interaction. We need two ways for the editor to signify changes: one that says "editing on this recipe is done" and a second that says "a property on this recipe has been edited." We have finishedEditingRecipe: to take care of the first. Let's use recipeChanged: for the second. Create a new protocol called PRPRecipeEditorDelegate and add these two methods:

```
Documents/DocumentRecipes_03/DocumentRecipes/PRPRecipeEditorDelegate.h
@class PRPRecipe;
@protocol PRPRecipeEditorDelegate <NSObject>

- (void)finishedEditingRecipe:(PRPRecipe *)recipe;
- (void)recipeChanged:(PRPRecipe *)recipe;

@end
```

Now we need to implement the new protocol. First, the PRPRecipesListViewController needs to adopt the protocol by adding PRPRecipeEditorDelegate in the header file like this:

```
Documents/DocumentRecipes_03/DocumentRecipes/PRPRecipesListViewController.h
@interface PRPRecipesListViewController :
UITableViewController <PRPRecipeEditorDelegate>

@property(nonatomic, strong) id <PRPRecipesListDataSource> dataSource;

@end
```

Don't forget to import the header file for the protocol.

Our PRPRecipesListViewController already implements the finishedEditingRecipe: method, so we are halfway there. Add an additional method implementation for recipeChanged:, like this:

```
Documents/DocumentRecipes_03/DocumentRecipes/PRPRecipesListViewController.m
Line 1 - (void)recipeChanged:(PRPRecipe *)recipe {
      -     [self.dataSource recipesChanged];
      -     NSUInteger row = [self.dataSource indexOfRecipe:recipe];
      -     NSIndexPath *path = [NSIndexPath indexPathForRow:row inSection:0];
      5     UITableViewCell *cell = [self.tableView cellForRowAtIndexPath:path];
      -
      -     if(nil != cell) {
      -         [self.tableView reloadRowsAtIndexPaths:[NSArray arrayWithObject:path]
      -                         withRowAnimation:UITableViewRowAnimationFade];
     10     }
      - }
```

On the first line we tell the data source that the recipes have changes. The next four lines of this code are the same as our implementation of finishedEditingRecipe:. On line 7 we check to see if there is a cell at this index. If so, we tell it to reload its contents.

The editor should no longer be using the list view controller directly and should instead be using the protocol. Specifically, find this line:

```
Documents/DocumentRecipes_03/DocumentRecipes/PRPRecipeEditorViewController.h
@property(nonatomic, weak) PRPRecipesListViewController *recipeListVC;
```

Change that line to this:

```
@property(nonatomic, weak) id<PRPRecipeEditorDelegate> delegate;
```

To rename the property, use the "Rename…" refactoring. When the refactoring is finished, the name will be updated in all the places it is used. Next, change the type to id<PRPRecipeEditorDelegate>. Now we can delete the forward declaration of PRPRecipesListViewController from the header file as well. The done: should have its implementation updated after the refactoring, like this:

```
Line 1 - (IBAction)done:(id)sender {
     2   [self dismissViewControllerAnimated:YES
     3                           completion:NULL];
     4   [self.delegate finishedEditingRecipe:self.recipe];
     5 }
```

Notice on line 4 that finishedEditingRecipe: is being called on self.delegate instead of on self.recipeListVC. Now we need to invoke recipeChanged: whenever a property is updated. The editor allows our users to change three properties: title, preparationTime, and image. The title is changed in textFieldDidEndEditing:, which should be updated to look like this:

```
- (void)textFieldDidEndEditing:(UITextField *)textField {
  self.recipe.title = textField.text;
  [self.delegate recipeChanged:self.recipe];
}
```

Once we add the call to recipeChanged: after setting the title, we are done with this method. The same basic approach applies to the other two methods. Add a call to recipeChanged: in changePreparationTime: and imagePickerController:didFinishPickingMediaWithInfo: to do the same.

What about the directions property? Since users are allowed to edit the directions property, why aren't we calling recipeChanged: when that property changes? To inform the document about a change in the directions property will require the same steps we took to define and use the PRPRecipeEditorDelegate. We need a delegate protocol defined for the directions editor. We need to update the recipe editor to implement that protocol and pass itself in as the delegate for the directions editor. And lastly, the recipes editor needs to inform the document about the change.

Since we just went through that when we defined PRPRecipeEditorDelegate for editing existing recipes, we are not going to go step by step through the process again. The downloadable code bundle has that change integrated into

DocumentRecipes_05 and all subsequent versions. Also, the list of things to try for further study at the end of the chapter has some hints on how to make this work. For now, we'll leave this as an open, known bug.

We've fixed the bug and got our recipes persisting properly. Along the way we've added the ability to edit existing recipes, which gave us the opportunity to develop and use a delegate protocol. It is hard to overstress the importance of defining our own protocols to formally capture the interaction between parts of our app. Just as having the protocol for our recipe list dataSource made it easy to replace the PRPRecipesSource with a PRPRecipesDocument instance, defining this new protocol makes it easy to change from the recipe list to some other view controller invoking the editor. Or even more importantly, it allows us to reuse the editor from different contexts.

Our app is in good shape. We've implemented just about every document-related feature that we specified at the beginning of this chapter. However, our users can't share their recipes with each other. Let's make that happen now.

7.3 Sharing Recipes

The concept of "document" is a useful abstraction for us. It gives us a nice neat package in which to group our users data. But documents can be a distraction for users. As our application currently stands, users are unaware that there is a document and instead think the app "just works." As we plan out this new feature to share recipes, we need to make sure that we don't unnecessarily add complexity by exposing documents. Instead, we should expose only what we must. As with any functionality on any app, we need to keep it as simple as possible and no simpler. With that in mind, let's plan out what our app will do when sharing recipes.

From our users' perspective, sharing involves two things: sending recipes to friends and receiving recipes from friends. To keep things simple from a user interaction perspective, when receiving recipes we will take any new recipes and add them to our existing document. To send recipes we'll allow our users to select which recipes to send and then package them up in a document and send that via email. This approach provides a simple interaction model—no need to expose multiple documents.

Technically we are going to send our recipes via email. The MFMailComposeView-Controller class built into iOS makes that relatively easy. To receive recipes our application must register a new document type. The bulk of that work is done via configuration in the DocumentRecipes-Info.plist. Let's start with the configuration.

Registering a New Type

The type system on iOS is based on uniform type identifiers (UTIs). UTIs are a way for us to describe the recipes data type so that iOS can understand enough to display meaningful info to the user without starting our application. In a UTI, we specify file name extensions, mime type, and a type description. iOS can then use this information to let the users know what kind of file it is so they can decide if they want to open it.

We can either use existing UTIs defined by Apple (such as PDF, JPG, and so on) or define a new one. Recipe data is very specific to our app, so we will define a new type in Xcode. Select the project at the top of the project navigator, select the target, and then select the Info tab within the target editor. Now click the disclosure triangle on the Custom iOS Target Properties to close that section, and click the disclosure on the Exported UTIs section to open it.

Tap the Add button on the bottom right side and choose Add Exported UTI. Specify the Description, Identifier, and Conforms To fields as "Recipe Data," "com.pragprog.adios.recipes," and "public.data," respectively. Description is a localizable, user-visible description of our document type. The Conforms To field allows iOS to try to open our file in other apps that understand that data type. Specifying "public.data" says that our files might be understood by other applications that know "public.data." The identifier is used by iOS as a unique identifier for this UTI, so we use the reverse DNS naming convention. On the right we can specify large and small versions of the icon for our file type. We don't have any artwork so we'll leave these two fields blank. The Xcode should look like Figure 64, *Add exported UTI*, on page 171.

UTI Hierarchy

It's unlikely that any other app is going to understand our file type. The UTI type hierarchy is really meant to allow the OS to fall back from a more specific type to a less specific type. For example, suppose we built an image editing application that allowed users to add custom keys to EXIF data. It's unlikely that another app would understand those extra keys and values. However, it's very likely that other image viewing applications would be able to display the image.

We need two more pieces of information to make our UTI definition complete, namely the file name extension and the mime type. Expand the Additional Exported UTI properties editor and click in there to add a new item. Change the new key to UTTypeTagSpecification and its type to Dictionary. Add a key and change it to "public.mime-type," its type to "String," and its value to

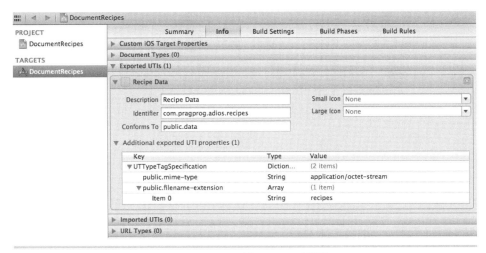

Figure 64—Add exported UTI

"application/octet-stream." This says that our application can open a binary stream of bytes. The next key is "public.filename-extension." It's an array with one value—recipes. Now that we have defined a new type, the file name extension "recipes" is tied to Recipe Data. With this Exported UTI in place, iOS will know that our app understands the UTI identified by "com.prag-prog.adios.recipes." Now we need to define a document type.

Define the Recipe Document

Collapse the Exported UTIs section and expand the Document Types section. In the bottom right side, click the Add button and choose Add Document Type. Expand the Untitled section that is created.

We need to specify three pieces of information here to complete the definition. The first is the name of the document type. Specify "Recipe Document" here. This text is used by iOS to display the document type to users. Next is the type, which must match the identifier we gave our UTI in the previous step. Specifically, put "com.pragprog.adios.recipes" into the Types field. The last item is the single key "LSHandlerRank" in the "Additional document type properties" area. LSHandlerRank tells iOS how your application relates to this document type. In our case we are the "Owner." When done, the Document Type area should look like Figure 65, *Add document type*, on page 172.

The Owner value is the appropriate choice for our application because we defined the "com.pragprog.adios.recipes" type. But if our application could open types that we did not define, image types for example, we'd want to specify Alternate for LSHandlerRank.

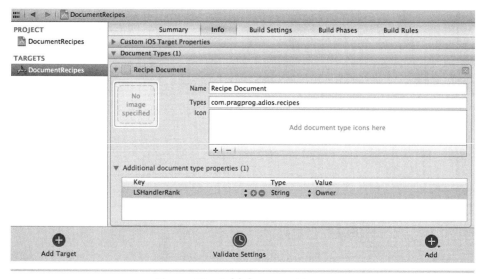

Figure 65—Add document type

When we specify Alternate, iOS understands that our app is one of many that can open and use a file type. But our app did not define that type; it merely understands the type.

It is extremely important that we get the LSHandlerRank value correct. Applications that specify Owner for a type are telling iOS that they should be the first app offered to the user when that document type is encountered. Again, in our case for the recipe document type, it is appropriate that DocumentRecipes be the first choice. But if an application understands PDFs, it should not claim ownership; that would supersede any other app in the system that understands PDFs. Users typically don't want apps doing that. Instead, if our app claims understanding of the document type with Alternate, then it would be added to the list of apps that can open PDFs.

Sending Recipes via Email

Now that our app can open recipe documents, we need a way for our users to send them to each other. The easiest way to do that is via email, so let's start there.

First, we need a button to do the initial composition of a new email. Add a new bar button item to the navigation bar on the recipes list view controller and change its identifier to Action. When that is done, the button should look like Figure 66, *Action button*, on page 173.

Figure 66—Action button

If we wanted to ship this app we'd want to have some custom artwork for this button, but for our sample app this icon looks great.

Next, we need to connect that button to some code. In the PRPRecipesListViewController.h file, add an IBAction called sendEmail:. In Interface Builder connect the Action button to the newly declared method.

Now that we declared and connected our button to sendEmail:, we need to implement the method. In order to implement sending email, we are going to use the MFMailComposeViewController to present the email to the users and allow them to hit Send or Cancel. Before we can use this class, though, we need to include the framework in our project. Looking in the documentation for MFMailComposeViewController, we see that the framework is called MessageUI. Select the project in the project navigator, click Build Phases, and open the "Link Binary with Libraries" item. Click the + button and type "MessageUI." Select that framework and click the Add button.

Our recipe document will be sent as an attachment. MFMailComposeViewController makes it easy to do that. All we need to do is call the addAttachmentData:mimeType:fileName: method. The first argument is the data for the attachment. We have a way to get data from our recipes document, but the PRPRecipesListViewController does not know about the document, only the data source. Rather than reimplement what the document does, we will expose a method to get at the data through the data source. Since we know the data source is really an instance of the document class, we could just cast it and call document methods. While that could work, it would be very bad for the design of our application and will end up causing problems. It is better to take the extra few minutes to do it correctly.

In the PRPRecipesListDataSource, add a new method called dataForRecipes: that returns an NSData or returns nil if there is an error. The single argument is a pointer to an NSError. Declare that method like this:

Documents/DocumentRecipes_05/DocumentRecipes/PRPRecipesListDataSource.h
```
- (NSData *)dataForRecipes:(NSError **)error;
```

Since we've added a method on the protocol, we need to add an implementation to PRPRecipesDocument. In the document class we need to place the document's contents into an NSData instance. Since we have the URL for the document, the initial first pass of this method could be very simple; just call dataWithContentsOfURL: and return that NSData. While that would work most of the time, we should take into account the multithreaded nature of UIDocument. Remember that UIDocument will read and write its content on a background thread. If we were to adopt this naive approach, we'd get bitten sooner or later by some very interesting and hard-to-find bugs. Instead, using an NSFileCoordinator makes sure that any writing that is currently happening finishes before we grab a copy of the file off disk. Here is the implementation:

Documents/DocumentRecipes_05/DocumentRecipes/PRPRecipesDocument.m

```
Line 1  - (NSData *)dataForRecipes:(NSError **)error {
     -      __block NSData *data = nil;
     -      NSFileCoordinator *coordinator = [[NSFileCoordinator alloc]
     -                                          initWithFilePresenter:nil];
     5      [coordinator coordinateReadingItemAtURL:[self fileURL]
     -                                       options:NSFileCoordinatorReadingWithoutChanges
     -                                         error:error
     -                                    byAccessor:^(NSURL *newURL) {
     -                                      data = [NSData dataWithContentsOfURL:newURL];
    10                                    }];
     -      return data;
     - }
```

On line 2 we declare the data object to be returned. We use the __block keyword to allow the block used later to be able to change the variable. Next, we create an instance of NSFileCoordinator, which will take care of coordinating access to the document on disk. On line 5 we ask the coordinator to coordinate reading our document's content from disk. This method prevents our program from proceeding until it is safe for us to read the file; when it is safe, the block that we pass in as the last argument will be executed. Notice that we do read the file on line 9 and that we use the newURL that was passed into our block. While doing the coordinating, some behind-the-scenes reorganization might be happening; the coordinator knows all about that and will tell us via this URL argument. It may or may not be the same URL we passed in on line 5. Always make sure to use the URL passed into this block to ensure the correct file is read.

If anything goes wrong during the coordination, the error object will be set and our block won't be executed. Otherwise, we'll load the content and return it.

With the infrastructure set up, we can implement the sendEmail: method. We need to create an instance of MFMailComposeViewController, become its delegate, set the subject, attach the document data from the dataForRecipes: method we just implemented, and then present the new compose view controller. We do that by adding this code to PRPRecipesListViewController.m:

```
- (IBAction)sendEmail:(id)sender {
  MFMailComposeViewController *mailVC =
  [[MFMailComposeViewController alloc] init];
  mailVC.delegate = self;
  [mailVC setSubject:@"Great Recipes"];
  NSError *error = nil;
  [mailVC addAttachmentData:[self.dataSource dataForRecipes:&error]
                   mimeType:@"application/octet-stream"
                   fileName:@"Recipes.recipes"];
  if(nil == error) {
    mailVC.mailComposeDelegate = self;
    [self presentViewController:mailVC
                       animated:YES
                     completion:NULL];
  } else {
    NSLog(@"error in coordinating read %@ - %@", error, error.userInfo);
  }
}
```

Make sure to import the <MessageUI/MessageUI.h> header file in the PRPRecipesListViewController.h.

Building now will lead to a compiler warning that self does not implement the UINavigationControllerDelegate and MFMailComposeViewControllerDelegate protocols. While at first blush it might seem daunting to implement two protocols, only one method, mailComposeController:didFinishWithResult:error:, is needed and the implementation is simple. All we have to do is dismiss the mail compose window. Add a method, like this:

```
- (void)mailComposeController:(MFMailComposeViewController *)controller
          didFinishWithResult:(MFMailComposeResult)result
                        error:(NSError *)error {
  [controller dismissViewControllerAnimated:YES
                                 completion:NULL];
}
```

Remember to also add both protocol declarations to the @interface in the PRPRecipesListViewController.h file. Add both protocols, comma separated, just after PRPRecipeEditorDelegate.

We can now compose and present an email message with our recipes attached as a document. Click the Run button in Xcode. Once the app starts, tap the Send button. The compose view controller is presented along with the recipes document attached. It looks like Figure 67, *Recipe document attachment*, on page 176.

Figure 67—Recipe document attachment

Unfortunately we can't send email in the Simulator, so we can't see the fruit of our labors. Let's perform a little trick on our Mac to get the same effect without having to deploy to a device. We are going to use the built-in python simple HTTP server to serve a document to Mobile Safari.

Web Sharing the Document

In Finder, select the "Go→Go to Folder..." menu item or use the ⌘⇧G keyboard shortcut. In the field that pops up, type ~/Library/Application Support/iPhone Simulator and hit Return. From that directory, select the version of iOS to which you are deploying your app, and then select the Applications folder. Applications contains all the apps that are deployed in the Simulator. This list might be quite long and all the folder names are UDIDs, making it tedious to find the DocumentRecipes application. To find the file quickly, click in the search box in the top right of the Finder window and type the name of the app, DocumentRecipes; then choose Applications from the "Search:" scope bar on the left. When done, the Finder window will look like Figure 68, *Searching in Finder*, on page 177.

Control-click the app and choose Open Enclosing Folder, which will bring up a new Finder window with the app selected. Click the Documents directory and notice the Recipes.recipes document. Finder will look like Figure 69, *Finding the Recipes.recipes document*, on page 177.

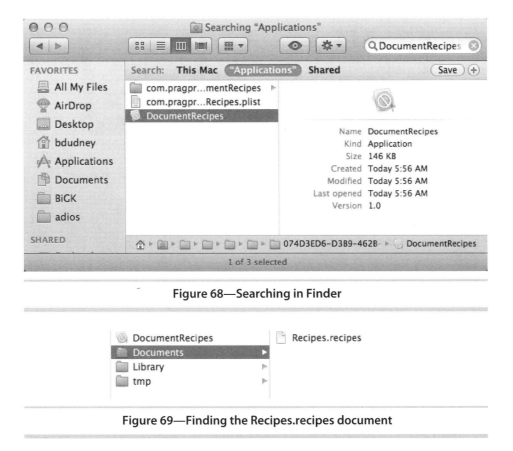

Figure 68—Searching in Finder

Figure 69—Finding the Recipes.recipes document

This document is equivalent to what we would have sent via that email.

Now we need to fire up the python HTTP server. Open Terminal.app and cd into the Documents directory. (You can launch Terminal via Spotlight by hitting ⌘Space and then typing "Terminal.") Once you have a Terminal window, type "cd" and then select the Documents directory in Finder and drag it into the Terminal window. Hit return so your current directory is the Documents directory. On the command line in Terminal, type "python -m SimpleHTTPServer" and hit return. You'll see a few diagnostic log messages from the server.

Back in the Simulator, tap the home button and open Mobile Safari. Type "http://0.0.0.0:8000/Recipes.recipes" into the location field. Tap the Go button, and Safari will download the file and present it to us as a document. The page should look like Figure 70, *Recipes document downloaded*, on page 178.

Recipes.recipes
177 KB

Figure 70—Recipes document downloaded

Mobile Safari offers us the "Open in DocumentRecipes" button, which when tapped will send this document to our app. All this works because of the configuration we did to share recipes back in Section 7.3, *Sharing Recipes*, on page 169. Since we specified the mime type as "application/octet-stream" and the filename-extension as "recipes," Mobile Safari makes the connection that this binary file named "Recipes.recipes" is associated with our DocumentRecipes app. If we were to deploy the app to a device and send an email, the recipient would have something very similar.

Now the time has come to tap the Open In button. And...nothing happens, a rather disappointing outcome. Since our app delegate class PRPAppDelegate does not implement the application:openURL:sourceApplication:annotation: method, iOS will not switch from Mobile Safari to our app. Let's go fix that now.

7.4 Opening Shared Recipe Documents

As we have seen, when an application specifies that it understands a document, iOS enables the Open In button. But if that application's delegate does not implement or does not return YES from the application:openURL:sourceApplication:annotation:, iOS assumes that something prevents that app from loading the document and does nothing. So we need to implement that method and return YES when we are done loading the document.

Copying Recipes

New documents delivered to an app by iOS through this sharing mechanism are placed in the applications sandbox. In order to pull the recipes out of this newly delivered document, we need to create a new PRPRecipesDocument instance, get the recipes from it, and copy them into our existing document. Let's update our code to make this possible.

First, we don't currently have a pointer to the existing doc. Fix that by adding a new property to the PRPAppDelegate and changing the application:didFinishLaunchingWithOptions: method to assign the document created there to the new property. In the demo code, the property is added in a class extension: since no other class needs to know about this new property, this is the best place to put it. Here is the new implementation:

```
Documents/DocumentRecipes_05/DocumentRecipes/PRPAppDelegate.m
Line 1 - (BOOL)application:(UIApplication *)application
   - didFinishLaunchingWithOptions:(NSDictionary *)launchOptions {
   -   UINavigationController *navigationController =
   -   (UINavigationController *)self.window.rootViewController;
5
   -   PRPRecipesListViewController *controller =
   -   (PRPRecipesListViewController *)navigationController.topViewController;
   -
   -   NSURL *docDir = [[[NSFileManager defaultManager]
10                       URLsForDirectory:NSDocumentDirectory
   -                     inDomains:NSUserDomainMask] lastObject];
   -   NSURL *docURL = [docDir URLByAppendingPathComponent:@"Recipes.recipes"];
   -   PRPRecipesDocument *doc = [[PRPRecipesDocument alloc] initWithFileURL:docURL];
   -   controller.dataSource = doc;
15
   -   [doc openWithCompletionHandler:^(BOOL success) {
   -     if(success) {
   -       [controller.tableView reloadData];
   -     } else {
20       NSLog(@"Failed to open document");
   -     }
   -   }];
   -   self.document = doc;
   -   return YES;
25 }
```

The only difference in this version of the method is the assignment of the new property on line 23.

The second change is to add a method we can call to add the recipes from the imported document to our existing document. We'll fix that by adding an addRecipesFromDocument: method to the PRPRecipesDocument class, like this:

Documents/DocumentRecipes_05/DocumentRecipes/PRPRecipesDocument.m

```
- (void)addRecipesFromDocument:(PRPRecipesDocument *)newDoc {
  [self.recipes addObjectsFromArray:[newDoc recipes]];
  [self updateChangeCount:UIDocumentChangeDone];
}
```

It is very important that we call the updateChangeCount: method so the document will know that it needs to write the recipes to disk.

Now we can properly implement the application:openURL:sourceApplication:annotation: method. Here is the code:

Documents/DocumentRecipes_05/DocumentRecipes/PRPAppDelegate.m

```
- (BOOL)application:(UIApplication *)application
          openURL:(NSURL *)url
  sourceApplication:(NSString *)sourceApplication
        annotation:(id)annotation {
  PRPRecipesDocument *newDoc = [[PRPRecipesDocument alloc] initWithFileURL:url];
  [newDoc openWithCompletionHandler:^(BOOL success) {
    if(success) {
      [self.document addRecipesFromDocument:newDoc];
    } else {
      NSLog(@"Failed to open new document - %@", url);
    }
  }];
  return YES;
}
```

iOS sends us the URL to the imported file, so creating a new document is easy. We pass the newURL variable to the initWithURL: method. Next, if the imported document is successfully opened, we need to copy its recipes into our existing document. So we send openWithCompletionHandler:, a block that calls addRecipesFromDocument: if opening was successful.

To test our changes, delete the existing app from the Simulator and then hit the Run button in Xcode. Once the application has started, hit the home button. The application is still running: it's just in the background. Now launch Mobile Safari and navigate to the URL that python is serving up (see *Web Sharing the Document*, on page 176) if Safari does not already have a window open on that URL. Tap the Open In button, and iOS switches us back to Document Recipes. But...no recipes! The issue is that the recipe has been loaded into the document but the view does not know that. Stop the app in Xcode and rerun it. The recipe appears in the list. Good to know our code works, but we really want the recipe to show up without quitting the app. Let's add a notification to let the view know that the recipe list has changed.

Notifying the List View

Notifications are a great way to let objects know about events without having to tightly couple the origin of the event to the code that needs to know about that change. The only thing the two pieces of code have to know about is the name of the notification. Since the document will be the source of this notification, we'll name the notification in the PRPRecipesDocument.m file, like this:

Documents/DocumentRecipes_06/DocumentRecipes/PRPRecipesDocument.m
```
NSString * const PRPRecipesDidChangeNotification =
@"PRPRecipesDidChangeNotification";
```

Next we need to send the notification. We'll do that in the addRecipesFromDocument: method, like this:

Documents/DocumentRecipes_06/DocumentRecipes/PRPRecipesDocument.m
```
- (void)addRecipesFromDocument:(PRPRecipesDocument *)newDoc {
  [self.recipes addObjectsFromArray:[newDoc recipes]];
  [[NSNotificationCenter defaultCenter]
   postNotificationName:PRPRecipesDidChangeNotification
   object:self];
  [self updateChangeCount:UIDocumentChangeDone];
}
```

Any time a document adds the recipes from another document we will post this notification. In order for other objects to receive this notification, all they need is the name. We'll expose it in the PRPRecipesListDataSource.h file so that every class that uses the protocol will know the name of the notification. The declaration looks like this:

Documents/DocumentRecipes_06/DocumentRecipes/PRPRecipesListDataSource.h
```
extern NSString * const PRPRecipesDidChangeNotification;
```

The extern tells the compiler that this name is defined elsewhere: in our case it's back in the PRPRecipesDocument.m file.

Finally, we want to have our list view controller listen to the notification and reload the table view when the list changes. We'll do that by making a method called recipesChanged:. We want the view controller to listen to the notifications only while its view is onscreen. So we'll register to listen in viewWillAppear: and stop listening in viewWillDisappear:. Here is the code for all three methods:

Documents/DocumentRecipes_06/DocumentRecipes/PRPRecipesListViewController.m
```
- (void)viewWillAppear:(BOOL)animated {
  [super viewWillAppear:animated];
  [[NSNotificationCenter defaultCenter]
   addObserver:self selector:@selector(recipesChanged:)
   name:PRPRecipesDidChangeNotification object:self.dataSource];
}
```

```
- (void)viewWillDisappear:(BOOL)animated {
  [super viewWillDisappear:animated];
  [[NSNotificationCenter defaultCenter]
   removeObserver:self
   name:PRPRecipesDidChangeNotification
   object:self.dataSource];
}

- (void)recipesChanged:(id)sender {
  [self.tableView reloadData];
}
```

We start listening by calling addObserver:selector:name:object:. The selector specifies the method we want called when the notification is posted. When the view leaves the screen, we remove the list VC from listening by calling removeObserver:name:object:. By passing in the object parameter to both the addObserver:selector:name:object: and removeObserver:name:object:, we are telling the notification center that we only want to listen to notifications from that object. The recipesChanged: method reloads the table view so that we can see the new recipes.

Delete the app from the Simulator and then run it again from Xcode. Tap the home button, go to Mobile Safari, and hit the Open In button. This time the new recipe is loaded into the document and displayed!

7.5 Storing Documents in iCloud

Storing our recipes in a document is an important step, but we really want to take advantage of the great iCloud feature introduced in iOS 5. One way to sum up what iCloud brings to users is "all your documents, on all your devices, all the time." Users might think that magically happens, but as developers we know better. Fortunately, since we have built Recipes using UIDocument, our work to migrate to iCloud is straightforward. We need to provide an entitlements file to tell iOS and the App Store that our app is going to participate in iCloud, move our document into the iCloud sandbox, and manage conflicts—three easy steps to make our users believe in magic. Let's get started.

A note of caution though. iCloud-enabled apps must be run on the device to be tested, so once you make the following changes the app won't work in the Simulator. Not to worry though—we will revert to a version of the app that can run on the Simulator when we are done with our iCloud work.

Setting up the entitlements for Recipes is as easy as flipping a switch. In Xcode, select the project in the Navigator, then select the DocumentRecipes target, which will display the target editor. Select the Summary tab and scroll to the bottom, where you'll see the Entitlements section. Check the box labeled

Enable Entitlements, and the editor will change to look like Figure 71, *Enabling iCloud with entitlements*, on page 183.

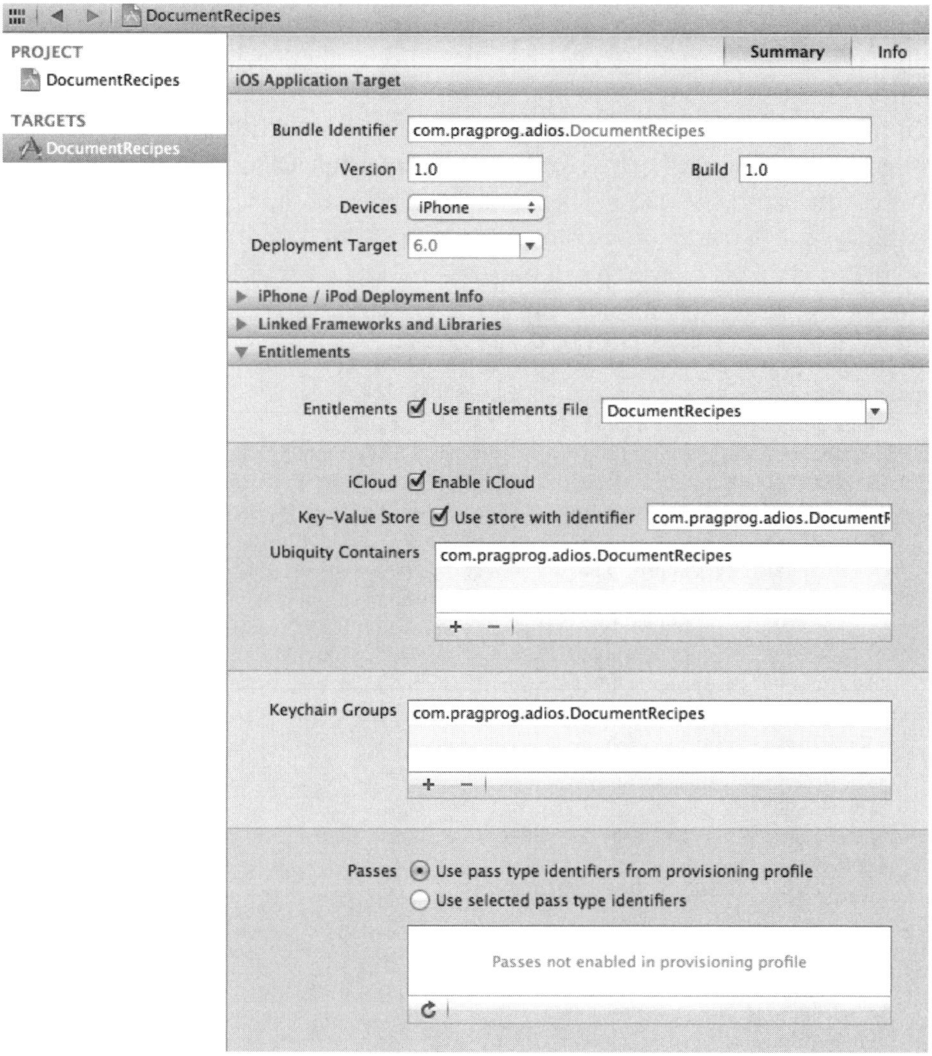

Figure 71—Enabling iCloud with entitlements

Xcode creates a file called DocumentRecipes.entitlements for us, which sets up several things that enable our app to work with iCloud. First, the Key-Value Store field becomes a way to distinguish this application's cloud-based key-value store. The Key-Value Store is used for small pieces of data, such as which level a player is on or what page of a PDF a user is reading. The next field, iCloud Containers, is a list of identifiers for each cloud-based directory that our application needs access to. The Recipes app only needs one, so we won't change this value. The last field is a way for applications to share information; we'll leave this value as is. Now Recipes has permissions to store its documents in iCloud. Let's go change the code to put the document into iCloud.

To tell iOS to store our recipes document in iCloud rather than the Documents directory, we just need to ask the NSFileManager for the iCloud-enabled directory. We do that with the URLForUbiquityContainerIdentifer: method. The argument can either be one of the identifiers we put into the iCloud Containers entitlements or nil. We will pass nil, which will use the first identifier in that list. Recall that we set up the recipes document in the application:didFinishLaunchingWithOptions: method. Change the code to look like this:

```
Documents/DocumentRecipes_07/DocumentRecipes/PRPAppDelegate.m
Line 1 - (BOOL)application:(UIApplication *)application
     - didFinishLaunchingWithOptions:(NSDictionary *)launchOptions {
     -   UINavigationController *navigationController =
     -   (UINavigationController *)self.window.rootViewController;
     5   PRPRecipesListViewController *controller =
     -   (PRPRecipesListViewController *)navigationController.topViewController;
     -   NSURL *docDir = [[[NSFileManager defaultManager]
     -                     URLForUbiquityContainerIdentifier:nil]
     -                     URLByAppendingPathComponent:@"Documents"];
     10  NSURL *docURL = [docDir URLByAppendingPathComponent:@"Recipes.recipes"];
     -   PRPRecipesDocument *doc = [[PRPRecipesDocument alloc] initWithFileURL:docURL];
     -   controller.dataSource = doc;
     -   [doc openWithCompletionHandler:^(BOOL success) {
     -     if(success) {
     15      [controller.tableView reloadData];
     -     } else {
     -       NSLog(@"Failed to open document");
     -     }
     -   }];
     20  self.document = doc;
     -   return YES;
     - }
```

On line 8 we call URLForUbiquityContainerIdentifer: passing nil, then append Documents to the returned URL. We end up with a directory called Documents in the iCloud enabled directory. Everything in the Ubiquity directory (that is, URLForUbiquityContainerIdentifer:) is stored in iCloud, but files in the Documents directory are exposed to our users individually. Everything else in the Ubiquity directory is grouped together as Data. Since we want our users to see the document, we'll put it here.

If we were to run the application now, our recipes document would be sent up to iCloud. Unfortunately, iCloud does not work in the Simulator, so you must deploy to a device to see it in action. If you can deploy to a device, do so now and load the Recipes.recipes from the web server on your Mac. After the file is loaded, hit the home button, launch settings, and tap iCloud. Then at the bottom, tap Storage & Backup, and finally tap Manage Storage. You'll see a list of all the backups you have enabled for iCloud as well as the data that each iCloud-enabled application is storing. Tap on the Unknown item. All apps during development appear in this group. Once the app is deployed to the App Store, it will get its own group. The page will look like Figure 72, *Recipes document in iCloud*, on page 185.

Figure 72—Recipes document in iCloud

Now that our document is in iCloud, it will be pushed to every device with the Recipes app installed.

Merging Changes from Multiple Devices

Users with a single device will have a great experience with our current implementation. Each change is saved locally and then pushed to iCloud. If anything happens to the device, the document is safe in iCloud. However, conflicts can arise when users have multiple devices. The next step in adding iCloud integration is to appropriately handle changes from iCloud.

As our users make changes on one device, the document is pushed to iCloud and then sent to all the other devices that have the app installed. As this new version of the file arrives, UIDocument does an evaluation of what the change means. In most cases there will be no conflict and we will have very little to do. However, if the document on the second device has changes, the document goes into a conflict state. It is very important that iCloud-enabled apps deal properly with these conflicts. Until the app marks a version as resolved, it will remain in the user's iCloud storage. Let's start with the easy case.

Update the UI on New Version Arrival

In the easiest-to-code scenario, a new version of a document will arrive from iCloud and the UIDocument will evaluate it, find no conflicts, and reopen the document. That will eventually end up in a call to loadFromContents:ofType:error: to reload the documents' contents. In our current implementation, the document reloads but the UI would not update. To fix that, we need to post the PRPRecipesDidChangeNotification as we did back in *Notifying the List View*, on page 181. Modify the code to look like this:

Documents/DocumentRecipes_08/DocumentRecipes/PRPRecipesDocument.m

```
Line 1 - (BOOL)loadFromContents:(id)contents
   -                    ofType:(NSString *)typeName
   -                     error:(NSError **)outError {
   -   BOOL success = NO;
5    if([contents isKindOfClass:[NSData class]] && [contents length] > 0) {
   -     NSData *data = (NSData *)contents;
   -     self.recipes = [NSKeyedUnarchiver unarchiveObjectWithData:data];
   -     [[NSNotificationCenter defaultCenter]
   -      postNotificationName:PRPRecipesDidChangeNotification
10       object:self];
   -     success = YES;
   -   }
   -   return success;
   - }
```

Notice on line 8 that we post the notification after the recipes array has reloaded. That ensures the UI will get updated when the new version of the file is loaded.

Resolving Conflicts in Incoming Versions

Cleaning up when a conflict arises can be handled in numerous ways. The best would be for us to do an automatic merge so no user-entered data is ever lost. For Recipes we would need to compare recipes, look for duplicates, and then merge changes from the most recent copy. We then need to add the recipes that are not there and somehow know which recipes to delete. That would provide the best user experience, but it is outside the focus of this chapter. Instead, we are just going to discard the conflict. Not nearly as elegant, but it ensures that we are not leaking files into the user's iCloud account.

Before we can discard the conflicted version, we need to know about it. We learn about conflicts by listening for the UIDocumentStateChangedNotification notification. Add the following statement to the application:didFinishLaunchingWithOptions: method just after opening the document.

Documents/DocumentRecipes_08/DocumentRecipes/PRPAppDelegate.m
```
[[NSNotificationCenter defaultCenter]
 addObserver:self
 selector:@selector(docChangedState:)
 name:UIDocumentStateChangedNotification
 object:doc];
```

Now we need to implement the docChangedState:. Here is the code:

Documents/DocumentRecipes_08/DocumentRecipes/PRPAppDelegate.m
```
Line 1 - (void)docChangedState:(NSNotification *)notification {
     2   NSURL *url = [[notification object] fileURL];
     3   NSArray *versions =
     4   [NSFileVersion unresolvedConflictVersionsOfItemAtURL:url];
     5   for(NSFileVersion *fileVersion in versions) {
     6     NSError *error = nil;
     7     [fileVersion removeAndReturnError:&error];
     8   }
     9 }
```

First we grab the file versions that are in conflict, and on line 7 we remove that version. Again, this is not a very elegant approach. In a more sophisticated app you'd want to do some type of merging.

If you have two devices to deploy to, push Recipes out to both and watch as changes are pushed between then. It is really amazing—with just these few changes our documents are going out to the cloud and down to another device.

7.6 Wrap-Up

Our Recipes application has gained a lot of features in this chapter, and along the way we have learned a lot. We started by making our recipes able to serialize themselves into an NSCoder. We learned how flexible key-based encoding is and how easy it is to write an object graph to a coder.

The work we did in subclassing UIDocument taught us about the new multi-threaded access to documents built into UIKit. We learned that saving and opening a document happen on a background thread, which is why we pass in a block to be invoked when the background I/O finishes. We also got to see how documents make it into iCloud, and thankfully most of the work is done for us via UIDocument.

We also learned how to send a copy of the recipes document via email. Since the Simulator is not able to send email, we copied the document and were able to interact with it through Mobile Safari via Web Sharing.

The recipes application is approaching full functionality. In the next few chapters we are going to add polish to the application via drawing and some performance work.

For Further Thought

Here are a few things to think about or try out to expand your understanding of the stuff we've covered in this chapter. The questions don't necessarily have "correct" answers. Please join us on the forums at http://forums.pragprog.com/ to discuss your ideas about them.

1. We had to copy code for the "editExistingRecipe" segue. Since copying code copies bugs, we'd rather not have copied code. Use the "Extract…" refactoring to place the copied code into a new method.

2. Adding a delegate to the directions editor is an important step in cleaning up the design of our application. To help solidify the ideas of delegate and protocols, define a new protocol for the directions editor to use. The delegate protocol needs only one method specifying that the user has finished typing in the new text and letting the delegate know what that text is. Have the recipe editor implement that protocol and set itself as the directions delegate in the prepareForSeque:sender: method.

3. Currently Recipes leaves the documents imported from Safari or other apps in the Incoming folder. Use the NSFileManager API to remove the document after we've imported the recipes from it.

CHAPTER 8

Drawing and Animating

To paraphrase Ernest Hemingway, "Every app's life ends the same way. It is only the details of how it worked and how it looked that distinguish one app from another."

Or to put that another way, the heart and soul of your application is how it works and how it looks. People will use an app if their experience with it is good, and otherwise they won't. Up to this point in the book we have worried little about the user experience of the Recipes app. The app functions, but it lacks refinement. We will begin to fix that in this chapter.

We will add a few interesting visual aspects to Recipes, but true usability polish is not the focus of this chapter or this book. The goal of this chapter is to point toward what is possible and where to look when the UX designer asks for the impossible. We will look at three things: drawing images to preserve memory, adding a frame and a shadow to our images to add a bit of visual appeal, and adding some animation to help our users keep what the application is doing in context.

The approach in this chapter is a bit different than in previous chapters. Instead of building toward an end, we will take many side trips to interesting destinations, turn around, start over, and find a new interesting trick. So much of the drawing capabilities in iOS come down to what looks the best, and often that requires trying a different approach. We'll be implementing several different possibilities in this chapter.

To start working on the examples in this chapter, download the code bundle and use the Recipes_start project from the Drawing directory. The iCloud-related code from Chapter 7, *Documents and iCloud*, on page 155, has been removed so the project runs in the Simulator again. The Core Graphics framework has also been added to the project.

8.1   Drawing Images

Currently when users add images to their recipes, we have to scale them to fit into the UIImageView. This default behavior from the image view is fine for getting started, but there are several reasons not to leave it like this.

First, it takes a lot of processing to get a really large image scaled down. Photos taken with the iPhone 4S camera are 3264 x 2448. When a user chooses one of these photos, our image view must scale that down to fit in a 43 x 43 area. Even though iOS is very efficient at scaling, an 8-megapixel image contains a lot of pixels to process every time that image is displayed onscreen.

Next, our app does not display differently sized images consistently. Instead of being centered and similarly sized, portrait images are flush against the left side and are only 32 points wide, while the landscape images are 57 points wide; we'll center the images so the layout of the table cells looks much better. The screenshot in Figure 73, *Before and after cells*, on page 190, shows how the screen changed with resizing.

Figure 73—Before and after cells

Finally, we'll discuss how to save memory when displaying large images by scaling them down to the correct size.

Drawing Thumbnail Images

First, redraw the images in a size that makes sense for the table view. For the recipes list that means 43 x 43. To keep track of this smaller image, let's add a property called thumbnailImage to the PRPRecipe class. Don't forget to synthesize the new property. Since we want this new property to be stored along with the rest of the recipes info, we also need to add this new property to the initWithCoder: and encodeWithCoder: methods. Change them to look like this:

```
Drawing/Recipes_01/Recipes/PRPRecipe.m
Line 1 - (id)initWithCoder:(NSCoder *)coder {
   -     self = [super init];
   -     if (self) {
   -         self.title = [coder decodeObjectForKey:@"title"];
   5         self.directions = [coder decodeObjectForKey:@"directions"];
   -         self.preparationTime = [coder decodeObjectForKey:@"preparationTime"];
   -         self.image = [coder decodeObjectForKey:@"image"];
   -         self.thumbnailImage = [coder decodeObjectForKey:@"thumbnailImage"];
   -     }
   10    return self;
   - }
   - - (void)encodeWithCoder:(NSCoder *)coder {
   -     [coder encodeObject:self.title forKey:@"title"];
   -     [coder encodeObject:self.directions forKey:@"directions"];
   15    [coder encodeObject:self.preparationTime forKey:@"preparationTime"];
   -     [coder encodeObject:self.image forKey:@"image"];
   -     [coder encodeObject:self.thumbnailImage forKey:@"thumbnailImage"];
   - }
```

On line 8 the thumbnailImage property is read from the coder, and on line 17 the property is written into the coder. The thumbnail image will now persist along with the rest of the recipe.

Next we will draw the chosen image at a 43 x 43 resolution. Open the PRPRecipeEditorViewController.m file and find the imagePickerController:didFinishPickingMedi-aWithInfo: method. Recall that this method is invoked by the image picker to let us know which image the user chose from the photo library. Here is the new code:

```
Drawing/Recipes_01/Recipes/PRPRecipeEditorViewController.m
Line 1 - (void)imagePickerController:(UIImagePickerController *)picker
   - didFinishPickingMediaWithInfo:(NSDictionary *)info {
   -
   -     UIImage *originalImage =
   5     [info valueForKey:UIImagePickerControllerOriginalImage];
   -
   -     CGSize cellViewSize = CGSizeMake(43.0, 43.0);
   -     CGRect cellViewRect = [self rectForImage:originalImage inSize:cellViewSize];
   -     UIGraphicsBeginImageContext(cellViewSize);
   10    [originalImage drawInRect:cellViewRect];
   -     self.recipe.thumbnailImage = UIGraphicsGetImageFromCurrentImageContext();
   -     UIGraphicsEndImageContext();
   -
   -     self.recipe.image = originalImage;
   15
   -     [self.delegate recipeChanged:self.recipe];
   -     [picker dismissViewControllerAnimated:YES
   -                                completion:NULL];
   - }
```

On line 4 we retrieve the image from the info dictionary just as we did previously. Then on lines 7 and 8 we initialize the rectangle in which we'll draw the image—we'll look at the implementation of rectForImage:inSize: shortly. On line 9 we create an image context to draw into. (An image context is like a canvas in memory; drawing commands apply paint to the canvas. Calling this function creates a new context and makes it the destination for our drawing calls.) Next, on line 10 we draw the image into the calculated rectangle. The drawInRect: method draws the image into the rectangle, stretching or squashing the image as needed to fill the whole rectangle. If the rectangle is not properly sized, the image will be distorted.

On line 11 we ask for an image from the current image context, and on line 12 we end the context, which frees up the memory and other resources allocated after calling UIGraphicsBeginImageContext(). This function also clears the current context so any drawing done after ending the context will do nothing. Make sure you call it when you are done drawing.

At first some of this might look a little odd; we are mixing Objective-C code with straight C code. The API for Core Graphics is based on C rather than on Objective-C, but the API is object-oriented with a slightly different syntax. Notice on line 7 where we create the cellViewSize. Instead of using alloc and init, we use CGSizeMake(). Even though we use different method names, we are doing basically the same thing: we are creating and initializing a new CGSize object. Some of the technical details are different to be sure, but the conceptual space is the same. So don't let the C-based nature of Core Graphics worry you.

The rectForImage: method that we used to scale and position our image's rectangle looks like this:

Drawing/Recipes_01/Recipes/PRPRecipeEditorViewController.m

```
Line 1  - (CGRect)rectForImage:(UIImage *)image inSize:(CGSize)size {
     -      CGRect imageRect = {{0.0, 0.0}, image.size};
     -      CGFloat scale = 1.0;
     -      if(CGRectGetWidth(imageRect) > CGRectGetHeight(imageRect)) {
     5          scale = size.width / CGRectGetWidth(imageRect);
     -      } else {
     -          scale = size.height / CGRectGetHeight(imageRect);
     -      }
     -
    10      CGRect rect = CGRectMake(0.0, 0.0,
     -                               scale * CGRectGetWidth(imageRect),
     -                               scale * CGRectGetHeight(imageRect));
     -      rect.origin.x = (size.width - CGRectGetWidth(rect)) / 2.0;
     -      rect.origin.y = (size.height - CGRectGetHeight(rect)) / 2.0;
    15      return rect;
     -  }
```

On lines 4–8 we calculate the scale factor, which we will use to scale the image so its longest side fits into our 43 x 43 image view. On lines 10 to 12 we use that scale factor in calculating the new size. And finally, on lines 13 to 14, we center the rectangle in the available space.

Now that we've created the thumbnail, we need to use it in the table view. That means we need to head over to the PRPRecipesListViewController.m and modify the tableView:cellForRowAtIndexPath: method to place the thumbnailImage into the image property of the cell's imageView, like this:

Drawing/Recipes_01/Recipes/PRPRecipesListViewController.m
```
- (UITableViewCell *)tableView:(UITableView *)tableView
        cellForRowAtIndexPath:(NSIndexPath *)indexPath
{
  static NSString *CellIdentifier = @"Cell";

  UITableViewCell *cell =
  [tableView dequeueReusableCellWithIdentifier:CellIdentifier];
  PRPRecipe *recipe = [self.dataSource recipeAtIndex:indexPath.row];
  cell.textLabel.text = [recipe title];
  cell.imageView.image = [recipe thumbnailImage];
  NSNumber *prepTime = [recipe preparationTime];
  cell.detailTextLabel.text = [NSString stringWithFormat:@"%@ %@",
                               prepTime, NSLocalizedString(@"minutes", nil)];
  return cell;
}
```

Now our table view has centered, scaled-down images like Figure 74, *Scaled images in table view cell*, on page 193.

Figure 74—Scaled images in table view cell

The benefit of using this approach is that much less memory and processing is required to draw each of the cells. We have not done much with large data sets yet, but the old approach of putting 8-megapixel images into a 43 x 43 space would totally kill our animation performance. Using these thumbnails will give us a butter-smooth 60 fps.

Drawing Full-Size Images

We have taken care of our table view; now let's scale down the images to better fit in the image view on the recipe details page. Basically, we need to do what we did for the thumbnails but for a larger size. Back in the imagePickerController:didFinishPickingMediaWithInfo: method, we need to add code to draw at 260 x 260, which is the size of our image view on the details page. Here is the new code:

```
Drawing/Recipes_02/Recipes/PRPRecipeEditorViewController.m
CGSize detailImageSize = CGSizeMake(260.0, 260.0);
CGRect detailImageRect = [self rectForImage:originalImage inSize:detailImageSize];
UIGraphicsBeginImageContext(detailImageSize);
[originalImage drawInRect:detailImageRect];
self.recipe.image = UIGraphicsGetImageFromCurrentImageContext();
UIGraphicsEndImageContext();
```

This needs to be added just after we end the image context used for the thumbnail. Now we have an image that is much smaller than the 8-megapixel image captured by an iPhone 4S. Take a look at the Recipes.recipes file in the ~/Library/Application Support/iPhone Simulator/5.0/Applications/.../Documents directory. The file is hundreds of kilobytes rather than several megabytes. This memory savings also translates into shorter load times and quicker saving, an overall better user experience.

Now that we have the images sized appropriately, let's look at some ways to liven up the user interface. First, we'll draw a frame around the image, and then to add a bit of depth we'll add a shadow.

8.2 Drawing Paths

To frame our image we'll draw a rectangle around the edge of the image. To do that we'll need a path, which is a geometric representation of a shape that we want to draw. A path consists of points, lines, arcs, and curves. We use these primitives to build up what we want to draw, and then we draw the path. The path is drawn with the state specified in the current graphics context. As we saw earlier in *Drawing Thumbnail Images*, on page 190, a context is the canvas where drawing takes place. It's also a holder of the state used to draw. We specify the width and color of paths. When we ask the context to fill or *stroke* (draw) the path, it uses the width and color we just specified to determine which pixels are drawn. We are going to create a path around our images and then stroke that path to get our frame.

Let's add a little texture to the background so we can see the path that we'll draw. We'll use the image titled wood.png from the code download as our background for both the edit and details view. Select that file and drag it into your project. Alternatively, you can use any image you'd like as the background. Make sure to specify that the file should be copied into your project.

We are going to add an image view to the recipe detail view first. Open the MainStoryboard.storyboard file. Select the detail view in the storyboard file, and then in the Object library (^⌥⌘3), select an image view and drag it into the scene. Open the Size inspector (⌥⌘5) and specify 0, 0, 320, 416 as the x, y, width, and height, respectively. The image view should cover the whole area of the detail view. In the Attributes inspector (⌥⌘5), specify the image for this image view as the wood.png image we previously added. For the wood image, the preparation time label and value are hard to see as black text, so change both of them to white. Or, if you are using your own image, change the text color to contrast with that image. When done, the view and controller should look like Figure 75, *Wood texture added*, on page 195.

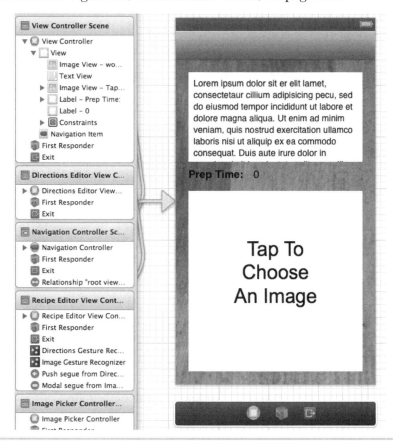

Figure 75—Wood texture added

Pay particular attention to the order of the views under the main view. Specifically, the image view needs to be at the top of this list for it to be behind all the other views. This needs to be repeated for the recipe edit view as well.

Now that we have a bit more texture in the UI, we can start to draw some interesting features into the images. First let's add a white frame around the image. To draw this frame, we'll use the UIBezierPath class. Paths are used to do vector-based drawing in Core Graphics. Here is the code in context of where we left off in the previous section:

Drawing/Recipes_03/Recipes/PRPRecipeEditorViewController.m
```
Line 1 CGSize detailImageSize = CGSizeMake(260.0, 260.0);
     - CGRect detailImageRect = [self rectForImage:originalImage inSize:detailImageSize];
     - UIGraphicsBeginImageContext(detailImageSize);
     - [originalImage drawInRect:detailImageRect];
     5
     - CGFloat frameWidth = 6.0;
     - CGRect frameRect = CGRectInset(detailImageRect, frameWidth / 2.0,
     -                                frameWidth / 2.0);
     - UIBezierPath *frame = [UIBezierPath bezierPathWithRect:frameRect];
    10 [frame setLineWidth:frameWidth];
     - [[UIColor whiteColor] setStroke];
     - [frame stroke];
     -
     - self.recipe.image = UIGraphicsGetImageFromCurrentImageContext();
    15 UIGraphicsEndImageContext();
```

We begin on line 6 by setting up the frame. We'll use this variable to specify how wide we want the frame's rectangle to be drawn. Next, on line 8 we create a rectangle that we'll use to specify the path we want to draw. We could draw the detailImageRect, but the graphics system on iOS draws paths straddling the geometric representation. In this particular case Core Graphics will draw three points over and three points under the line specified by the rectangle. If we just used the image's rectangle, that would mean the frame's drawing would be beyond the edge of the image by three points. So instead, we inset the rectangle by half of the desired frame width. Then on the next three lines we create a UIBezierPath for the rectangle around the image and set the width and the color of the line.

It might seem a little odd that we send the setStroke method to a UIColor instance instead of sending something like setStrokeColor: to the path object. After all, we send setLineWidth: to the path, and both stroke color and line width are state variables on the graphics context. The UIBezierPath holds onto some of the state that will be applied when it's drawn and leaves other elements of the state to be specified in other ways. The only way to tell whether you should set a state value on the path or somewhere else is to look at the documentation.

Now that we have configured all the state variables for drawing our path, we call stroke on line 12. The image now has a white border around it. Run the app in the Simulator and either create a new recipe or edit an existing one. Choose a new image, and the edit screen will look like Figure 76, *Image in white frame*, on page 197.

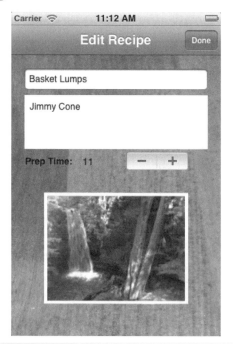

Figure 76—Image in white frame

The photo in a frame looks pretty cool, but it still looks a bit flat. A shadow is one of the most common approaches to add depth to a scene. Let's do that next.

8.3 Using Shadows

There are multiple ways to apply shadows in iOS. As with the use of any API, we should look to the highest-level approach possible. We should use lower level APIs only when performance concerns or additional flexibility requirements force us to.

The easiest way to get a shadow under a view's content is to use the layer's shadow-related properties. To do that we need to add the QuartzCore framework to the project. The QuartzCore framework is where we find Core Animation: in addition to the shadow properties, it also provides easy-to-use animation API.

Select the project in the project navigator, click the Build Phases tab, then expose the list of linked frameworks. Click the + button near the bottom and search for QuartzCore.framework.

After adding the framework to the project, we need to import the header file at the top of the PRPViewController.m and the PRPRecipeEditorViewController.m files. Then in the viewWillAppear: method on PRPRecipeEditorViewController, add the following:

Drawing/Recipes_04/Recipes/PRPRecipeEditorViewController.m
```
self.recipeImage.layer.shadowRadius = 5.0;
self.recipeImage.layer.shadowColor = [[UIColor blackColor] CGColor];
self.recipeImage.layer.shadowOffset = CGSizeMake(8.0, 8.0);
self.recipeImage.layer.shadowOpacity = 0.75;
```

This code sets various shadow properties required to get a shadow. The shadowRadius property sets the amount of blur to apply to the shadow. The offset is how far from the content the shadow will extend. Since Core Animation layers deal exclusively with Core Graphics types, we have to convert our UIColor to a CGColor before we can set the shadowColor. Once applied, the shadow will look like Figure 77, *Shadowed image*, on page 198.

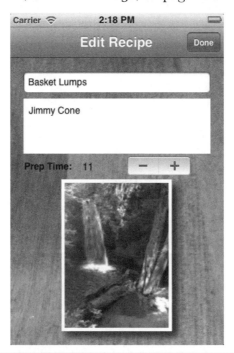

Figure 77—Shadowed image

We need to apply these same changes to the PRPViewController as well. In the implementation file, add the import statement and then apply the four layer properties to the imageView's layer.

This shadow looks great, and it's super easy to add via the Core Animation API. However, the simplicity of the approach can lead to some major performance problems if the graphic being shadowed is animating. In order for Core Animation to know how to cast that shadow, it first has to render the graphic offscreen, cast the shadow, and then pull the graphic and the shadow onto the screen. The operation by itself is fast, but if the shadowed graphic is animating, that has to be done again for each frame. At 60 Hz we only have 16.7 milliseconds to render each frame, and that's not much time. Rendering offscreen and then shuttling the data back onto the screen can take a big chunk of that per-frame time.

Fortunately, there is another way that we will look at shortly. But first let's add the ability to change the orientation of our image by rotating it with a tap.

8.4   Rotating and Animating Images

Let's add the ability for our users to rotate images with a tap by adding a gesture recognizer to the image view. In the MainStoryboard.storyboard, select the recipes detail view. From the Object library (^⌥⌘3), select a tap gesture recognizer (GR) and drag it onto the image view. Once placed, the scene should look like Figure 78, *Gesture recognizer placed*, on page 200.

We used gesture recognizers back in Chapter 6, *Storyboards and Container Controllers*, on page 119, to kick off our segues. Gesture recognizers (GR) are objects that process touch events and look for gestures. Once recognized, the gesture recognizer sends a message to its target.

The great thing about using gesture recognizers is that every app on iOS feels the same for our users. A swipe feels the same in any application that uses a swipe gesture recognizer.

To use gesture recognizers we need to turn on user interaction for the image view. Most views have user interaction turned on by default but not image view. If user interaction is turned off, the GR will fail to fire. After selecting the image view, open the Attributes inspector (⌥⌘4) and check the box labeled User Interaction Enabled.

The work in Interface Builder is done for the moment. Open the PRPViewController.m file and add a method called rotateImageView:, like this:

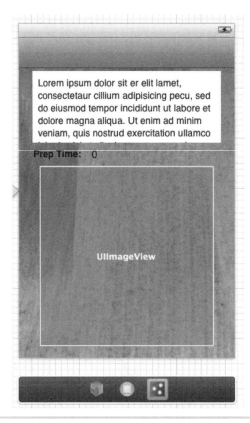

Figure 78—Gesture recognizer placed

Drawing/Recipes_05/Recipes/PRPViewController.m
```
- (IBAction)rotateImageView:(UITapGestureRecognizer *)tapGR {
  self.imageView.transform = CGAffineTransformRotate(self.imageView.transform,
                                        M_PI / 2.0);
}
```

Now that we have a method to connect the gesture recognizer, we need to go back to Interface Builder and connect the GR to the rotateImageView:.

In this method we are changing the view's transform property to append a new transform matrix that is 90 degrees more than it previously was, so with each tap the image will rotate another 90 degrees.

Build and run the app and tap on the image for a recipe. It looks great rotated, but the lack of animation is a bit jarring. We definitely want to clean that up by animating the rotation. The UIView animation API makes that a snap. Change the code to use the animatedWithDuration:animations:completion: method, like this:

Drawing/Recipes_06/Recipes/PRPViewController.m
```
- (IBAction)rotateImageView:(UITapGestureRecognizer *)tapGR {
  [UIView animateWithDuration:0.5
                   animations:^{
                     self.imageView.transform =
                     CGAffineTransformRotate(self.imageView.transform,
                                        M_PI / 2.0);
                   }
                   completion:^(BOOL finished) {
                   }];
}
```

Any animatable properties we change inside the animations block will be animated. We first saw blocks back in Chapter 3, *Asynchronicity and Concurrency*, on page 57—recall that a block is just a simple way to wrap up a bit of code that we want run by another object. In this case the UIView will call this block for us after it has set up the animation. Once the animation is finished, the completion block will be invoked. Since we don't need to do anything upon completion, we will leave that block empty.

Build and run the app now. When you tap on the image, the rotation animates over a half a second. It is really simple to get animation with UIKit.

Using a tap gesture recognizer is sufficient for the detail view. In the editor view, however, a tap indicates we want to choose a new image. So let's switch from a tap gesture recognizer to a two-finger rotate gesture.

Two-Finger Rotation

To make this switch, change the rotateImageView: method to accept a UIRotationGestureRecognizer, and then go back to the storyboard and replace the tap GR with a rotation GR. The rotation GR needs to be connected to the rotateImageView: method. Now we have a rotation GR instead of a tap GR.

Let's update the code to use the angle of rotation from the GR. Back in the PRPViewController's implementation of rotateImageView:, change the creation of the transform to look like this:

Drawing/Recipes_07/Recipes/PRPViewController.m
```
- (IBAction)rotateImageView:(UIRotationGestureRecognizer *)gr {
  [UIView animateWithDuration:0.5
                   animations:^{
                     self.imageView.transform =
                     CGAffineTransformMakeRotation(gr.rotation);
                   }
                   completion:^(BOOL finished) {
                   }];
}
```

Instead of always rotating by a constant 90 degrees, we make a new rotation transform with the values from the GR.

Build and run the app, and try rotating it. To get two touches on the Simulator, hold down the ⌥ key while dragging around on the screen. The image rotates with the two touches. This is a great time to deploy the app to your device. Look in Chapter 10, *The App Store and Beyond*, on page 233, for the details.

Now we can add this same functionality to the recipe editing scene. Copy the code over to the PRPRecipeEditorViewController implementation and then add the rotation GR to the image view. This scene is a little tricky to test in the Simulator because holding down the ⌥ key always centers on the middle of the iOS screen. It is much easier to test this on a device.

Our image is shadowed and our users can rotate the image to match their preferences—we even got the rotation animated. We've added a lot of polish to this part of the application. But as we alluded to earlier, this approach to shadowing can have some serious performance implications. Each frame of this animation has to be rendered offscreen and then composited back onto the screen. That process takes quite a few of the 16.7 milliseconds that we have for each frame. Let's look at an approach to get rid of this offscreen render pass.

8.5 Drawing Shadows

Now that we have an animation, we need to look at the performance of our shadow. Recall that using the shadow API from Core Animation is easy but requires an offscreen rendering pass, which can be expensive. As promised in this section, we are going to learn how to draw a shadow with the Core Graphics API so we only pay that shadowing cost once.

Let's start by removing the code we added to set the Core Animation shadow on our image view's layer. In PRPRecipeEditorViewController and PRPViewController, delete the following code from the viewWillAppear: method:

```
self.imageView.layer.shadowRadius = 5.0;
self.imageView.layer.shadowColor = [[UIColor blackColor] CGColor];
self.imageView.layer.shadowOffset = CGSizeMake(8.0, 8.0);
self.imageView.layer.shadowOpacity = 0.75;
```

Now let's go back to where we draw the image in PRPRecipeEditorViewController's imagePickerController:didFinishPickingMediaWithInfo: method and use Core Graphics to create our shadow. Setting up the shadow is similar to what we did with Core Animation. Here is the shadow code in context:

```
Drawing/Recipes_08/Recipes/PRPRecipeEditorViewController.m
Line 1 CGSize detailImageSize = CGSizeMake(260.0, 260.0);
   -   CGRect detailImageRect = [self rectForImage:originalImage
   -                                       inSize:detailImageSize];
   -   detailImageRect = CGRectInset(detailImageRect, 8.0, 8.0);
   5   UIGraphicsBeginImageContext(detailImageSize);
   -   CGContextRef context = UIGraphicsGetCurrentContext();
   -   UIColor *color = [[UIColor blackColor] colorWithAlphaComponent:0.75];
   -   CGContextSetShadowWithColor(context, CGSizeMake(8.0, 8.0), 5.0,
   -                               [color CGColor]);
```

Setting up the context is the same. We specify the size and then call the UIGraphicsBeginImageContext() function to create a new context. However, we set up the image's rectangle a bit differently. On line 4 we inset the image by the shadow's offset. Core Animation is able to draw the shadow outside the context's bounds, but Core Graphics is not. Since we need to call other Core Graphics functions, we need the context, which we do on line 6. Then on line 8 we set the shadow parameters on the context with the CGContextSetShadowWith-Color() function.

With the shadow set on the context, all drawing that happens from this point forward will be shadowed. That is not exactly what we want, since we are drawing two things—the image and the frame—and we only want one shadow. If we were to continue to draw as we were in the previous examples, we'd end up with a shadow under the image and also under the frame. To fix that we will use a CGLayer object to draw the image and the frame. Then we'll draw the layer into the context, and the shadow will be cast under the frame and image together.

As we discussed earlier, a context is the canvas on which all drawing takes place. When we create the layer, we'll get the graphics context from the layer and then use that to draw on. Here is the code to create the layer and get its context:

```
Drawing/Recipes_08/Recipes/PRPRecipeEditorViewController.m
Line 1 CGLayerRef layer = CGLayerCreateWithContext(context,
   2                                             detailImageSize,
   3                                             NULL);
   4   CGContextRef layerCtx = CGLayerGetContext(layer);
```

The first parameter is the context we want to create the layer in. The next parameter is the size of the context, and the third is always NULL. Then on line 4 we get a graphics context from the layer.

The default coordinate system of Core Graphics is upside down from the default UIKit system, so we need to swap the *y*-axis. We do that with a coordinate transform, like this:

Drawing/Recipes_08/Recipes/PRPRecipeEditorViewController.m
```
CGContextTranslateCTM(layerCtx, 0.0, detailImageSize.height);
CGContextScaleCTM(layerCtx, 1.0, -1.0);
```

Next we want to draw the image and the frame into the layer's context. In the previous code we used the UIKit methods on UIImage and UIBezierPath to draw, but these methods only draw into the *current* context. We want to draw into the layer's context, like this:

Drawing/Recipes_08/Recipes/PRPRecipeEditorViewController.m
```
Line 1 CGContextDrawImage(layerCtx, detailImageRect, [originalImage CGImage]);
     2 CGFloat frameWidth = 6.0;
     3 CGRect frameRect = CGRectInset(detailImageRect, frameWidth / 2.0,
     4                                 frameWidth / 2.0);
     5 UIBezierPath *frame = [UIBezierPath bezierPathWithRect:frameRect];
     6 CGContextSetLineWidth(layerCtx, frameWidth);
     7 CGContextSetStrokeColorWithColor(layerCtx, [[UIColor whiteColor] CGColor]);
     8 CGContextAddPath(layerCtx, [frame CGPath]);
     9 CGContextStrokePath(layerCtx);
```

This might look a bit spooky since it's mostly C function calls rather than message sends. But take a minute to look at how this code is structured. On line 1 we call CGContextDrawImage(). The first argument is the context, the next specifies which rectangle to draw the image into, and the third is the image to draw. That's not all that different than a call to UIImage's drawInRect:. The parameters are in a different order, and the context is assumed, but it's basically the same thing. On line 6 we set the line width with a call to CGContextSetLineWith(), which is very similar to the setLineWidth: method call on the path. On line 7 we set the color to use when stroking the path. Then on lines 8 and 9 we add the path to the context and then stroke it. Some of this is happening in a little different order, but it's all basically the same as what we did before. The context is not assumed. We have to explicitly state which context by passing it in as the first argument to each of these functions. Now we have our image and path drawn into the layer's context.

Next, we need to draw this layer back in our original context, which is done like this:

Drawing/Recipes_08/Recipes/PRPRecipeEditorViewController.m
```
        CGContextDrawLayerAtPoint(context, CGPointMake(0.0f, 0.0f), layer);
CGLayerRelease(layer);
```

Since we made our layer the same size as the parent context, we just draw it at 0.0, 0.0. Now our image and frame will have only one shadow and our animation performance will be great. Build and run the app and look at the images. Except for being a few points smaller, they look the same as when we drew the shadows with Core Animation, but no offscreen rendering pass is required.

8.6 Wrap-Up

Drawing with Core Graphics is a huge topic and we have barely scratched the surface. We have learned how to draw images into the default context as well as into an explicit context, and we have seen how much memory we can save by scaling images down. We also added a bit of depth to our scene with a frame and a shadow.

For Further Thought

Here are a few things to think about or try out to expand your understanding of the stuff we've covered in this chapter. The questions don't necessarily have "correct" answers. Please join us on the forums at http://forums.pragprog.com/ to discuss your ideas about them.

1. Experiment with different stroke colors and widths for the frame.

2. Set the fill color to a semitransparent color and fill the path we used for the frame.

3. Spend some time changing the shadow offset and color parameters when using a CGLayer.

4. Try drawing a different shape as the path, and clip the image to that path.

CHAPTER 9

Testing and Fixing Apps

It's great when code compiles and runs right the first time. It's even better when it all keeps working, never affected by changes elsewhere in an ever-expanding, evolving code base. As the app gains new features and is put to new uses, it's awesome that all the work we've already done never regresses into crashes, bugs, or other misbehavior.

At least it would be awesome if any of this were true. But the fact is, *this never happens.*

As we build out our apps, our code often needs to be reworked or run in an environment that has subtly (or obviously) changed from its initial form. Assumptions we made when we created the project and wrote the first few classes cease to be accurate, implicit contracts get broken, and the app fails, sometimes in ways we don't expect.

In this chapter, we're going to look at how to keep this from happening in our apps: how to use testing to give us confidence that our code continues to behave as expected, and how to fix things when they do break.

9.1 Unit Testing

How do we know our code really works? Is it enough to say "it works for me"? That doesn't mean much if we just haphazardly try out new features as we write them and just assume everything else is fine. It's entirely possible that our new code will create side effects that break existing functionality in the app.

For professional development, we should have a formal system of testing the app, and that begins with spelling out what we want to test. A *unit test* is a piece of code that calls into the application code to check some behavior, such as executing a calculation or performing a task, like reading in some sample data. Based on what the application code does, a given test either passes or fails. By assembling a large number of tests and running them consistently, developers can gain a high level of confidence that the application works and will continue to work as expected.

Unit testing is not as entrenched in desktop and mobile programming as it is on the server and in web apps. iOS reflects this reality: there are multiple testing frameworks available—some included with Xcode and others supplied by third parties like the open-source community—each of which serves different purposes and works somewhat differently. In this chapter, we are going to work with the testing facilities provided by Xcode, but that shouldn't keep you from looking elsewhere if you're dissatisfied. Testing on iOS is certainly a work in progress.

Xcode's unit testing features are based on the open-source OCUnit, which is short for "Objective-C Unit Testing Framework."[1] OCUnit offers two kinds of tests: logic tests and application tests. Logic tests check the behavior of our code in isolation, not in the context of the app, letting us focus on our data models and algorithms. Logic tests run only in the iOS Simulator. Application tests are meant to test the app as a whole and can run on the device and address issues specific to the device, like location awareness and low-memory conditions. We will be focusing on logic tests in this section and set aside OCUnit in favor of a new framework when we're ready to test the application and its UI.

Creating a Unit Test Target

To get started, let's take our Recipes app as it stood at the end of the last chapter and make it testable. We could have done this in the beginning, way back in Section 4.1, *Practicing MVC*, on page 78. When we created the project, a check box offered us the opportunity to set up unit tests. Since we didn't do it then, we need to add them now.

To add unit testing to an existing project, add a new target to the project. Click Recipes.xcodeproj at the top of the file navigator to see the overview of the project and its targets. Way back in *Projects, Targets, and Schemes*, on page 21, we learned that a target represents the sources, resources, and actions needed to produce a certain product. So far, our targets have just been the app; now we're going to add a new target that consists of unit tests and the scripts to run them.

---

1. http://www.sente.ch/software/ocunit/

Find the Add Target button at the bottom left of the Content area and click it. This shows the sheet in Figure 79, *Adding a Cocoa Touch unit testing bundle target*, on page 209. Choose Cocoa Touch Unit Testing Bundle and click Next. In the next screen, set the product name to RecipeUnitTests, and click the Use Automatic Reference Counting check box.

Figure 79—Adding a Cocoa Touch unit testing bundle target

Now our project has two targets: Recipes, the app itself, and RecipeUnitTests, the unit tests. But we're not quite done, since the unit test bundle has no idea what to test. Select the new target and click its Build Phases tab. We want the Recipes project to always be built and be up-to-date with its sources before we run any tests. We can do this by expanding the Target Dependencies section, clicking the plus (+) button, and selecting the Recipes target. This tells Xcode that the RecipeUnitTests' build depends on the Recipes target being built first.

Creating the unit testing target automatically included SenTestingKit.framework in its list of libraries to link; this is OCUnit's Objective-C framework package. However, there are a few manual steps that we need to perform now to get our tests to run against the existing code. Under Build Settings, find the Linker entry called Bundle Loader and add the value $(BUILT_PROD-UCTS_DIR)/Recipes.app/Recipes. Then find the Unit Testing entry for Test Host and set it to ${BUNDLE_LOADER}. These two steps allow the tests and the app code to be linked and run together. If it seems like drudgery—and it is—then one way to avoid it is to just enable unit tests when creating the project in the first place, which sets up everything nicely to begin with.

At this point, we can run our unit tests by changing the current scheme to RecipeUnitTests and using the menu command Product→Test (⌘U). Try it, and the Xcode heads-up displays will show Build Succeeded, followed shortly thereafter by Test Failed. You can use the log navigator (⌘7) to show the build and run history: click the topmost item ("Test RecipeUnitTests") and you'll get a hierarchical list of all the tests that were run, as seen in Figure 80, *Log of default unit test failure*, on page 210. The message logged by the test is Unit tests are not implemented yet in RecipeUnitTests.

Figure 80—Log of default unit test failure

So where does that come from? Return to the file navigator and we notice that adding the Unit Test target also created a new group, RecipeUnitTests, initially containing a single RecipeUnitTests class. And in RecipeUnitTests.m, we find the following method:

```
- (void)testExample
{
    STFail(@"Unit tests are not implemented yet in RecipeUnitTests");
}
```

This lets us know that running the tests works, since the only functionality of the default test is to fail. In fact, comment out the STFail() call, test again, and you get Test Succeeded.

Configuring the Recipes Target to Run Tests

By adding unit testing after creating the project, we have two targets, one for building and running the app and the other for building and running the tests. Had we set up tests in the beginning, we would have just a single target, one that can both run the app and test it. This can be more convenient, as the two-target arrangement sometimes leads us to run the wrong command for the current target: running the app (⌘R) from the test target or testing (⌘U) from the app target will beep or pop up an error that the scheme isn't configured for that command.

To enable the test command in the app target, select the Recipes target in the Scheme menu in the toolbar, and then select "Edit Scheme…" from the same menu. The left pane of the scheme editor shows the possible commands for a scheme, one of which is Test. Click Test to bring up a list of tests that the command will run, as shown in Figure 81, *Configuring the Recipes target to perform unit tests*, on page 211. Click the plus (+) button at the bottom of the list to bring up a sheet listing the test targets in the project. When you click RecipeUnitTests, it gets added to the list with a white building-block icon. Open its disclosure triangles to discover that the building-block item contains a list of test cases (classes), which in turn contains lists of tests (methods), all of which can be enabled or disabled with check boxes.

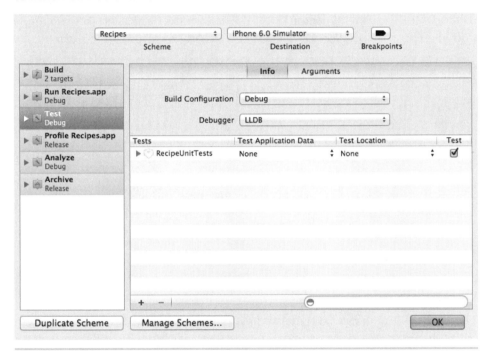

Figure 81—Configuring the Recipes target to perform unit tests

Once we've done this, the Test command (⌘U) will work in the Recipes project, and we won't need to flip back to the RecipesUnitTests target any more.

Writing Unit Tests

Now that we have a testing infrastructure set up, we are ready to start writing tests to exercise our code. What's provided in this class helps us see what we need to do. The RecipeUnitTest class is a subclass of SenTestCase and comes with three methods by default: setUp, tearDown, and testExample. The way it works is that any method that begins with the word test, returns void, and takes no parameters is recognized as a test to be performed. There can be any number of these methods in a SenTestCase subclass. Prior to running each test method, the setUp method is called, and the corresponding tearDown is called when the test has completed.

We can create as many tests as we like in this class or create additional test cases with "File→New File…" (⌘N) and selecting the Objective-C Test Case Class template. One catch though: when adding new test case classes, we will need to add them only to the RecipeUnitTests target, not the main Recipes target, which doesn't link against SenTestingKit.framework. We would set this with the Target check boxes in the file-selector sheet when creating the test class or later with the File inspector (⌥⌘1). But for now, let's keep things simple and just edit the RecipeUnitTests class we've already been provided with.

Joe asks:
Can I Write the Tests First?

In the doctrine of test-first development, we write the tests *before* writing any code, and all tests fail until the code they test is correctly implemented, typically via the "simplest thing that could work" approach. This is possible in iOS development, subject to the limitations of logic testing in OCUnit.

To do it, we would want to use the Include Unit Tests check box when creating the project in the first place. In a sense, the starting point of such a project is what a test-first developer would expect: there's one test and it fails, using STFail() to log a "testing has not been set up" message. From here, we would add more test methods that effectively define the programmatic interface to the application code, all of which would fail until we then go and start writing the real app.

The Recipes app doesn't do a lot of particularly tricky work, but there are a few of its behaviors we want to make sure keep working. We did a lot of work in Chapter 7, *Documents and iCloud*, on page 155, to get the recipes to persist, and it would be a disaster if that suddenly broke, so let's write a test to make sure that keeps working. In short, we'll write a test that creates a recipe, saves it, reloads the saved recipes, and makes sure we got back what we put in. If any of those steps fails, the whole test case fails.

In RecipeUnitTests.m, delete the dummy testExample method, and start a new test-Persistence. Since we'll be using PRPRecipe and PRPRecipeDocument, be sure to #import them at the top of the file.

Fixing/Recipes_01/RecipeUnitTests/RecipeUnitTests.m
```
-(void) testPersistence {
  NSURL *docDir = [[[NSFileManager defaultManager]
              URLsForDirectory:NSDocumentDirectory
```

```
                inDomains:NSUserDomainMask] lastObject];
NSURL *docURL = [docDir URLByAppendingPathComponent:@"Recipes.recipes"];
PRPRecipesDocument *recipesDocForSaving =
[[PRPRecipesDocument alloc] initWithFileURL:docURL];
PRPRecipe *recipeToSave = [recipesDocForSaving createNewRecipe];
```

This method duplicates how we created the PRPRecipesDocument in the earlier chapters: we create the path to the Recipes.recipe file in the application's document directory and create the recipesDocForSaving document with the file's URL. From that, we can create a single PRPRecipe called recipeToSave.

What if that doesn't work? This is something we should test for: if recipeToSave is nil, our test should fail now. In the template code, failure was signaled by a call to the macro STFail(), so we could use that. However, it's more elegant to use some of the more descriptive macros defined in SenTestCase.h, such as the various asserts. So we write the next line as follows:

Fixing/Recipes_01/RecipeUnitTests/RecipeUnitTests.m
```
STAssertNotNil(recipeToSave, @"Failed to create recipe from document");
```

Using the STAssertNotNil() macro, we pass through if recipeToSave is not nil and fail with the message Failed to create recipe from document if it is. Unlike many programmatic assertions, the STAssert... and other SenTestKit macros do not throw exceptions, return prematurely, or terminate the app in failure cases. Instead, program flow will just continue into the next test case.

Speaking of which, let's continue our test. If recipeToSave is created successfully, we want to set properties like its title and directions, and then save the entire PRPRecipesDocument. We do that by marking the change and closing the document. When we close, the completion handler block will receive a BOOL that indicates whether the close succeeded. Of course, that's another thing we want to test: if the success parameter passed into the completion handler is NO, then our test should fail.

Performing Asynchronous Tests

There's just one problem here: asynchronicity. The closing of the PRPRecipesDocument and the completion handler block will complete at some point in the future. In the meantime, testPersistence will continue on, and if it reaches the bottom, the test will be considered a success...before we know whether or not closing the document worked. We need the test to wait a little bit before continuing. Actually, more than a "little" bit; in our experience, it takes up to 30 seconds for the UIDocument to close.

We can't just explicitly suspend the current thread with C's sleep() or usleep(), because then the thread's run loop won't start the I/O that we're waiting for:

sleeping would actually just make our problem worse. What we need to do is to tell the thread to come back to us later. Fortunately, this is pretty easy, because Foundation provides an API for equipping threads with run loops and interacting with them. The method -[NSRunLoop runUntilDate:] gives us an easy way to say "do all your other stuff and come back to us at a future date." So now we can get our test to wait for the results of the document's closeWith-CompletionHandler:.

```
Fixing/Recipes_01/RecipeUnitTests/RecipeUnitTests.m
recipeToSave.title = NSLocalizedString(@"Nachos", nil);
recipeToSave.directions = NSLocalizedString(
  @"Open bag\nOpen jar of salsa\nEnjoy", nil);
recipeToSave.preparationTime = [NSNumber numberWithInt:1];
[recipesDocForSaving recipesChanged];
[recipesDocForSaving closeWithCompletionHandler:^(BOOL success) {
  STAssertTrue(success, @"failed to save recipes doc");
}];
[[NSRunLoop currentRunLoop] runUntilDate:
  [NSDate dateWithTimeIntervalSinceNow:30.0]];
```

By creating a resume date 30.0 seconds in the future, we can be pretty confident the close will have finished by then. This is admittedly inelegant: it would be better to use the completion handler block to signal that the save has finished. This worked in iOS 5, but the completion handler isn't consistently called in iOS 6, so we can't count on it anymore. If the block does get called like it's supposed to, we can use STAssertTrue() in the block to fail the test if the success variable passed to us is NO.

Finishing the Test

Now that we've created a PRPRecipe and saved it inside an instance of PRPRecipesDocument, we want to finish the test by reading into a new document and verifying we got back what we put into it in the first place. Loading a UIDocument finishes with a call to a completion handler, and that's where we can check that the document has just the one recipe, with the properties that we set on it earlier. Since loading is asynchronous, we need to have the NSRunLoop wait for us again. So here's how we finish up the testPersistence method:

```
Fixing/Recipes_01/RecipeUnitTests/RecipeUnitTests.m
  PRPRecipesDocument *recipesDocForLoading = [[PRPRecipesDocument alloc]
                                              initWithFileURL:docURL];
  [recipesDocForLoading openWithCompletionHandler:^(BOOL success) {
    STAssertTrue(success, @"failed to open recipesDocForLoading");
    NSInteger recipeCount = [recipesDocForLoading recipeCount] ;
    STAssertEquals(recipeCount, 1, @"Wrong number of recipes: %d", recipeCount);
    if (recipeCount > 0) {
      PRPRecipe *recipeToLoad = [recipesDocForLoading recipeAtIndex:0];
```

```
        STAssertNotNil(recipeToLoad, @"Couldn't load first recipe");
        if (! [recipeToLoad.title isEqualToString:
              NSLocalizedString(@"Nachos", nil)]) {
          STFail (@"First recipe has wrong title: %@", recipeToLoad.title);
        }
      }
    }];
    [[NSRunLoop currentRunLoop] runUntilDate:
      [NSDate dateWithTimeIntervalSinceNow:2.0]];
}
```

The tests in the completion handler block give us a chance to exercise several of the SenTestingKit assert macros. However, since there isn't an equivalent to -[NSString isEqualToString:]—STAssertEquals() works with scalars and pointers, and STAssertEqualObjects() calls -[NSObject isEqualTo:]—we do our own string comparison on the keyword's title property and call STFail() if the value is wrong.

Running Unit Tests

Now that we've written our test, we can run it with the menu command Product→Test (⌘U). Right now, since our code works, we pass our one and only test and get the Test Succeeded message as an Xcode heads-up display.

For testing, failure is much more interesting, so let's break our application code and see what a failed test looks like. Breaking the persistence engine we're working with would be a hassle, but one thing we can easily break is our last test, the one that checks if the value we read in from the opened recipe is Nachos. Go over to PRPRecipe.m and add the following method:

Fixing/Recipes_01/Recipes/PRPRecipe.m
```
-(NSString*) title {
  return NSLocalizedString(@"Onion Rings", nil);
}
```

By overriding the property's getter method, we make the title of every recipe Onion Rings regardless of what we originally set it to. Test again and we fail, with Xcode automatically switching to the issue navigator (⌘4) to show us a list of warnings and failures, as shown in Figure 82, *Issue navigator showing failed test in code*, on page 216. Click the first issue and it will take us to the failed test, with a red arrow containing our log message, First recipe has wrong title: Onion Rings. This is different than the log navigator (⌘7) viewer seen earlier in Figure 80, *Log of default unit test failure*, on page 210, since clicking on items in the issue navigator will show the failed test in the test source code, whereas the log navigator provides more of an overview that's useful once we have a large number of tests written and want to drill down into specific test failures and not into the test code itself.

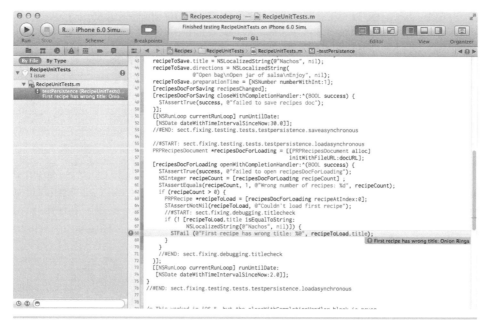

Figure 82—Issue navigator showing failed test in code

Automating Xcode Unit Tests

Once we write a lot of tests, one thing we might naturally want to do is to automate our tests and run them frequently. Ideally, we'd like to have a server check out our code, build it, run all the tests, and let us know if something breaks.

Strangely, this is not fully practical with Xcode 4. There is a command-line utility, xcodebuild, that can build a specific target or scheme in an .xcodeproj file. In theory, a continuous integration system could call this from a shell script to build and test the code. xcodebuild implements several "build command" arguments, such as the usual clean and build. Xcode 4.3 added test as a build command, which can only be used with the -scheme flag (as opposed to -target, the other way of telling xcodebuild what to build). Unfortunately, it's barely documented in the man page for xcodebuild, and we haven't heard of anyone getting it working in Xcode 4.5 without extraordinary hackery, such as workarounds that involve calling Xcode's test runner from shell scripts via the Run Script portion of Xcode's build phases. You can look these up via search engines, Stack Overflow, and the like if you need a solution now. You can also join us in filing feature requests at http://bugreport.apple.com/ to get automated unit testing better supported in Xcode.

Let's step back to the big picture: we've written tests and are surprised at some point in the future when a test fails. That means our code is now known to have a bug. Let's look at how we can track it down.

9.2 Debugging Our App

Xcode comes with integrated debugging support, which means we use Xcode to inspect what's going on inside an app while it runs, either in the Simulator or on the device. One of the most common features provided by debuggers are breakpoints, which indicate where program execution should pause and allow us to inspect the app's state. Since we know we're in trouble when the test fails, we'll set a breakpoint there.

In RecipeUnitTests.m, go to the if statement to check the recipe title, as shown here:

```
Fixing/Recipes_01/RecipeUnitTests/RecipeUnitTests.m
  if (! [recipeToLoad.title isEqualToString:
        NSLocalizedString(@"Nachos", nil)]) {
    STFail (@"First recipe has wrong title: %@", recipeToLoad.title);
  }
}
```

To the left of this line, Xcode has two narrow vertical strips. The leftmost and wider one is called the *gutter* and is where line-specific error and warning icons will appear. If you have turned on line numbering in Xcode's preferences, the numbers will be shown in the gutter as well. To set a breakpoint, just click once in the gutter, next to the line that you want to pause on. The blue pointer, as seen in Figure 83, *Setting a breakpoint*, on page 217, shows the newly created breakpoint.

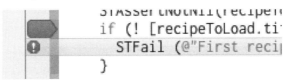

Figure 83—Setting a breakpoint

We can drag the breakpoint up and down in the gutter to change the line that we will pause on, or we can drag it out of the gutter to delete it. We can also disable the breakpoint with a single click (which turns it translucent) and reenable with another click. While clicking, be careful not to hit the strip just to the right with the varying bands of gray; this is the focus ribbon, and while its intended purpose is to collapse parts of code that aren't currently of interest, we're always freaked out when it makes our source disappear while we're messing with breakpoints.

To see all the breakpoints in the project, visit the breakpoint navigator (⌘6) on the left side of the workspace window. This makes it easy to jump around to source files where we've set breakpoints, disable or delete old breakpoints we're not using anymore, and so on.

Once the breakpoint is set on the if statement, test again. This time the Simulator starts up, but control returns to Xcode and the Debug area is automatically opened at the bottom of the window. The Content area shows the code with the breakpoint and a green arrow on the same line, which indicates that's where the app's execution has been paused.

Down in the Debug area, shown in Figure 84, *Debug area while stopped on a breakpoint*, on page 218, the toolbar buttons are now enabled. Equally importantly, the Variables view is populated (to see it, use the view split buttons to the right of the Clear button if you're currently showing only the Log view). While stopped on a breakpoint, we can use this view to inspect any of the variables in scope. We can also mouse over variables in the source code to see their values and members.

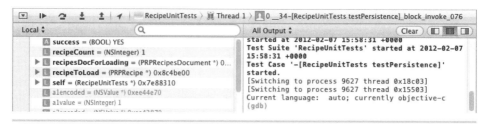

Figure 84—Debug area while stopped on a breakpoint

Still, we may conclude there is nothing obviously wrong with the state of the app when it reaches the breakpoint, so we want to go step by step until we can see what's going on. This is where we make use of the Debug area toolbar buttons. Moving left to right, the buttons are as follows: Hide Debug Area, Pause/Continue, Step Over, Step Into, Step Out, and Simulate Location. The step commands are what we need now. With Step Over, we can continue just long enough to reach the next statement in this source file, allowing us to iterate through it one step at a time. With Step Into, we go into whatever method or function this line of code calls and pause again there. Step Out does the opposite: it runs until we exit the current method or function, and it pauses when control returns to the caller.

Click Step Into, the button with the arrow pointing down into a line, to see what's happening inside this call that causes the if statement to return NO. The first part of the line to be evaluated is the call to recipeToLoad.title, so stepping into that call takes the Content area to PRPRecipe.m and its overridden title getter method. And from here, we should realize that this getter method is the problem and that we never should have written it in the first place. We can clean up by stopping the test, commenting out or deleting the method, disabling or deleting the breakpoint, and testing again. Now we should pass the test just fine.

This is just a taste of what we can do by setting breakpoints and inspecting the app's state. One particularly common use for breakpoints is to diagnose problems where UI actions don't seem to do anything. If we set a breakpoint on the method that's supposed to be called on a button tap and we don't stop there, that's a pretty good sign that we have a missing or miswired connection in a .xib or .storyboard file and should turn our attention to Interface Builder.

Testing and fixing the logic of our app is well and good, but it's not all our app does. Think about how users interact with our application: they scroll through the list of recipes, press the plus button to create new recipes and edit various properties, navigate between the list and editor views and the image picker, and so on. So far, we haven't exposed *any* of that to automated testing.

9.3 User Interface Testing

GUIs have long been difficult to test, and that probably accounts for much of the reason why the testing religion is so much more established among server-side and web developers than their desktop and mobile counterparts. Mock an HTTP POST, grep the response, and your test code has programmatic visibility into the entire client-server conversation. But when the user interacts via touches and swipes with a UI that's set up in a .storyboard file, where do we begin? GUIs don't get tested as much because they're a lot harder to test.

The outlook for GUI testing is getting better. The UI Automation framework, introduced in iOS 4 and greatly enhanced since then, makes testing iOS GUIs much more practical. In this section, we'll prove it by creating recipes with the UI, capturing that interaction, and replicating it as a test case.

Using the Automation Instrument

UI Automation is not part of OCUnit or the other Xcode testing facilities. In fact, it runs in a completely different application. *Instruments* is a profiling tool that monitors a running Mac or iOS application and can perform many different kinds of analyses, some of which we'll investigate in Section 9.4, *Testing Performance with Instruments*, on page 228. Instruments can work with an app running in the Simulator or on the device and is separate from Xcode, though it is usually launched directly from Xcode via the Profile command (⌘I).

To start using it, switch back to the Recipes target and use the Profile command to launch Instruments. Once launched, it shows a sheet with templates of its various profiling tools, which themselves are commonly called "instruments." From the iOS Simulator group, choose Automation, as shown in Figure 85, *Choosing the Automation template in Instruments*, on page 220.

Figure 85—Choosing the Automation template in Instruments

Instruments sets up its GUI and launches the Recipes app in the Simulator. The Instruments app is similar to Xcode in many ways, with a large toolbar and a multipaned main view. The main content pane uses a timeline metaphor, similar to media apps like GarageBand, where each track is one instrument.

In our case, the one track is called Automation, and it doesn't really do anything because we haven't yet told it what to do. The left pane includes controls for the Automation instrument, while the bottom pane contains an initially empty log view.

In the left pane, click the Add button and choose the "Create..." option. This switches the detail pane into Script view and sets up an initial automation script, as seen in Figure 86, *Starting an automation script in Instruments*, on page 221.

The default script contains a single line of code: var target = UIATarget.localTarget();

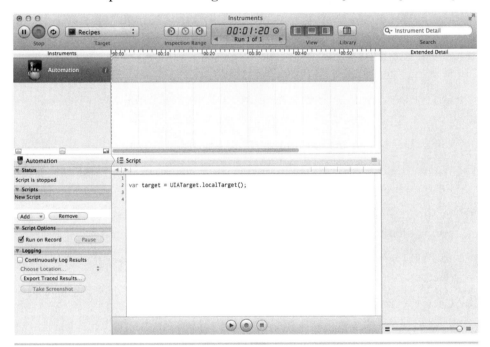

Figure 86—Starting an automation script in Instruments

Wait a minute...var? Is this JavaScript?

Why yes, yes it is. UI Automation scripts are written in JavaScript and interpreted by Instruments, which then calls into the running application. The use of a scripting language is fortuitous: instead of requiring a rebuild of the app, we can rewrite and rerun our automation scripts repeatedly, even during a single run of the app.

The obvious question is how we go about writing scripts to test the app. Back in Xcode, we can search the documentation for "UI Automation Reference

Collection" and find documentation on a couple dozen JavaScript classes. These classes offer a programmatic interface to the elements of our UI. For example, there's a UIAButton class we can use to tap(), doubleTap(), or touchAndHold() to simulate user input. So we could think through what views are visible on what screen, come up with calls in this API to access those views, and then programmatically work with them.

And that would be a lot of learning and a lot of work.

Recording Automation Scripts

Fortunately, we can cut to the chase. Notice the script editor has a round red button at the bottom. That is a record button. Just like with AppleScript, the Automation script editor allows us to record our UI interactions and capture them as a runnable script. The resulting script may not be perfect, but it's a quick way to get started.

Click the record button and switch over to the Simulator. With the Recipes app running, perform the following actions in order:

1. Click the plus (+) button on the right side the navigation bar.

2. When the Edit Recipe view flies in, tap in the name field (initially "New Recipe") and enter a recipe name.

3. Tap in the directions field. When the editor view comes up, type in the recipe directions.

4. Tap the back button on the left of the navigation bar (labelled "Edit Recipe").

5. Click the Prep Time plus (+) button five times.

6. Tap the Done button at the right side of the navigation bar.

7. Back in Instruments, tap the stop button at the bottom of the script editor.

When we're done, our script will look something like this:

```
var target = UIATarget.localTarget();

target.frontMostApp().navigationBar().rightButton().tap();
target.frontMostApp().mainWindow().textFields()[0].tap();
target.frontMostApp().mainWindow().textViews()[0].tapWithOptions(
        {tapOffset:{x:1.43, y:2.00}});
target.frontMostApp().navigationBar().leftButton().tap();
target.frontMostApp().mainWindow().buttons()["Increment"].tapWithOptions(
        {tapCount:5});
target.frontMostApp().navigationBar().rightButton().tap();
```

The target that was set up when we created the script represents the system being tested, and from this, we can get the frontMostApp(), as every line of the recorded script does. Within the app, we can get the navigationBar(), mainWindow(), or other high-level UI containers. Each of these contains arrays of UIAElements (and are themselves UIAElements), a superclass of all UI elements exposed via Automation.

Some of the methods in the script are surrounded with blue balloons and have disclosure triangles. This shows that the recorded call has several valid forms. For example, click the rightButton() on the first line. This pops up the menu shown in Figure 87, *Method variants in recorded Automator script*, on page 223. The choices are all ways of getting the add button from the navigation-Bar: as its rightButton(), as the button with the name Add, as the button at index 1, and so on. All of them are valid; we can choose whichever one best represents what we mean.

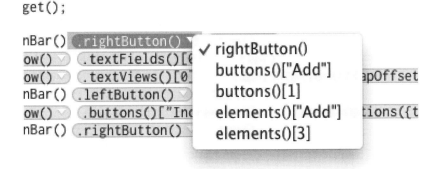

Figure 87—Method variants in recorded Automator script

Now that we've got a script, let's re-create our recipe by running it. In the Simulator, swipe right across the table row to delete the recipe we just created. Then, in Instruments, click the play button at the bottom of the script editor to run the script.

The result is likely a disappointment. The recorded script doesn't type in our title or instructions. Depending on the timing of the view transitions, it might even perform taps that don't work and end up running on the wrong screen or kick up a JavaScript error.

Recording a script is a start, but it's just that: a start.

UI Automation Is Not UIKit

Despite some similarities, keep in mind that UI Automation and UIKit are very different APIs for very different purposes. In UIKit, the top-level view class is UIView, with logic often coordinated by a UIViewController. In UI Automation, there is no controller class at all. That's because UI Automation represents the UI as a user would see it: it's about what can be done with the UI widgets, not about the behavior behind them. So instead of a UIView possibly backed by a UIViewController, we get a UIAElement: a generic UI element that we can interact with.

Another way to think of it is that UI Automation is a client making requests of the GUI, just the way that a user would be.

What's interesting about how this works is that UI Automation uses the accessibility APIs to get access to the UI controls. The same methods that allow buttons and labels to be read aloud or activated through gestures other than location-specific taps are also the ones that Instruments uses to fetch the names or labels of UI elements and programmatically tap them.

Writing Automation Scripts

To fully script our test, we're going to have to write some of the automation script manually. The obvious deficiencies are that the script doesn't always wait for transitions, and it doesn't know how to type into text components. Those are two things we're going to want to write by hand.

Let's start simple by defining constant strings for the recipe title and description. We'll need to set them as the contents of the text elements and then test their values later against these strings.

Fixing/Recipes_02/Create new recipe UIA test.js
```
var target = UIATarget.localTarget();
var recipeTitle = 'Pepperoni Pizza';
var recipeInstructions = 'Call pizza shop.\nOrder pizza.\nWait for delivery.';
```

The first line of the recorded script, the tap on the navigation bar's right button, works well enough to take us to the recipe editor view, so we can leave that in. What we need to do is to enter the title into the title text field when we get there. So how do we find the text field, considering that the recorder missed it? Every UIAElement—including the UIAWindow that many of the recorded lines get via target.frontMostApp().mainWindow()—expose their subelements as arrays. We can get all the subelements with the elements() method or get specific kinds of elements, such as buttons(), switches(), textFields(), and so on. In other words, buttons().[0] returns the first button and elements().[0] returns the first element of any kind. For our needs, we just need the first text field, the one at index 0.

```
     Fixing/Recipes_02/Create new recipe UIA test.js
Line 1  UIALogger.logStart ("Adding a recipe");
     2  target.frontMostApp().navigationBar().rightButton().tap();
     3  target.delay(1);
     4  target.frontMostApp().mainWindow().textFields()[0].setValue (recipeTitle);
```

After tapping the navigation bar's plus button, we delay for one second on line 3 to make sure the next view has time to appear. That lets us get the title text field on 4 and call its setValue() method to set its value directly, rather than simulating the typing (which the script recorder didn't capture in the first place).

Also notice how we use the logStart() method of the UIALogger class to leave a trail of what our test is doing, so later we will be able to tell how far our test got.

Now we're ready to set the instructions. Our recorded script managed to capture the tap on the text view, which takes us to the directions editor view and the back button when we finished typing the directions, but that's it. We can save those two lines and write some code to set the instructions. Along with target.delay() calls to wait out the view transitions, these are the same kind of things we did before.

```
     Fixing/Recipes_02/Create new recipe UIA test.js
UIALogger.logMessage ("Set text field value");
target.frontMostApp().mainWindow().textViews()[0].tap();
target.delay(1);
target.frontMostApp().mainWindow().textViews()[0].setValue (recipeInstructions);
UIALogger.logMessage ("set recipe text");
target.frontMostApp().navigationBar().leftButton().tap();
target.delay(1);
```

Finally, the last part of the recorded script tapped the prep time button five times and then clicked the right nav button to return to the list of recipes. This is all fine; let's just add another delay to make sure the table has time to reload before we do anything else.

```
     Fixing/Recipes_02/Create new recipe UIA test.js
target.frontMostApp().mainWindow().buttons()["Increment"].
        tapWithOptions({tapCount:5});
target.frontMostApp().navigationBar().rightButton().tap();
target.delay(1);
```

Notice, by the way, that the recorded script accesses the Prep Time plus (+) button via the string Increment rather than by its index in the buttons() array. This generally works for elements that have names or labels and are accessed via the accessibility API. We saw this earlier with the blue balloons and how the navigation bar's plus button could also be accessed by its name (Add) rather than by its index. Depending on how a UI is changing, accessing elements by name or by index may make more sense for different automation scripts.

So now we have a script that can perform all of the UI actions we need for our test. By setting the text components' values directly and putting in a few delays, our script duplicates our original gestures. Try running the script with the play button. The Instruments debug pane will switch to Editor Log mode and log each JavaScript call as the Simulator or device performs each of the steps. At the end, we get back to the table view with the new recipe as the first row.

Testing in Automation Scripts

The only problem when we run like this is that the Editor Log (use the pop-up menu to see if if you're still in Trace Log) concludes with the message Script ended without explicitly closing this test. And it has a point: we started a test with UIALogger.logStart ("Adding a recipe");, but we never finished it. To do so, we have to log either success or failure.

What's going to constitute success? Let's say that when we get back to the table, there should be one row, and its cell's contents need to match our expected recipeTitle.

Fixing/Recipes_02/Create new recipe UIA test.js
```
var recipesTable = target.frontMostApp().mainWindow().tableViews()[0];
var rowCount = recipesTable.cells().length;
if (rowCount != 1) {
        UIALogger.logFail ("Wrong number of rows in table: " + rowCount);
```

This is pretty easy: we get the first member of the window's tableViews() array, get its cells() array, and fail if it's not equal to 1. Notice how we end the test with a call to logFail(), which balances the earlier logStart(). Of course, before we run this test, we'll have to clear out any recipes that the app has stored or else we'll have more than one recipe after we create the new one and the test will fail.

Once we know the table has just the one row we created, we want to make sure that row is displaying the same text we entered. Digging into an element takes a little discovery; it may help to call recipesTable.logElementTree while writing the test to see what the subelement tree looks like. In the case of table cells, the subelements are of type UIAStaticText, which combine the UITableViewCell's textLabel and detailTextLabel into a single comma-separated string, like Pepperoni Pizza, 5 minutes. This represents how the accessibility API presents the cell content for a nonvisual context, such as the VoiceOver screen reader. At any rate, we just have to get the first cell's first static text subelement and check that it starts with our recipeTitle. So here's the rest of the test:

```
} else {
        // verify that the one cell has the proper contents
        var firstCell = recipesTable.cells()[0];
        var recipeLabel = firstCell.staticTexts()[0];
        if (recipeLabel == null) {
                UIALogger.logFail ("Didn't get first cell");
        } else if (recipeLabel.value().indexOf(recipeTitle) != 0) {
                UIALogger.logFail ("Table cell title incorrect: " +
                                                recipeLabel.value());
                } else {
                        UIALogger.logPass ("Added recipe " + recipeLabel.value());
        }
}
```

The if-else logic provides either a logFail() or a logPass() for every possible path through this test, matching the original logStart(). So now we're ready to go. In the Simulator, delete any rows in the table (since they'll cause the number-of-rows test to fail), and then run the test from Instruments. Again we see the Simulator navigate back and forth and programmatically enter our text. When it's done, the Editor Log shows Pass in the Log Type column.

The logging methods also do something interesting in failure cases. Without deleting the new row, run again. This time the test fails with the Wrong number of rows in table: 2 message. And there's a tiny icon in the Screenshot column. Expand the tree of log messages and select the failure row; the detail pane on the right will show the text of the log message and a screenshot of the app in the failure state, as seen in Figure 88, *Automation test failure with screen-shot of failing application*, on page 228. The "eye" button under the screenshot allows us to open it full size in its own window for detailed inspection. If the test fails, we'll be able to really see what happened.

It hasn't taken a lot of work to get the user interface of our application pretty significant test exposure. Consider that if we were to make a major storyboard change that broke, the script would fail, probably with a JavaScript error when an expected element wasn't found, and we'd know right away that we had a problem. Writing the scripts is a manual process and requires studying UI Automation's JavaScript API, but the ability to use the record button to capture most of our interaction with the app saves a lot of time when getting started, and it exposes a lot of the JavaScript API to boot.

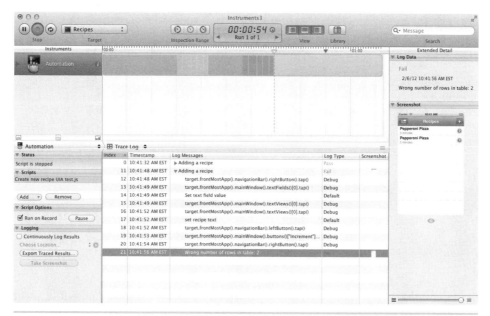

Figure 88—Automation test failure with screenshot of failing application

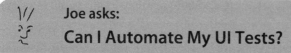

Joe asks:

Can I Automate My UI Tests?

As with xcodebuild, Instruments has a command-line equivalent, instruments, which can be run from something like a shell script or a cron job. So, in theory, we could package up all our UI tests in an Instruments Automation "Template" file and invoke it automatically.

However, the instruments program doesn't exit with a nonzero Unix status code when tests fail, as would be expected by a shell script or continuous integration system. That means we'd have to use hacky workarounds, like logging "magic" strings to indicate success or failure and having the calling script grep for those.

Supposedly Apple uses UI Automation internally. Maybe they know some neat tricks that we don't.

9.4 Testing Performance with Instruments

Automator is a recent addition to Instruments and isn't quite typical of how the application is usually used. It's worth pausing for a second to see what the rest of this application offers us.

The command to launch Instruments from Xcode is called "Profile" for a reason. When Instruments runs our app, it samples what the app is doing many times a second and logs it all in a run of the app that can then be inspected with the Instruments timeline, even after the app has been stopped. By profiling the app's behavior, particularly in response to user interactions, we can find performance hotspots.

To try it out, close the Instruments document with the Automator script, return to Xcode, and profile the code (⌘I). This brings us back to Instruments's template selector. This time, choose the Time Profiler instrument. Use the app in the Simulator as you normally would, and when you've finished, click Instruments's record button to stop profiling. The display will look like Figure 89, *Instruments's time profiler trace*, on page 229.

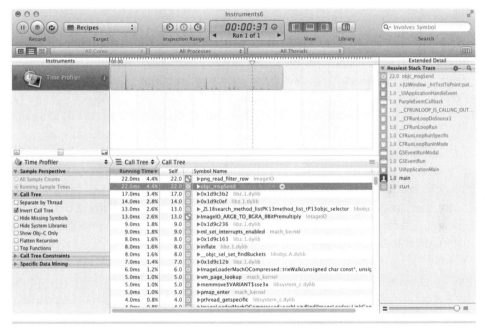

Figure 89—Instruments's time profiler trace

The timeline at the top of the window shows us the app's CPU activity, while the table at the bottom shows us where the app has spent most of its time. In this brief run, the most expensive activity is a system call to png_read_filter_row(), presumably part of our loading the wood panel background for the editor view, since loading that view accounts for the activity spike seen early in the timeline.

The next most expensive call in this figure is objc_msgSend(), which is the C function that actually performs Objective-C message dispatch. This doesn't mean that there's something wrong with our message calls; it's just the nature of the language that every Obj-C method call will go through objc_msgSend(), so this function will naturally account for a lot of our CPU time. And that's the thing about Instruments: making sense of what's normal and what isn't is something of an art learned in time. Not every CPU expense is unwarranted, after all.

Available iOS instruments allow us to monitor CPU and filesystem activity, Core Data I/O, and Objective-C object allocations. Two of the instruments that were critical in earlier versions of iOS are largely irrelevant in the age of ARC. Leaks and Zombies, respectively, are instruments that can catch the underrelease and overrelease of objects when using manual memory management in Objective-C. This used to be critical, as an overreleased object (one whose memory has been freed but to which there is still a pointer reference) was a crash waiting to happen. As long as we use automatic reference counting, our code can't make these kinds of mistakes, and thus we don't need to diagnose them with Instruments.

9.5 Wrap-Up

In this chapter, we've stopped adding to the Recipes app and instead focused on how to make sure it keeps running as expected. We exposed the app to two different forms of unit testing. With Xcode and OCUnit, we were able to create logic tests that verify that our models and program logic behave as expected. Since that only goes so far, we turned to Instruments and UI Automation to create UI tests in JavaScript that simulate a user's interaction with the UI, providing programmatic taps and typing to ensure that the app continues to work as expected. We also took a brief look at how Instruments probes a running app and stores a history of what the app was doing during its run. This lets us identify performance hotspots and ask ourselves if our code is as efficient and "performant" as it could be.

Taking care of our code base as it matures and changes is an important duty for a professional programmer. In the next chapter, we'll complete the journey to professional programmer by managing our source code properly and submitting the app to the App Store.

For Further Thought

Here are a few things to think about or try out to expand your understanding of the stuff we've covered in this chapter. The questions don't necessarily have "correct" answers. Please join us on the forums at http://forums.pragprog.com/ to discuss your ideas about them.

1. If you've used unit-testing frameworks on other platforms, how do you think OCUnit measures up, given what we've seen in this chapter. What do other testing frameworks offer that you'd most want to use in iOS development?

2. Imagine we wrote the Recipes app in a test-first manner. How would we have done that? What would the tests look like, and at what point would we start writing application code?

3. In a SenTestCase, should there ever be a case where a testFoo calls a testBar, where both methods are in the test case class?

4. Scenario: a UI Automation script reveals an error. You fix it in Xcode and build (⌘B), then go back to Instruments and run the script. The problem is still there. What has happened?

5. If we replaced the list of recipes with a custom view of our own creation that showed a scrolling view of recipe icons, how would we make our view testable with UI Automation?

CHAPTER 10

The App Store and Beyond

We've come from no code, no tools, and no plan, and now we've got a working, testable Recipes manager and a Twitter client. That's great! However, they only run in the Simulator and only then as a result of an Xcode build. The point of writing iOS apps is to run them on iOS devices, and now it's time to take that final step.

As we start thinking of our app in terms of getting it to end users, we're going to want to begin accounting for the app's life cycle and its life beyond the Simulator. How do we get it onto our devices and into the hands of testers? How do we get it up on the store, and once it is, what happens when people start downloading and using it? What if they turn up bugs or ask for new features?

When we write the last line of code, we're not really done—we may really just be getting started.

In this chapter, we're going to add some "grown up" processes to our development: taking care of our source, testing it on the device, getting it on the store, and managing the app's life after it ships.

10.1 Protecting Our Code with Source Control

So far, we've made the implicit assumption that our code could live just fine as one collection of source files and resources on one computer, used by one developer. By and large, this isn't realistic: apps are often created by multiple developers working together, and even solo developers often move their projects between desktops and laptops.

To make this more practical, many developers use source control systems (also known as *revision control*). Source control systems exist as both network services and client-side applications, and they allow us to manage multiple versions of the files in our project. This means if we introduce an error in some version of a given source file, we can roll back to an earlier version of the file. Most such systems are also meant to be used by multiple developers, allowing us to get a copy of the code, add to or change it, and send those changes back to other developers.

Xcode offers support for two popular source control systems: Subversion and Git. The two have deep differences in design and philosophy—Subversion is based on a single canonical repository for a code base, while Git's more distributed mindset allows for many differing instances of a project—but Xcode works with a subset of features that both systems implement in similar ways.

Source-Controlling an Existing Project

Let's add the benefits of source control to our project. When we created the Recipes project, we could have set up a local Git repository for it. Since we didn't then, we will do so now. However, Xcode's Git support doesn't include the ability to create new repositories once a project has been created without one, so we need another application to do that. The most universal approach is to use the /usr/bin/git command-line program from the Terminal.

Unfortunately, as of Xcode 4.3, neither git nor svn (the Subversion command-line program) is installed by default. To install them, go to Xcode's Preferences and select the Downloads tab. As seen in Figure 90, *Installing Xcode's command-line tools*, on page 235, one of the items is Command-Line Tools. Click its Install and wait for the install to finish. This will install git, svn, and many other developer-oriented command-line programs.

Now we're going to add source control to our existing application. This is easier to do in Git because of its distributed nature: we can convert any folder to a Git repository, and if we decide later to share it with other developers, we can let them clone our repository (or connect our repository to a remote, usually a networked repository like GitHub), then push our changes out to partners and pull others' changes from them. With Subversion, we would have to set up a single, authoritative server first. In practical terms, Git encourages us to adopt source control early, which is one reason Xcode offers to set up a Git repository for new projects when we create them.

Launch the Terminal application from /Applications/Utilities. We need to change our working directory to the Recipes directory via the cd command. If you're not familiar with the command line, just type cd, a space character, and then drag the Recipes folder to the Terminal window—this will type out the filesystem path as the next part of the command. So, if Recipes is on the Desktop, we

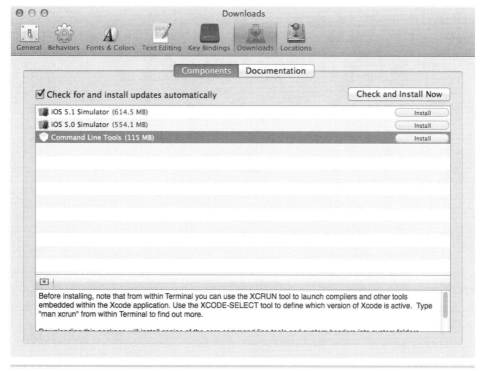

Figure 90—Installing Xcode's command-line tools

change directories with cd /Users/yourname/Desktop/Recipes or cd ~/Desktop/Recipes, which uses the Unix home directory shortcut, ~.

Prior to using git on the Mac, we need to perform a one-time-only fix, telling Git to not perform an automatic conversion from default OS X line endings (the LF character) to Git's Windows-like default (CRLF). Type the command as follows:

⇒ `git config --global core.autocrlf input`

If we don't do this, every line will go into the repository with CRLF line endings, and then when Xcode writes a new version of the file with LF endings, Git will think *every line* of the file has changed. We avoid this by setting Git's core.autocrlf configuration prior to creating any repositories. We only need to do this once per machine prior to running other git commands.

To have Git start source-controlling our code now, we issue three commands: one to create the Git repository, one indicating we have files to add, and one to actually commit our changes (that is, to add the files). On the command line, it looks like this:

```
⇒ git init
《 Initialized empty Git repository in /Users/cadamson/Desktop/Recipes/.git/
⇒ git add .
⇒ git commit -m "Created new Recipes repository"
《 [master (root-commit) c947cd6] Created new Recipes repository
  44 files changed, 2298 insertions(+), 0 deletions(-)
  create mode 100644 .DS_Store
  create mode 100644 Create new recipe UIA test.js
  create mode 100644 NewRecipeAutomationTest.tracetemplate
  create mode 100644 RecipeUnitTests/RecipeUnitTests-Info.plist
  create mode 100644 RecipeUnitTests/RecipeUnitTests-Prefix.pch
  create mode 100644 RecipeUnitTests/RecipeUnitTests.h
  create mode 100644 RecipeUnitTests/RecipeUnitTests.m
  《Many more output lines omitted.》
```

The git init creates the actual Git repository, which is stored in an invisible .git directory. git add . tells Git we want to add all the files from the current directory (.) to the repository. Finally, git commit actually performs the add, along with providing a log message (via the -m flag) that we can check later. Every time we make a change, we should provide a useful log message saying what we did so that we can understand in the future what changes were made in each commit.

Now we have our project under source control. Let's see what that does for us.

Working with a Source-Controlled Project

Our first commit has set up the Git repository with initial versions of all the project files. Let's make a change and see what that looks like. Go to any source file and add a comment, then save the file. As soon as we save, the file explorer puts a dark gray box with an *M* the right of the file name. The *M* means the file has local modifications. If we add a file to the project, it will show an *A* icon, and if our code comes from a networked repository that has changes waiting for us, we'll see a *U* (for "update"). One icon we don't want to see is the exclamation point ("!"), which means that our local copy of the file and a pending update have both changed the file, which means Xcode will have to merge the changes into one version, something that will require careful editing if the same lines of the file have been updated. We avoid this in team situations by pulling updates and pushing commits frequently.

So, we know the file is modified, but if we work across a bunch of files and make lots of changes, it would be nice to know exactly what has changed. We can do this by clicking the third button on the toolbar's editor control, which puts us into the Version editor. This view has three modes, selected by buttons at the bottom, the default being Comparison mode. In this mode, shown in Figure 91, *Version editor, comparison mode*, on page 237, we see our locally modified version of the file on the left and the most recently committed version from the repository on the right, with blue swooshes in the middle divider indicating where lines have been added or removed between the two revisions. The clock icon in the bottom center lets us bring up a pair of vertical sliders so we can switch either side to show as new or as old a revision as we like. This may be helpful in the future if we discover we've introduced a bug and we want to look at old versions of the code to figure out exactly which change introduced the bug.

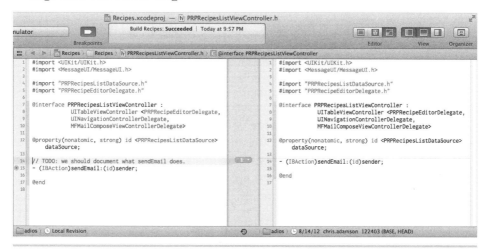

Figure 91—Version editor, comparison mode

Now that we've made a change, and assuming we want to keep it (or, in a team environment, assuming that we want our teammates to have it), we should commit the change. Right-click or control-click the file and choose "Source Control → Commit Selected Files…" from the pop-up menu. To commit many files at once, we could command-click to select all the changed files, but we only have the one for now. Xcode slides out a sheet that shows all the files to commit with a comparison view like we saw in the project workspace. This sheet, shown in Figure 92, *Committing changed files*, on page 238, gives us one last chance to review the changes (the *diffs*)—and make further changes if we like—prior to committing. The sheet also has a comment area at the bottom to add a log message to send to the repository with the commit. Enter a comment and click the Commit button to make the commit. The sheet dismisses and the second version of the file is now in the repository.

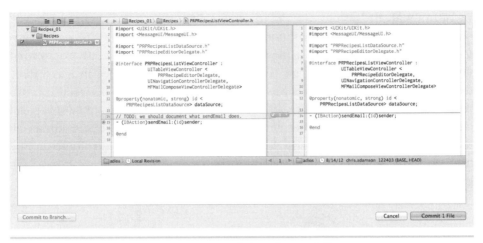

Figure 92—Committing changed files

The Version editor has two other modes that help us in long-term projects. The middle button is the Blame mode, which annotates each line or group of lines with the last revision of the file that edited those lines. In Figure 93, *Version editor, Blame mode*, on page 238, we can see the log comments and revision numbers are different for the comment line that we just added as the second revision of the file. A third choice for the Version editor, Log mode, lets us see a scrolling list of commit dates, revision numbers, and log comments for the file without corresponding to individual lines like Blame mode does.

Figure 93—Version editor, Blame mode

As we've seen, the project workspace shows the source control status of files for the specific project we're working with. In the Organizer (⌘⇧2), we can get a look at source control for *all* our projects. Click the Repositories tab and we'll see a list of every source-control repository that this copy of Xcode knows about, whether local projects for which we enabled Git or projects that we downloaded from Git or Subversion servers. Any time we open a project that's under source control, it gets added to this list. The view includes a file browser for the project and lets us look through commits for the whole project or for individual files without actually opening the project for editing.

Taking care of our code over the lifetime of the app is an important habit for the professional developer. As our project grows and matures, having the code under source control gives us the ability to keep track of what changes we made, when, and why. To really work, it requires some discipline; we won't have a good log of changes if we're not committing regularly and writing useful log messages that we will understand months from now. In a team environment, where we also use source control to share code between team members, this becomes even more important. Everyone needs to commit their code when new features and fixes are working (and *not* commit broken code that doesn't work or even build) and to pull updates from teammates so our code will integrate as expected.

10.2 Running on the Device

The next step on our path to getting the app into users' hands is to move beyond the Simulator and get the app running on actual iOS hardware. Doing this is going to require a real device and the spending of real money, but if you're not in a position to do that yet, feel free to follow along.

Running an app on the device requires joining Apple's iOS Developer Program at a paid level. There are several different programs; the Standard program allows individuals and companies to distribute apps on the App Store, while the Enterprise and Education programs are for developing and distributing apps through internal, non–App Store channels. For this book, we'll limit ourselves to the Standard program, which currently costs US$99 (and similar values in other currencies) for a one-year membership.

The two essential benefits of standard program membership are the ability to install apps onto test devices and to distribute through the App Store. Since the former is a prerequisite for the latter—we shouldn't try to sell an app on the store until we've ensured it works on a real device—we'll start there.

Overlooked Developer Program Benefits

Joining Apple's Developer Program isn't just about signing apps. There are several other benefits you get for your $99. For starters, membership in this program is a requirement if you want to attend Apple's World Wide Developer Conference (WWDC).

In our opinion, the most overlooked and valuable perk of membership is support incidents. With these, members can send questions and code to an Apple support engineer and get detailed, code-level support with their problems. Members get two of these per year as part of the program membership and can purchase more if they run out. For problems that can't be solved with a web search or a forum post, it can be a great way to get unblocked.

Provisioning the App

Members of the iOS Developer Program have access to the *iOS Provisioning Portal*, the part of the http://developer.apple.com/ website where we manage test devices and identify the apps we will run on them. First, though, we have to set up our signing certificate, a document that will allow Xcode to cryptographically sign apps, authenticating them for installation on test devices and for submission to Apple.

There are two ways we can get a signing certificate. We can either go through a multistep process within the Portal website, or we can let Xcode do it for us. Let's take the easy route and do the latter. Open the Xcode Organizer, select the Devices tab, and choose Provisioning Profiles from the Library section. We're asked to sign in with our Apple ID, and since we don't have a development certificate, we're asked if we want to create one, as shown in Figure 94, *Requesting a development certificate*, on page 241. Click Submit Request. We'll also be asked about creating a distribution request. We'll need it later, so go ahead and send that request too.

Once we have a certificate for app signing, we have several tasks to perform on the Portal website. First, in the Certificates section, look for the link to the WWDR Intermediate Certificate, download it, and import it into the keychain by double-clicking it or dragging it to the Keychain Access application. This certificate authenticates your Apple-issued certificates, and app-signing won't work if it's not present in the keychain.

Next, we can start registering test devices. These are the actual iPhones, iPod touches, and iPads we want to test our apps on. In the Portal's Devices section, click Add Devices and enter a descriptive name (like "Bill's iPad 2") and the device ID. We can get the device ID by connecting the device via the dock cable and launching iTunes: click the device in the left column and then click

Figure 94—Requesting a development certificate

its serial number, which will change to its identifier (UDID), as shown in Figure 95, *Getting a device identifier (UDID) from iTunes*, on page 241 (note that we have intentionally blurred a few digits of the ID and phone number in this screenshot). Once the UDID is showing, it can be copied to the clipboard with a ⌘C. Paste this value in the Portal's Device ID field and click Submit.

Figure 95—Getting a device identifier (UDID) from iTunes

It's also possible to add a device with the Xcode Organizer via an Add To Portal button under the Devices tab, but that requires the developer to have access to the test devices. For distributed testers, using the Portal website is the way to go.

The next step on the portal is to create an App ID, a string that uniquely identifies a single app or a group of apps. For a single app, the App ID allows use of certain APIs, such as Push Notifications and In-App Purchase. For a group of apps, a shared App ID allows them to share sensitive information with each other via the iOS keychain. For apps that don't use these features, the App ID is supposedly optional, but enough app-signing steps require an App ID that we should just go ahead and create one. To create an App ID for one app, we enter a description like "Demo Recipes app" and leave the Bundle Seed ID as Use Team ID. For the bundle identifier, we can either enter a reverse-domain name format string, like com.company.appname, to identify one app to sign or use the wildcard character (*) to sign any app for testing. For now, let's use the wildcard.

Finally, we create a provisioning profile, which identifies a combination of certificate, App ID, and devices, and represents the certification for specific apps to run on specific devices. There are two kinds of profiles we can create; for the moment, we only care about development profiles, which are used for testing on devices that will be directly connected via Xcode. To create a new development profile on the Portal, we click New Profile, enter a name for the profile, select an App ID and which certificate to sign with, and select some or all of the devices we have configured. After a few seconds or minutes, the profile will be available to download as a .mobileprovision file. Once downloaded, drag it to Xcode to add it to the Organizer's list of profiles.

Creating a provisioning profile is also a task we can perform within Xcode—provided we have already set up the App ID and devices on the Portal—as shown in Figure 96, *Creating a provisioning profile in Xcode Organizer*, on page 243. The Organizer also maintains an iOS Team Provisioning Profile, which is a wildcard signing profile that Xcode automatically keeps up-to-date and which can be used to sign most apps (those that don't require App ID-dependent features) for local testing.

Setting up app signing is a lot of steps, and it's nobody's favorite thing to do, but once we have the .mobileprovision, we're *this close* to running the app on our iOS device.

Signing and Running the App

Now that we've got a .mobileprovision file that identifies what we want to run, what devices we want to run on, and the fact that we're certified to do so, we're ready to run our app on an actual iOS device. Both of the examples in the book use the iPhone form-factor and don't use model-specific features like GPS, so they can run on any current iPhone, iPod touch, or iPad that you happen to have.

Now that we've set up Xcode with the provisioning profile for our iOS device, we can connect the device itself via the dock cable to the Mac. When we do

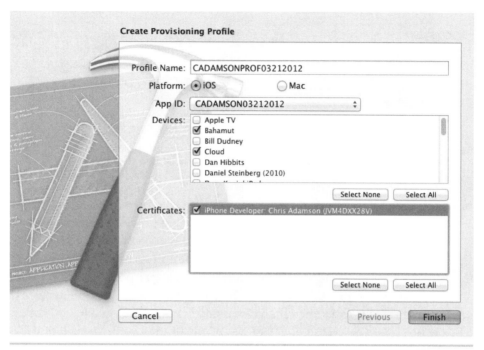

Figure 96—Creating a provisioning profile in Xcode Organizer

this, the Organizer adds it to its list of devices and displays a "Use for Development" button. We need to click this to authorize Xcode to sign and install development apps on the device. Once we've added a device, we will be able to use the Organizer to collect screenshots, console logs, and crash reports from the device.

With development enabled on the device, we should be able to build and run the app on the device. Back in the project workspace, pop up the right side of the scheme selector. In addition to the available simulators, we should now see all devices that are capable of running the current project. In Figure 97, *Changing scheme to build and run on the device*, on page 244, we are selecting an iPhone called Zidane to run the current project. If the device isn't in the list, check the sidebar *How Come My App Won't Run on My Device?*, on page 245, for some common causes.

Prior to running, let's take a look at how all these app-signing pieces have come together. Click the project icon in the file explorer, select the Recipes target, and choose the Build Settings tab. Find the entry for Code Signing Identity (typing "sign" into the filter helps), and expand the spin-disclosure arrows to expose the Debug and Release settings. The pop-up menu, shown

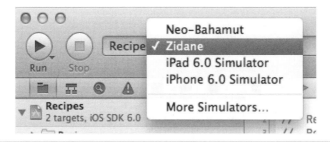

Figure 97—Changing scheme to build and run on the device

in Figure 98, *Code signing identity*, on page 244, includes an automatically-selected profile, selectable menu items for installed provisioning profiles, an option to not code-sign, and an "Other..." that takes a string for a profile name that will presumably become valid by build time (perhaps on a different machine). Whatever certificate was used to create the profile on the Portal site must be in the current keychain (as indicated by the Keychain Access application). This creates the chain of trust: the Portal and Xcode both know who we are from the certificate, and the provisioning profile associates that identity with the identifiers of devices in the profile, one of which is the one we want to install the app on.

Figure 98—Code signing identity

With the device set in the scheme selector, click the Run button to build and run the app. The code builds, and after a brief pause, it starts running on the iPhone, iPod touch, or iPad. At this point, our testing experience is basically no different from running in the Simulator: we could set breakpoints and view log messages as in the last chapter, run logic tests with the Test command, or use the Profile command to have Instruments profile the app while it runs on the device.

So what do we test on the device? For starters, we try out the features that aren't supported in the Simulator, like storing our documents in iCloud, the code for which we wrote back in Section 7.5, *Storing Documents in iCloud*, on

> ### Joe asks:
> ### How Come My App Won't Run on My Device?
>
> You and everyone else, Joe...you *and everyone else*.
>
> The challenges of app signing for iOS are legendary and are the cause of much pain among developers. Usually, there's some kind of coherent reason for the problem, although some of the cases are so aggravating!
>
> If a device doesn't appear in the scheme selector, the causes are usually pretty sensible: the device hasn't been enabled for development, the device is running an older version of iOS than the target's iOS Deployment Target, the device is an iPhone and the project uses the iPad form-factor, and so on.
>
> The really troublesome problems are errors when code signing at the end of a build. These can come from a bad automatic choice of code signing identity, an expired certificate or provisioning profile, or Keychain Access being set to a different keychain than the one the signing certificate was imported into. Sometimes, Xcode will just do stupid things, like copying expired certificates from a device into Keychain Access and announcing that there are two copies of the signing certificate when there can only be one. Xcode will also import expired profiles from the Portal into the the Organizer, so it's wise to delete expired profiles via the Portal site.
>
> Fighting through this stuff takes a combination of perseverance, logic, and more than a few trips to Apple's developer forums or other online resources. Apple Tech Note TN2250, "iOS Code Signing Setup, Process, and Troubleshooting," also has a collection of common problems and their solutions. It can still be a hassle for long-time iOS developers, but in time, it's at least possible to anticipate and avoid a lot of the common problems and understand what might be causing the more esoteric errors.

page 182. We also use the device for features that the Simulator can't realistically support, like motion sensing and location awareness. And even for less exotic features, we want to make sure that the app behaves well under real-world conditions. iOS devices have slower CPUs and less memory than desktop Macs, and cellular data connections have higher latency and lower throughput than wired ethernet, so testing the app on real devices will let us see if it works well enough or if we need to make changes.

Ad Hoc Distribution

Testing on our own device is good, but it's probably not good enough. Each of us comes to an app with our own ideas of how it should work, and as developers of the app, we're hardly unbiased. To really test the app rigorously before we send it out into the world, we need other people to run it. But how do we get it to them? We're certainly not going to have all our testers come over to our place and connect their iPhones to our copy of Xcode, right?

To support testing on multiple devices, Apple offers *Ad Hoc distribution*. This allows us to build a version of our app that our testers, reviewers, and other trusted parties can install and run on their iOS devices without needing Xcode or our signing certificate.

Creating the Ad Hoc Distribution Profile

For an Ad Hoc build, we need a distribution certificate. This is different from the development certificate because it's used to send the app to others or to submit it to Apple rather than install the app on our own devices. Also, in developer teams, only the team leader has access to the distribution certificate, while all team members can have developer certificates. We requested the distribution certificate earlier, after requesting the development certificate, but if there isn't an entry in Keychain Access called "iPhone Distribution: *Your Name*," then click the Refresh button in the Xcode Organizer's list of Provisioning Profiles to be asked again to submit a request for a distribution certificate.

We need to collect the device IDs of our testers' devices and add them to the list of devices in the Portal, like we did for our own devices earlier. Keep in mind that we can only add one hundred devices per year to this list. Once these are ready, we go to the Provisioning section of the Portal, select the Distribution tab, and click New Profile. The New Profile page has radio buttons to indicate whether we want an App Store or Ad Hoc distribution profile (we want the latter), a field for the profile name, an App ID selector, and check boxes for devices. The Ad Hoc build will run only on those devices, so we add any device we think we'll want to run on (including our own).

After clicking Submit, the distribution profile will appear in the list of profiles —if it's "pending," give it a few seconds and then refresh. Once it's there, click the Download button to download the .mobileprovision file and then drag it to Xcode to add it to the list of profiles in the Organizer (or just click the "Refresh" button in the Provisioning Profiles to fetch all profiles from the Portal). Now we're ready to build and distribute an ad hoc version of our app.

Using an Ad Hoc Distribution

Now that we've got our distribution profile, we're ready to build the Ad Hoc version. We don't use the usual build (⌘B) or build-and-run (⌘R) for this. Instead, any build meant to be distributed is considered an *application archive*, so named because it's something we're going to want to keep track of.

To create an archive, we use the Product→Archive command. But before we do, we should head off a possible error. Go over to the target's build settings and look up the code signing identity again. For developer builds, we checked the Debug value of this setting. For archival builds, we need to verify that the Release line is set to "iPhone Distribution: *Your Name*."

This brings up something we've been ignoring up to this point: Xcode builds our code differently based on whether we're going to just be running and testing it locally ("debug" builds) or whether we're going to be distributing it to others ("release" builds). For debug builds, Xcode defaults to build settings that will enable testing and debugging, even at the expense of code performance. For a release, Xcode turns up compiler optimizations that may take longer to build and make the code less fit for debugging but also speed it up by a significant degree. The scheme determines which kind of build we perform for a given task: by default, Profile and Archive are the only build actions that use the Release settings.

Once we create an archive with Build→Archive, Xcode automatically opens up the Organizer's Archives tab, shown in Figure 99, *Application archives in Xcode Organizer*, on page 247. This view shows all the archives of all applications built on this Mac and lets us enter a comment to help organize multiple archives of a single app.

Figure 99—Application archives in Xcode Organizer

Now that we have an archived build, we're ready to hand it out to our testers. In the Organizer's Archives pane, select the row with the archive we just created and click the "Distribute…" button. This slides in a sheet asking if we want to submit to the App Store, save for Enterprise or Ad Hoc deployment, or export the archive. Choose the second option and click Next. After this, we're asked to choose a signing identity, for which we should choose the distribution profile we created earlier. Click Next to get a file selector of where to place the resulting file. Once we select this, Xcode signs the archive for the devices in the distribution profile and writes an .ipa file.

At this point, we can send this .ipa file to our testers. All a tester needs to do is drag the file into the iTunes Library (on OS X or Windows) and then either add the app to the list of files to sync to a given device or just drag the app icon from the library to the device icon. Either of these techniques will install the app to the device. Figure 100, *Ad Hoc build of Recipes app running on iPhone 4S*, on page 248, shows an Ad Hoc build of the Recipes app running on an iPhone.

Figure 100—Ad Hoc build of Recipes app running on iPhone 4S

Now that we can run the app on many devices, we can have our testers bang on the app and send us feedback. We'll work through the bug reports and feature requests, send out new Ad Hoc builds, and eventually reach a point where we're ready to send the app on to the world. To the App Store we go!

10.3 Submitting Apps for Review

Once we've rigorously tested our app, we're ready to submit it to the App Store to send it out to the public. Or are we?

It turns out there are a bunch more steps to get our app up on the store. First off, we need to answer two questions: "What are we offering?" and "How do we communicate that?"

App Metadata

Submitting to the App Store requires a lot more than just a rigorously tested code base and an attractive visual design (see *Don't Ship Programmer Art*, on page 250). We will be submitting an extensive collection of metadata, including but not limited to the following:

- A 1024 x 1024 icon for the App Store, which should match the icon in the Xcode project. Since Apple may come back and ask for art at varying sizes to promote the app in the store, it's useful to have graphic designers create icons and other art for the app at very high resolutions (or with vector graphics tools) so they can turn out new graphic assets at arbitrary sizes.

- At least one (and up to five) screenshots showing the app in action. These need to be in the Retina Display resolutions, meaning 640 x 920 or 640 x 960 for iPhone (depending on whether the status bar is visible) for portrait orientation and 960 x 600 or 960 x 640 for landscape. If we explicitly support the iPhone 5, then we must submit screenshots in its dimensions (portrait 640 x 1136 or 640 x 1096, landscape 1136 x 640 or 1136 x 600); same goes for the iPad (with dimensions representing any of the eight possible combinations of landscape/portrait, status bar present/absent, Retina / non-Retina). Screenshots can be generated from the iOS Simulator's Save Screen Shot (⌘S) command or by using the Organizer's Devices tab, which offers a New Screenshot button when a device is connected.

- A description of the app and keywords to help find it. The description needs to be translated into every language for which we have localized the app.

- A decision about what price to charge for the app. For non-free apps, we also have to agree to an online sales contract with Apple and provide banking information to receive payments. These steps can take days or even weeks to complete, so they should be worked out well before we need to launch the app.

- A SKU number, meaning an arbitrary string by which we will track sales of the app.

- A support URL and support email address.

Don't Ship Programmer Art

Deadlines are a fact of life. We have all been forced by one deadline or another to do something we didn't want to do. But when that happens, skip features; don't skip design. The biggest mistake developers make is not having a designer in the loop from the beginning. The design of your app is the way that users will perceive it. After spending countless hours thinking about the internal workings of your app, you don't want to leave the users' interaction left to chance. Just as classes need to be designed, user experiences need to be designed.

Interfaces designed by programmers tend to look like programming languages: specific and detailed but tedious. Users don't want tedious, they want it to *just work*. If you expose the switch to toggle the 20 percent feature, that leaves 80 percent to wonder at the complexity of the app.

Programmers fight for control; designers fight for the user. Make sure your app has someone fighting for the users. Don't ship an app that has not been designed from start to finish. If the idea is worth your time and energy, then it's worth getting a designer involved.

Once all of this metadata is ready, we can create an entry for the app on iTunes Connect, the website for the commercial aspects of our app. This is where we prepare the app's sales information for the store and where we'll track it after it goes on sale. Log in at http://itunesconnect.apple.com/.

From the iTunes Connect front page, click Manage Your Applications, and then click the Add New App button. From here (Figure 101, *App summary page on iTunes Connect*, on page 251), we choose whether we're adding an iOS or Mac app and then enter the app's name, default language, SKU number, and bundle ID (which is the reverse-domain name part of the App ID we set up on the Portal). If the name is already in use, we'll be returned to this screen and asked to pick another. For example, while taking screenshots for this chapter, we found that "Recipes" was taken (not a surprise, really), so we had to change the name to "Pragmatic Recipes."

Figure 101—App summary page on iTunes Connect

Next, we are asked to set an availability date, which defaults to today. We can set the date to one in the future if we want to coordinate launch-day publicity, or we can leave it set to today in order to be released as soon as Apple finishes its review. At this point, we also need to enter the app's "price tier." The App Store works with a tiered pricing system, currently with 87 tiers that range from free to US$999.99. A pricing matrix on this page offers current prices in several international currencies, showing both the price users will be charged and what we'll get after Apple takes its 30 percent cut.

The page after this asks for most of the metadata we collected earlier: app description and keywords, support URL and email, screenshots and 1024 x 1024 icon, and so on. We also have to provide a version number and copyright holder and click radio buttons in a "content descriptions" grid to indicate the prevalence of factors like violence, nudity, and profanity, which are combined to set an age rating for the app.

When we're done with all this, we get a version summary page that lists the app's status as Prepare For Upload and has a Ready To Upload Binary button. By clicking this button, we indicate that we are done in iTunes Connect and can move on to uploading the binary. If we want to make any changes before then, we can return to the app summary (shown in Figure 101, *App summary page on iTunes Connect*, on page 251) and click View Details in the Current Version section.

With the app metadata settled, it's time to build and upload the app binary.

Uploading an App Binary

Once the metadata on iTunes Connect is ready, we need to use the distribution tools we already know about to prepare a distribution build for the App Store.

First, we go back to the Provisioning Portal to create a new distribution profile. We already created one of these, but it was for Ad Hoc distribution and specified a set of devices it could run on. To submit to the store, we need to go through this process again (described in *Creating the Ad Hoc Distribution Profile*, on page 246), but this time we click App Store instead of Ad Hoc. We also need to verify that if we're using an App ID the bundle identifier we enter on the Portal website matches the bundle identifier shown in the target's summary in Xcode. Download the distribution profile and drag it to Xcode to add it to the Organizer's list of profiles.

Now we can build the application archive that we will submit to the App Store. In the target settings, change the value for "Code Signing Identity→Release" to the new distribution identity and create a new archive with Product→Archive. In the Organizer, this adds a new entry to the list of archives. Select that entry and click the "Distribute…" button.

Like before, this takes us to a wizard-style sheet to ask what kind of distribution we want to perform. This time, we click "Submit to the App Store." This asks for our Apple ID and then checks with iTunes Connect to see if we have any applications set as Ready To Upload Binary. This test may fail if we forgot to set that button or if there's a mismatched version number or bundle identifier between iTunes Connect and the archive we just built. The version and bundle identifier are set in the target's summary; check there if the test indicates an error.

Assuming the organizer finds at least one app record on iTunes Connect waiting for an upload, we see the sheet shown in Figure 102, *Uploading archive to App Store*, on page 253, which asks which app (on iTunes Connect) we're uploading and which distribution identity should be used to sign the app for submission to Apple. Choose the distribution identity we created earlier and click Next.

Choose an application record and an identity to sign with:

Application: Pragmatic Recipes 1.0 (iOS App)

Code Signing Identity: Chris Adamson

Cancel   Previous   Next

Figure 102—Uploading archive to App Store

At this point, Xcode will run a series of validations on the app archive to ensure it meets certain minimum criteria, like whether the version number and bundle identifier are what iTunes Connect is expecting. If this validation and the upload to Apple succeed, we see the message shown in Figure 103, *Successful app validation and upload*, on page 254, which tells us that the app is now in line for review.

And now we wait.

If we check the app on iTunes Connect at this point, the status will say "Waiting for Review." After some time (usually days, sometimes longer), the status will change to "In Review," meaning that it has reached the front of the review queue and is being reviewed by Apple's testers.

At this point, two outcomes are likely: either the app will be approved or it will be rejected for some reason. If it's rejected, we'll get an email detailing the cause for the rejection, which is usually a crash in testing but is sometimes a violation of an Apple policy. At this point, it's back to the beginning: we

Figure 103—Successful app validation and upload

need to fix the bug or resolve whatever issue Apple has brought up, tell iTunes Connect we're ready to submit a new binary, build a new app archive, and resubmit via Xcode.

On the other hand, if the app is approved, then it will appear on App Stores around the world in a few hours (or on our release date if we told iTunes Connect to hold it). Either way, we dance the happy dance of actually getting our app through the App Store process and get ready for the users.

10.4 After We Ship

So, we've shipped our app and users around the country or around the world are using and enjoying it. Now what?

With iTunes Connect, we can use the "Sales and Trends" page to see how many people are downloading the app—whether the trend is positive or negative. "Payments and Financial Reports" lets us check Apple's transfers to our bank account with our cut of the app's sales if it's a paid app.

But are our users actually happy? We can check the reviews in the App Store, and hopefully users with a problem will send an email to the support address we provided, though it's also possible they left a one-star review in lieu of a bug report or just quit using the app altogether. It definitely helps to have feedback channels other than the App Store, like a Twitter account, Facebook page, or website, so it's easy for users to contact us if they need to.

Retrieving and Analyzing Crash Reports

What if—heaven forbid—the app is actually *crashing* out in the field? Actually, Apple gives us big help with that. In iTunes Connect, select the app and then click the button for its current version. In the version summary page, there's a link for Crash Reports. If we click this button, we'll get a summary of crash reports that have been collected from devices in the field and returned to Apple, a feature that users have to explicitly enable when they set up their devices. Figure 104, *Crash reports on iTunes Connect*, on page 255, shows the crash reports page for an old game Chris put on the App Store and hasn't kept up-to-date (Bad Developer! Bad!). Under iOS 5 — there are no iOS 6 reports shown because iOS 6 hadn't been released to the public when we collected these crashes — there are two common crashes identified by the names of the methods that crash. Reading further down the page, we see that the app has not been killed by the system for being too slow to start up, for becoming unresponsive (by blocking the main thread), or by running out of memory. So at least the problems are limited only to a few specific bad calls.

Figure 104—Crash reports on iTunes Connect

The crash entries have a Download button. If we click this, we get a folder containing one or more .crash files. We can double-click the crash file to open it in the Console application (/Applications/Utilities/Console.app), but it's potentially more useful to open the file with Xcode.

We say "potentially" because of what Xcode may or may not be able to do with the crash log. By default, the crash log will start with some general identifier information, like the time and date of the crash, the version of iOS running at the time, and the thread that crashed. If we look at that thread later in the crash log, we get a *stack trace*, a listing of the function and method calls that led to the crash, like this (word-wrapped to fit book formatting):

```
Thread 4 name:  Dispatch queue: com.apple.root.default-priority
Thread 4 Crashed:
0    libsystem_kernel.dylib      0x3112f32c __pthread_kill + 8
1    libsystem_c.dylib           0x33c12f54 pthread_kill
2    libsystem_c.dylib           0x33c0bfe4 abort
3    libc++abi.dylib             0x30fdcf64 0x30fd6000 + 28516
4    libc++abi.dylib             0x30fda346 0x30fd6000 + 17222
5    libobjc.A.dylib             0x31acb2dc _objc_terminate
6    libc++abi.dylib             0x30fda3be 0x30fd6000 + 17342
7    libc++abi.dylib             0x30fda44a 0x30fd6000 + 17482
8    libc++abi.dylib             0x30fdb81e 0x30fd6000 + 22558
9    libobjc.A.dylib             0x31acb22e objc_exception_rethrow
10   MediaPlayer                 0x319a33e8 -[MPMediaLibraryDataProviderML3
                                     performBackgroundTaskWithBlock:]
11   MediaPlayer                 0x319a191a -[MPMediaLibraryDataProviderML3
                                     loadItemsUsingFetchRequest:]
12   MediaPlayer                 0x3199f350 __56-[MPMediaEntityStreamArray
                                     _onQueueStartLoadingEntities]_block_invoke_0
13   libdispatch.dylib           0x324a3d4e _dispatch_call_block_and_release
14   libdispatch.dylib           0x324af79c _dispatch_worker_thread2
15   libsystem_c.dylib           0x33bcf1c8 _pthread_wqthread
16   libsystem_c.dylib           0x33bcf09c start_wqthread
```

The hexadecimal values are the memory addresses. Where we see two values added together is an entry point into a library or our code and a memory offset. Unfortunately, this does almost no good whatsoever, because we don't know which of them refer to our code or what methods in our code are involved.

However, *if* this build is still archived in Xcode, then the crash log can be *symbolicated*, meaning that Xcode can correlate what it knows about the binary submitted to Apple with the memory offsets in the crash log and change the address references to method calls with line numbers. This means that we won't see a line like this:

```
1    Recipes                     0x0009513c 0x93000 + 8508
```

We will instead see a much more useful stack entry:

```
1    Recipes                    0x0009513c -[PRPAppDelegate
                                    applicationDidFinishLaunching:withOptions:]
                                    (AppDelegate.m:32)
```

Just knowing the line number may not be enough for us to fix the error, but knowing that the app is crashing in some specific way on that particular line should at least give us some good hypotheses to try out. And it's certainly far better than where we stood with just a memory offset.

10.5 Onward!

With an app up on the App Store, we've achieved what we set out to do: we've written an app, fine-tuned its performance and appearance, found and fixed its bugs, and made it available to users around the world.

Now what do we do?

For every app we ship, we watch the sales and downloads, check the reviews, collect crash logs, and put out new versions with new features and bug fixes.

And then we decide what we want to do next. In this book, we've limited ourselves to the essential frameworks of iOS and the best practices of iOS development. We left out some really interesting stuff, and that material offers a sensible place to seek the next challenge. We could dig further into UIKit by developing custom UIViews and master gesture recognizers to allow interaction with them. Or we could try out the various media frameworks—Media Player, AV Foundation, Core Audio, and the like—that let our apps use the cameras, microphones, and music library. Or maybe we want to write a productivity app that will need to store the user's data in a relational database, something that Core Data could help with. Or make use of the accelerometer and gyroscope via Core Motion. Or...

There's too much neat stuff in iOS to fit in one introductory book anymore. What we've done in this book is to establish a core base of knowledge and a set of strong practices. We now know how to build apps well, test them, release them, and manage them throughout their life cycle. From here, it's a matter of choosing our path for the next app.

What shall we try to do next?

For Further Thought

Here are a few things to think about or try out to expand your understanding of the stuff we've covered in this chapter. The questions don't necessarily have "correct" answers. Please join us on the forums at http://forums.pragprog.com/ to discuss your ideas about them.

1. Try remoting your Git repository to a Git hosting site like GitHub; most will have online instructions to walk through the process. Commit a change locally and then push it to the remote site. Can you see the change on the site? If you clone the server's repository to another Mac (or another directory on your current machine), what does it take to get a change from one repository to the other?

2. Compare the app metadata in iTunes Connect to what the App Store shows. What kinds of things can you do to make your app more appealing and its public listing more useful?

3. Do you think you will ever need to develop on multiple machines, like on a desktop and a laptop? How do you suppose you would manage your certificates and profiles between them?

4. What iOS feature would you most like to learn more about? How soon will you be looking up its documentation and trying it out?

Wait! I Forgot (or Never Learned) C!

Most iOS code is written in Objective-C, a language that many new iOS developers typically don't have experience with. Apple's *The Objective-C Programming Language* tries to put developers' minds at ease with the following introduction:

> The Objective-C language is a simple computer language designed to enable sophisticated object-oriented programming. Objective-C is defined as a small but powerful set of extensions to the standard ANSI C language. Its additions to C are mostly based on Smalltalk, one of the first object-oriented programming languages. Objective-C is designed to give C full object-oriented programming capabilities, and to do so in a simple and straightforward way.

This reminds us of an exchange from the movie *The Adventures of Buckaroo Banzai: Across the Eighth Dimension*, in which Buckaroo and his alien ally, John Parker, have just escaped in a flying "pod car" that they don't know how to fly:

> **BUCKAROO BANZAI:** *John Parker, take this wheel. And hold this. It flies just like a truck.*
>
> **JOHN PARKER:** *Good…What is a truck?*

In other words, saying that Objective-C is just a set of extensions to C isn't much comfort for developers who aren't familiar with C in the first place. If this is you, or if your C experience is so far in the past that the thought of pointers or malloc() scares you, this appendix will serve as a very short crash course in C programming.

A1.1 C: The Basics

Most measurements of programming language popularity have shown C as a top-five language, if not *the* top language, since its development in the early 1970s. It has been highly influential on most popular languages created since then, so most programmers will find familiar concepts in C. Here are some of the traits that specifically distinguish C.

- *Primitive types*—C only provides a handful of numeric types: integers at various bit-depths (short, int, long) and floating points (float, double). char represents a single character and a bool that can be true or false. In evaluating conditionals, C actually uses ints, with 0 meaning false and any other value meaning true. A void keyword indicates the absence of type. Everything interesting is built on this simple base.

- *Flow control*—A handful of simple constructs perform basic looping and branching of code. while*(condition) { ... }* and do *{ ... }*while*(condition);* to loop while some condition is true, for*(initialization statement; continue condition; iteration statement) { ... }* to count over a block while a continue condition is true, if*(condition) { ... }* and if*(condition) { ... }*else *{ ... }* to execute code if a condition is true (and to do something else if it is false), and switch*(int)* {caseint: ...;caseint: ...; ...} for executing code based on the value of an int. There are also two short-circuit statements: continue returns to the top of the closest enclosing loop, while break exits the nearest enclosing loop or case.

- *Variables*—Variables must be explicitly declared and typed prior to use and have lexical scope, meaning they exist within the context of the function they're declared in. Variables can be declared outside of any function: these are global variables and should be used sparingly, if at all.

- *Function Declarations*—Functions explicitly declare their parameter types and return type and must appear in source prior to their being called; for unpredictable or circular cases a *forward declaration*, consisting of a function header with no body, can be used as a promise that the compiler will encounter the function's code eventually.

- *Source Files*—C code usually uses two kinds of files. *Header files*, with file extension .h, expose the public interface to code: function declarations, global variables, and constants. *Implementation files* import the headers for functions they implement as well as the headers for any third-party code they need to call and include the actual implementation of publicly declared functions as well as any other functions they need.

- *Creating New Types*—enum defines enumerations, associating int values (starting with 0 and counting up by default, though this can be overridden) with lexical constants. struct creates structures that have several fields of potentially different types. Members of a struct are accessed with the dot operator, as in *variable.member*. The typedef keyword declares an enum or struct as a new primitive type. Putting it all together, here's how to define and use a new PlayingCard variable type:

```
typedef enum {SUIT_CLUB, SUIT_DIAMOND, SUIT_HEART, SUIT_SPADE} CardSuit;
typedef enum {CARD_VAL_ACE = 1,
        CARD_VAL_2, CARD_VAL_3, CARD_VAL_4, CARD_VAL_5,
        CARD_VAL_6, CARD_VAL_7, CARD_VAL_8, CARD_VAL_9, CARD_VAL_10
        CARD_VAL_JACK, CARD_VAL_QUEEN, CARD_VAL_KING} CardVal;
typedef struct {
        CardSuit suit;
        CardVal value;} PlayingCard;

PlayingCard aCard;
aCard.suit = SUIT_SPADE;
aCard.value = CARD_VAL_ACE;
```

- *Arrays and Strings*—A C array is declared with square braces and the number of members in the array. For example, PlayingCard hand[5] declares hand as an array of up to five PlayingCards, the first of which is hand[0]. There is *no* bounds-checking: getting or setting hand[100] will not cause a build error, but it may lead to chaos or crashes at runtime. Basic C strings are simply arrays of type char, with a NULL character as the last member. Quote marks can be used to create string literals, as in char[] foo="bar";. C strings do not specify a character encoding.

A1.2 Pointers

If this were all that C provided, it would be a simple (indeed, primitive) language that wouldn't have its reputation for difficulty. The "hard parts" of C begin with pointers. In somewhat simplistic but concrete terms, a pointer is the memory address of a variable. We define a variable with the * operator, like this:

```
int *count;
```

This means that count is not itself an int but rather a *pointer* to an int. Once we populate this pointer (so far, we have only declared it), if we print out the value of count with C's default logging function, printf(), we will see the memory address of count, not its value. To get or set the value, we dereference count by preceding the variable with the * operator, like this:

```
*count = 100;
```

There is great danger in getting pointers wrong. For example, what if we forgot the leading *, like this:

```
count = 100;
```

Then we would now be asserting that there is an int at memory address 100, something that is almost certainly not true. Indeed, address 100 is probably not available to our application. So if we then try to read or write the value, like with *c = 100, the system will see this as a security violation and crash our app with the dreaded EXC_BAD_ACCESS message.

Pointers open up some interesting abstractions. C arrays and strings are actually just syntactic sugar over pointers. The array variable is the address of the first member of the array, and any member can be obtained by multiplying the array index times the size of an array member. Given int foo[], we can get the tenth member as either foo[9] or *(foo + (9 * sizeof(int))), though the array syntax is obviously far simpler. And the C string is just an array of chars, so it, too, is just a pointer.

Pass-by-Value Versus Pass-by-Reference

Pointers let us do interesting things. For one, they let us break out of C's pass-by-value system. Let's do an experiment. Here's a C program that uses the PlayingCard type defined earlier.

NeverLearnedC/cardexample01.c
```
#include <stdio.h>
#pragma mark - private methods
typedef enum {SUIT_CLUB, SUIT_DIAMOND, SUIT_HEART, SUIT_SPADE} CardSuit;
typedef enum {CARD_VAL_ACE = 1, CARD_VAL_2, CARD_VAL_3, CARD_VAL_4, CARD_VAL_5,
  CARD_VAL_6, CARD_VAL_7, CARD_VAL_8, CARD_VAL_9, CARD_VAL_10,
  CARD_VAL_JACK, CARD_VAL_QUEEN, CARD_VAL_KING} CardVal;
typedef struct {
  CardSuit suit;
  CardVal value;} PlayingCard;

void convertToAce (PlayingCard card) {
  card.value = CARD_VAL_ACE;
}

int main(int argc, char *argv[]) {
  PlayingCard originalCard;
  originalCard.value = CARD_VAL_KING;
  convertToAce (originalCard);
  printf ("originalCard.value=%d\n", originalCard.value);
}
```

It's obvious what the convertToAce() function is supposed to do, right? It changes the value of a PlayingCard to CARD_VAL_ACE. Compile and run the code in Terminal, like this:

```
$ gcc cardexample01.c -o cardexample01
./cardexample01
```

When we run this, it prints originalCard.value=13, meaning our card's value is the thirteenth member of the enum, meaning it's still CARD_VAL_KING. What happened?

C passes parameters by value, even multimember types like the PlayingCard. So the local variable, card, is a *copy* of the caller's originalCard, and it expires when the function returns.

Pointers give us a way out of the pass-by-value trap. Let's rewrite convertToAce() as follows:

NeverLearnedC/cardexample02.c
```
void convertToAce (PlayingCard *card) {
  card->value = CARD_VAL_ACE;
}
```

This is different only in that it takes the pointer to a PlayingCard. This in turn changes the syntax for how we access a member, requiring us to replace the dot operator with ->. The arrow operator is really just syntactic sugar for dereferencing the variable and then using the dot operator, like (*card).value. Obviously, the arrow operator is easier to read and write.

We also have to change how we call the function, since it now takes a pointer to a PlayingCard, not just the PlayingCard itself. So we change the call to convert-ToAce(), like this:

NeverLearnedC/cardexample02.c
```
convertToAce (&originalCard);
```

This uses the & operator, which is C's "address-of" operator. That gives convert-ToAce() the pointer it expects.

Now run again and the output is originalCard.value=1, which means convertToAce() actually modified originalCard to CARD_VAL_ACE. And it was able to do this because by using pointers, we changed our function's idiom from pass-by-value to pass-by-reference. Instead of sending the function a copy of the PlayingCard, we told it where originalCard lives in memory and let the function modify the structure there.

Lots of modern object-oriented languages are pass-by-reference only. It's a common and useful idiom, and Apple uses it frequently in its low-level C APIs too.

A1.3 Dynamic Memory Management

Still, outside of pass-by-reference, it would be a fair question to ask if pointers are really worth the tricky syntax, confusion, and danger they add. And the answer is yes. Where pointers really come into their own is when using dynamic memory management. After all, it would be very limiting to be able to use only whatever variables we explicitly declared in the program code; older languages, including many flavors of BASIC, had this problem.

In C, when we need a new PlayingCard, or anything else, we can just ask the system to set aside some memory for it. We do this with the malloc() function:

```
PlayingCard *anotherCard = malloc (sizeof (PlayingCard));
```

This allocates enough memory for a new PlayingCard and returns a pointer to the newly allocated memory. With the pointer, we could now start using it like any other variable:

```
anotherCard->suit = SUIT_HEART;
anotherCard->value = CARD_VAL_QUEEN;
```

When we're done with the memory we've allocated, we need to give it back to the system via the free() function:

```
free (anotherCard);
```

Simple enough...until we start to pass pointers around between different parts of an application. The whole problem of memory management is knowing when to free a pointer we've allocated. In complex software, a given pointer could be used in many different places, so the software needs a way to coordinate the use of memory, to know when no part of the program still needs it and it is thus safe to free. Not only is there no built-in way to figure that out for us, but the consequences of getting it wrong are dire: fail to free memory we've allocated and we leak, bloating the app's memory footprint; bloat too much, and the system will terminate us. But, free it too soon, try to access memory that's been freed, and crash instantly with EXC_BAD_ACCESS.

Dynamic memory management is great...when it works. Part of the point of C's various successors (C++, Objective-C, Java, and so on) is to make that process easier to manage.

Wrap-Up

Having covered pointers and malloc()/free(), we've worked through the prerequisites for the primary language for iOS development, Objective-C. We're now ready to return to Chapter 2, *Programming for iOS*, on page 27.

C Preprocessor Trickery

iOS code isn't just about executable instructions. The C preprocessor allows us to perform some actions before the compiler even begins to convert our C source to binary.

C preprocessor directives begin with the # character. One of the simplest is #define, which simply performs a macro substitution. Consider the following line:

```
#define PRAGS_URL http://www.pragprog.com
```

If we add this to our code, then anywhere that PRAGS_URL appears in our source, the preprocessor will replace it with http://www.pragprog.com. This happens prior to compilation, so we can insert anything: strings, numeric values, even keywords and method/function calls.

#define is often used for what's called *conditional compilation*. By using the #ifdef-#endif block, we can indicate that part of our program is to be built only if a given term is #defined. To not build that code, we just comment out the #define (or perform other Xcode build magic). Apple uses this a lot and defines availability macros like _IPHONE_6_0 in the Availability.h header, which we implicitly import from the Foundation framework.

Another handy directive is #pragma mark. This causes the rest of the text on that line to be added to the method pop-up menu at the end of the Jump Bar. We can also precede the text with a - to create a separator line.

Starting a comment line with // TODO: or // FIXME: also creates a menu item with whatever text follows the colon.

Bibliography

[WD11]   Paul Warren and Matt Drance. *iOS Recipes: Tips and Tricks for Awesome iPhone and iPad Apps*. The Pragmatic Bookshelf, Raleigh, NC and Dallas, TX, 2011.

[Zar12]   Marcus S. Zarra. *Core Data*. The Pragmatic Bookshelf, Raleigh, NC and Dallas, TX, Second, 2012.

Index

More on iOS Programming

Ready to learn more on iOS? We've got you covered.

Take your iPhone and iPad apps to the next level. You've seen cool features and tricks in other apps, but haven't had the time to really look into how they're done. We've got the answers for you. This book walks you through clean, reusable solutions to a wide variety of problems and patterns common to iOS development with Cocoa Touch and Objective-C. With these recipes in your arsenal, your next apps will be more polished and more maintainable than ever.

Paul Warren and Matt Drance
(200 pages) ISBN: 9781934356746. $33
http://pragprog.com/titles/cdirec

Core Data is Apple's recommended way to persist data: it's easy to use, built-in, and integrated with iCloud. It's intricate, powerful, and necessary—and this book is your guide to harnessing its power.

Learn fundamental Core Data principles such as thread and memory management, discover how to use Core Data in your iPhone, iPad, and OS X projects by using NSPredicate to filter data, and see how to add iCloud to your applications.

Marcus S. Zarra
(250 pages) ISBN: 9781937785086. $33
http://pragprog.com/titles/mzcd2

Seven Databases, Seven Languages

There's so much new to learn with the latest crop of NoSQL databases. And instead of learning a language a year, h ow about seven?

Data is getting bigger and more complex by the day, and so are your choices in handling it. From traditional RDBMS to newer NoSQL approaches, *Seven Databases in Seven Weeks* takes you on a tour of some of the hottest open source databases today. In the tradition of Bruce A. Tate's *Seven Languages in Seven Weeks*, this book goes beyond a basic tutorial to explore the essential concepts at the core of each technology.

Eric Redmond and Jim Wilson
(330 pages) ISBN: 9781934356920. $35
http://pragprog.com/titles/rwdata

You should learn a programming language every year, as recommended by *The Pragmatic Programmer*. But if one per year is good, how about *Seven Languages in Seven Weeks*? In this book you'll get a hands-on tour of Clojure, Haskell, Io, Prolog, Scala, Erlang, and Ruby. Whether or not your favorite language is on that list, you'll broaden your perspective of programming by examining these languages side-by-side. You'll learn something new from each, and best of all, you'll learn how to learn a language quickly.

Bruce A. Tate
(328 pages) ISBN: 9781934356593. $34.95
http://pragprog.com/titles/btlang

Be Agile

Don't just "do" agile; you want to *be* agile. We'll show you how.

The best agile book isn't a book: *Agile in a Flash* is a unique deck of index cards that fit neatly in your pocket. You can tape them to the wall. Spread them out on your project table. Get stains on them over lunch. These cards are meant to be used, not just read.

Jeff Langr and Tim Ottinger
(110 pages) ISBN: 9781934356715. $15
http://pragprog.com/titles/olag

You know the Agile and Lean development buzzwords, you've read the books. But when systems need a serious overhaul, you need to see how it works in real life, with real situations and people. *Lean from the Trenches* is all about actual practice. Every key point is illustrated with a photo or diagram, and anecdotes bring you inside the project as you discover why and how one organization modernized its workplace in record time.

Henrik Kniberg
(176 pages) ISBN: 9781934356852. $30
http://pragprog.com/titles/hklean

The Pragmatic Bookshelf

The Pragmatic Bookshelf features books written by developers for developers. The titles continue the well-known Pragmatic Programmer style and continue to garner awards and rave reviews. As development gets more and more difficult, the Pragmatic Programmers will be there with more titles and products to help you stay on top of your game.

Visit Us Online

This Book's Home Page
http://pragprog.com/titles/adios
Source code from this book, errata, and other resources. Come give us feedback, too!

Register for Updates
http://pragprog.com/updates
Be notified when updates and new books become available.

Join the Community
http://pragprog.com/community
Read our weblogs, join our online discussions, participate in our mailing list, interact with our wiki, and benefit from the experience of other Pragmatic Programmers.

New and Noteworthy
http://pragprog.com/news
Check out the latest pragmatic developments, new titles and other offerings.

Save on the eBook

Save on the eBook versions of this title. Owning the paper version of this book entitles you to purchase the electronic versions at a terrific discount.

PDFs are great for carrying around on your laptop—they are hyperlinked, have color, and are fully searchable. Most titles are also available for the iPhone and iPod touch, Amazon Kindle, and other popular e-book readers.

Buy now at *http://pragprog.com/coupon*

Contact Us

Online Orders: *http://pragprog.com/catalog*
Customer Service: *support@pragprog.com*
International Rights: *translations@pragprog.com*
Academic Use: *academic@pragprog.com*
Write for Us: *http://pragprog.com/write-for-us*
Or Call: +1 800-699-7764